Purnell's Family Atlas

Authenticator: Keith Lye

Editor: Wendy Hobson

SBN 361 05156 5
Copyright © 1981 Vallardi Industrie Grafiche
Text copyright © 1981 Purnell and Sons Limited
Published 1981 by Purnell Books, Berkshire House,
Queen Street, Maidenhead, Berkshire
Made and printed in Italy

Purnell's Family Atlas

Contents

Photographic Sources: Arch. Vallardi: 9cr, 10l, 13r, 16l, 19t,bl, 23l, 33bl,41cl, br, 43, 47, 53l, 54c, 56blc, 66bl, 78clr, 85bl, 90c,br, 91, 94cbr, 95cbr. Atlas-Photo: 74bl. Balletto: 82bl. Barone: 27t. Blauel: 54tr, Coleman: 34t, 40t, cbr, 41t,cr. Diamante: 72br. Fiore: 15, 71, 72cl, 80c. Freelance: 76c. Jeiter: 46b. Maffei: 95t. Mairani: 75. Marka: 2-3, 4-5, 6-7, 9cl,b, 10c,r, 11, 12, 13l,c, 16c,r, 17c, 18b, c,r, 19c,r, 21l,cb,rb, 22c,r, 23c,r, 25, 26, 28c, 29, 30, 31, 32, 33t,bc,r, 34b, 35, 40cl, 42cbr, **44bc, 45, 46t,c, 48tr,b, 50, 51, 52cr,b, 54tl, 56t,br, 58, 59, 60t,mr,br, 62t,csr, 64, 65, 66t, clr,br, 67, 68t,c,br, 69, 70, 72t,cr, 76t,b, 77, 78c, 79, 80t,b, 82c, 83, 84, 86, 87, 88t,c,bl, 89, 90t,bl, 92, 94t,cbl, 95cbr, 96. Nasa: 72bl. Pedone: 20ct, 21tr, 52t. Prato Previde: 18t, 20l,cb,r, 28l,r, 42blc, 44t, 48t, 60cl,bl, 62b, 74t,br, 82t, 85br, 93. Publiaerfoto: 27c, 42t. Regaldi: 17r, 21ct, 53r, 78t, 82br. Ricatto: 17l, 18bl, 22l, 44bl, 74c, 88br. Sauli: 9t. Stutte: 68bl. Zefa: 44cr.**

The Earth

Volcanic and seismic phenomena give the strongest indications that the Earth's surface is changing, something which, to the casual observer, does not seem to happen. However, if we consider the crust of our Earth in terms of geological time, it becomes clear that our planet is in a continuous process of evolution, with mountain chains rising out of the sea, oceans being swallowed up, and ice caps forming and dispersing. For us, all these are landmarks in Earth chronology, taking place over millions of years.

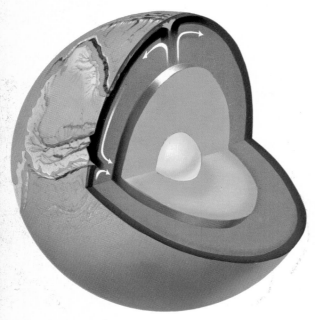

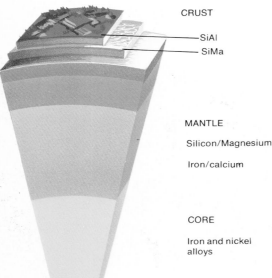

CRUST
- SiAl
- SiMa

MANTLE
Silicon/Magnesium
Iron/calcium

CORE
Iron and nickel alloys

Inside the Earth
The various natural phenomena, and what we know about them from geology, géophysics and geochemistry, lead us to suppose that Earth's structure takes the form of a series of concentric shells (see diagram on the left). There is a marked difference between the density in the core of the planet (12-13 g/cm²) and that of the solid crust (2-7 g/cm². Temperature increases by 3°C per 100 metres of depth. Seismic waves are deflected and change speed according to the depths they reach. Three fundamental areas may be distinguished – the continental crust, designated SiAl because of the abundance of silicon and aluminium, and the oceanic crust called SiMa, because of the presence of silicon and magnesium; the mostly rigid mantle; and the core, the inside of which is thought to be solid due to the very high pressures prevailing, while the outer part is liquid. The Earth's crust and upper part of the mantle form a rigid band, known as the lithosphere. This covers a lower, plastic layer called the asthenosphere.

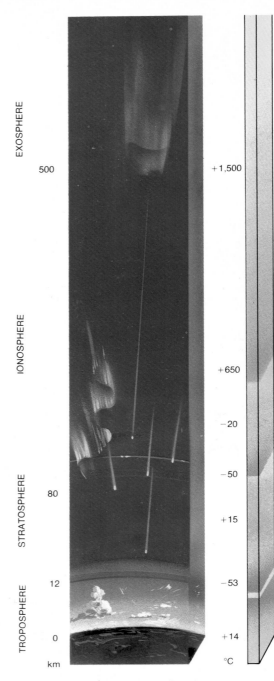

EXOSPHERE

IONOSPHERE

STRATOSPHERE

TROPOSPHERE

500
80
12
0
km

+1,500
+650
-20
-50
+15
-53
+14
°C

The atmosphere
The atmosphere is made up of a series of gaseous zones encircling our planet. The layer in immediate contact with the crust and known as the troposphere, varies in height from 8 kilometres above the Poles to about 18 kilometres above the Equator. It is from here that rain, snow and hail originate. The troposphere is made up of certain known gases in constant percentages: nitrogen, 78.09 per cent; oxygen, 20.95 per cent; and carbon dioxide, 0.03 per cent, along with argon (0.93 per cent) and other rare gases and specks of salt and dust. Above the troposphere lies the stratosphere, where density and humidity are considerably reduced. The temperature, which drops in the troposphere down to −50°C, remains constant at first but then tends to rise in the stratosphere, forming the so-called warm layer. This stratosphere contains an ozone layer, which is responsible for filtering much of the potentially harmful solar radiation. At more than 90 kilometres up, is the ionosphere, consisting of electrically-charged particles. Above the ionosphere is the exosphere which merges into space.

Formation and destruction of the crust
The lithosphere, consisting of the crust and the upper stratum of the mantle, has an average thickness between 30 kilometres beneath the continents to 5 kilometres beneath the oceans. Its main feature is that it is split vertically into rigid plates or blocks which are able to move over the more flexible underlying asthenosphere, probably as a result of convective movements (indicated by arrows in the diagram below) within the asthenosphere itself. It is along the edges of the plates that the main phenomena of the Earth's crust occur: the expansion of ocean beds along the oceanic ridges where plates diverge; orogenesis, or mountain building, with the formation of ridges and mountain chains; and volcanic and seismic activity, where plates converge and pile on top of or slide alongside one another.

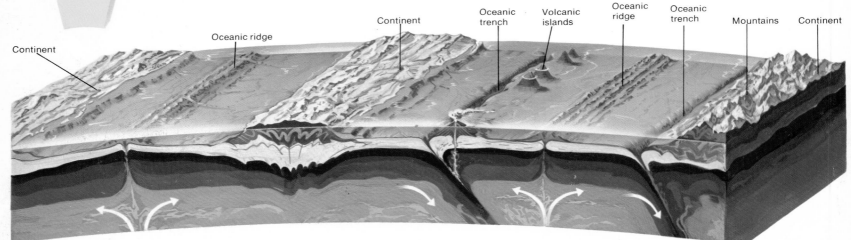

Continent — Oceanic ridge — Continent — Oceanic trench — Volcanic islands — Oceanic ridge — Oceanic trench — Mountains — Continent

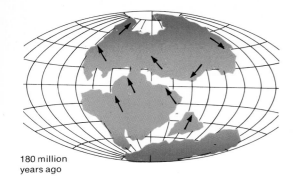

180 million years ago

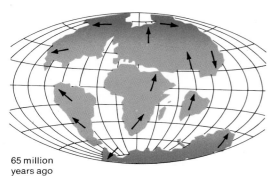

65 million years ago

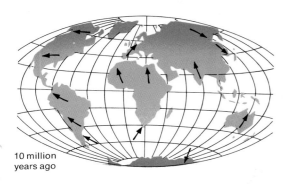

10 million years ago

The origin of the continents

The rigid plates or blocks of the lithosphere are able to move over the soft asthenospheric layer beneath. The plates which support the continents have moved around with the passage of geological time. The German scientist Alfred Wegener postulated his theory of the origin of the continents in the early part of this century, though he was not able to identify their true origin on account of the limited scientific equipment available at the time. It is only recently that geologists have obtained reliable evidence of the Earth's structure, and have evolved the theory of 'global tectonics'. They have, for instance, found evidence of considerable heat-flow along the oceanic ridges, and a reduced heat-flow along the trenches, which in all probability indicates convection currents within the mantle. Palaeomagnetic anomalies have been discovered on the ocean beds, providing conclusive proof of their expansion.

Erosion

The Earth's landscape is shaped by a complex series of physical and chemical phenomena. This shaping of the landscape is known as erosion. One of the most powerful eroding agents is water, in its various physical states: in rivers, in glaciers, which erode mountains, and in sea waves, which eat into coastlines. The wind too erodes the land in dry areas, forming rocky peaks and arches.

Volcanic activity

The map below enables us to compare the distribution of seismic activity with that of volcanic areas. There is obviously a considerable degree of coincidence. Earthquakes and volcanoes are in fact two phenomena linked with the dynamics of the Earth's crust. The areas of greatest incidence, as recorded since the 1950s, coincide with the distribution of plate edges, namely oceanic ridges, transform faults and oceanic trenches. Volcanoes are situated mainly near the edges of the plates, and these volcanoes are evidence both of the formation of fresh crustal rock (along the oceanic ridges, as the ocean beds expand) and of the destruction of the crust, by melting, within the mantle. This occurs in the subduction zone, where one plate slides beneath its neighbour. The diagram on the far right shows a section through an active volcano. The magma collects in a pocket between lithosphere and asthenosphere, and comes to the surface through fissures or areas of low resistance. On contact with the atmosphere, it solidifies along with ash and other types of ejecta to form a volcanic cone.

Stromboli type (right) Small flows of lava, accompanied by intermittent eruptive activity.

Hawaiian type (left) Characterised by a continuous flow of very liquid lava.

Vulcanic type (right) Violent eruptions of volcanic ash and small stones, accompanied by a characteristic plume of smoke.

DISTRIBUTION OF VOLCANIC AND SEISMIC AREAS

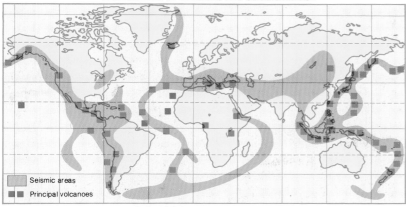

Seismic areas

Principal volcanoes

Earthquakes (right) Earthquakes are caused by movements of rocks along faults, and by friction along the edges of the plates. They are thus located in the regions characterised by instability in the Earth's crust (ridges, trenches and recent mountain chains). Tremors are violent also along the edges of two plates running sideways in opposite directions (transform faults).

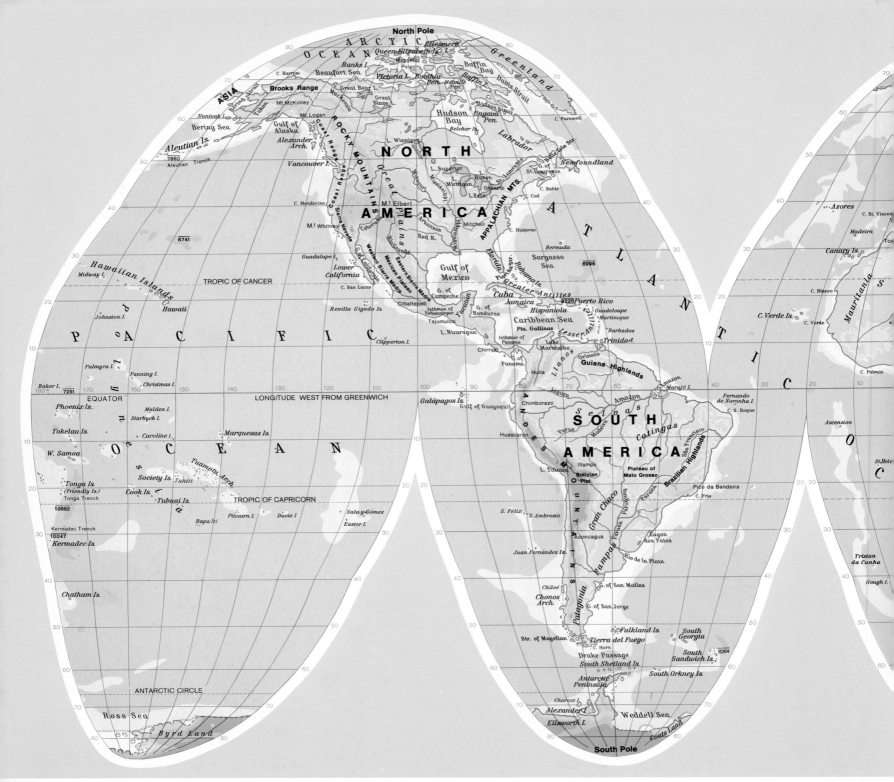

Ice

Ice currently covers a surface area of more than 15 million square kilometres, corresponding to 10 per cent of the land masses. Most of this is found in the Antarctic ice sheet (13 million square kilometres) and in the Greenland ice sheet (1.7 million square kilometres). Small ice caps and valley glaciers account for the remainder. The picture shows the snout of a Greenland glacier.

Mountains

The most marked features of continental relief are fold mountain ranges. There are two great chains of comparatively recent origin. The first stretches from the Atlas to the Alps and on to the Himalayas, where it takes in Everest (8,848 metres), the highest point on Earth, and from there into Indonesia. The second runs lengthwise down the western side of both the North and South American continents.

Rivers

The River Amazon discharges into the Atlantic Ocean. The vast river system of the Amazon and its tributaries covers about 6½ million square kilometres. It is the second longest river in the world at 6,440 kilometres, but it has the greatest flow. The Nile, the world's longest river, flows into the Mediterranean, but much of its water is evaporated by the hot sun before reaching the sea.

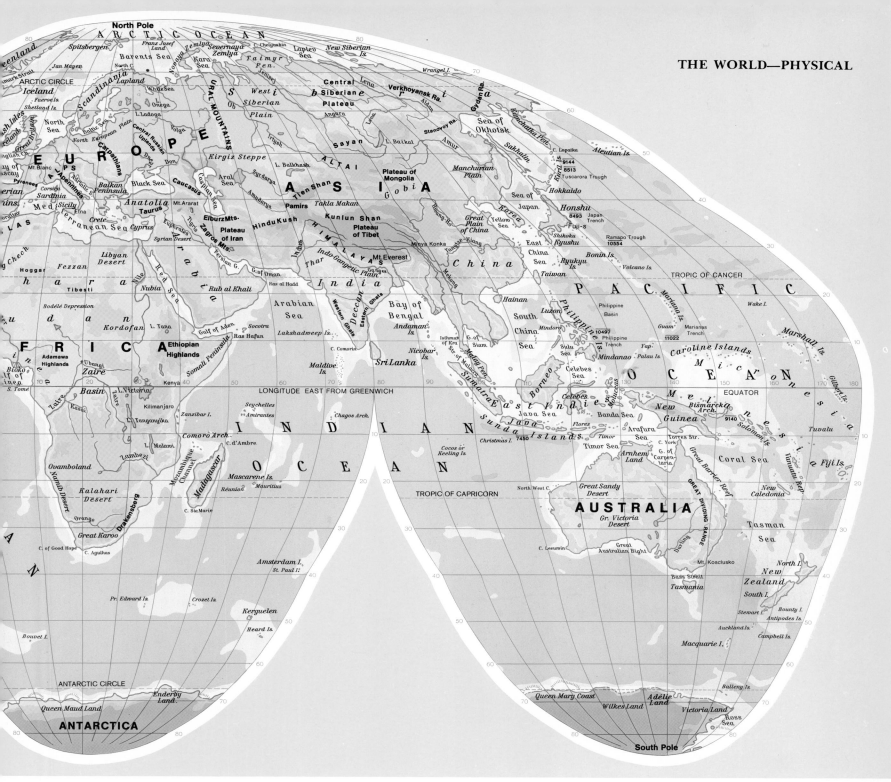

Map labels include: North Pole, ARCTIC OCEAN, Spitsbergen, Franz Josef Land, Severnaya Zemlya, Novaya Zemlya, Taimyr Pen., Laptev Sea, New Siberian Is., C. Chelyuskin, Wrangel I., Barents Sea, Kara Sea, Jan Mayen, ARCTIC CIRCLE, Iceland, Faeroes Is., Shetland Is., North Sea, Scandinavia, Lapland, White Sea, Onega, L. Ladoga, Ob, West Siberian Plain, Central Siberian Plateau, Lena, Verkhoyansk Ra., Gydan Ra., Central European Plain, Carpathians, Central Russian Uplands, Volga, Ural Mountains, Irtysh, Yenisei, Angara, Sayan, L. Baikal, Stanovoy Ra., Amur, Sea of Okhotsk, Kamchatka Pen., C. Lopatka, Aleutian Is., EUROPE, Mt. Blanc, ALPS, Apennines, Balkan Peninsula, Black Sea, Caucasus, Caspian Sea, Aral Sea, Kirgiz Steppe, L. Balkhash, Syr Darya, Amu Darya, ALTAI, Tien Shan, Plateau of Mongolia, Gobi, Manchurian Plain, Sakhalin, Hokkaido, Sea of Japan, Korea, 9144, 8513, Tuscarora Trough, Pyrenees, Corsica, Sardinia, Sicily, Etna, Anatolia, Taurus, Crete, Cyprus, Mediterranean Sea, Mt. Ararat, Elburz Mts., Zagros Mts., Plateau of Iran, Hindu Kush, Pamirs, Takla Makan, Kunlun Shan, Plateau of Tibet, HIMALAYAS, Mt. Everest, Minya Konka, Hwang-Ho, Great Plain of China, Yellow Sea, Yangtze Kiang, China, East China Sea, Honshu, Fuji-s 8493, Japan Abyssal, Shikoku, Kyushu, Ramapo Trough 10554, Bonin Is., Volcano Is., TROPIC OF CANCER, ATLAS, Sahara, Libyan Desert, Tibesti, Hoggar, Fezzan, Bodélé Depression, Nile, Red Sea, Arabia, Rub al Khali, Persian G., G. of Oman, Ras al Hadd, Indus, Thar, Indo-Gangetic Plain, Ganges, India, Deccan, Western Ghats, Eastern Ghats, Bay of Bengal, Andaman Is., Hainan, South China Sea, Luzon, Philippines, Mindoro, Philippine Trench 10497, Mariana Is., Guam 11022, Marianas Trench, Wake I., Marshall Is., Caroline Islands, Micronesia, PACIFIC OCEAN, AFRICA, Adamawa Highlands, Bioko, S. Tomé, Ubangi, Zaire, Zaire Basin, Kasai, Kordofan, L. Tana, Nubia, Ethiopian Highlands, Somali Peninsula, Gulf of Aden, Socotra, Ras Hafun, Arabian Sea, Lakshadweep Is., Maldive Is., Sri Lanka, Nicobar Is., Isthmus of Kra, G. of Siam, Malay Pen., Str. of Malacca, Sumatra, East Indies, Sulu Sea, Celebes Sea, Borneo, Mindanao, Palau Is., Yap, Celebes, Moluccas, New Guinea, Bismarck Arch. 9140, Solomon Is., EQUATOR, C. Comorin, Seychelles, Amirantes, Chagos Arch., Kenya, Kilimanjaro, Zanzibar I., L. Victoria, L. Tanganyika, Comoro Arch., Reunion, Mauritius, Mascarene Is., INDIAN OCEAN, Java Sea, Sunda Islands, Flores, Banda Sea, Timor, Arafura Sea, C. York, Gulf of Carpentaria, Torres Str., Coral Sea, Vanuatu Rep., Fiji Is., Tuvalu, Melanesia, Polynesia, Gilbert Is., Ovamboland, Namib Desert, Kalahari Desert, Orange, Drakensberg, Great Karoo, C. of Good Hope, C. Agulhas, Zambezi, L. Malawi, Madagascar, Mozambique Channel, C. d'Ambre, C. Ste Marie, Christmas I. 7450, Cocos or Keeling Is., TROPIC OF CAPRICORN, North West C., Great Sandy Desert, AUSTRALIA, Gr. Victoria Desert, Great Dividing Range, Great Barrier Reef, Arnhem Land, Timor Sea, Darling, New Caledonia, Tasman Sea, Amsterdam I., St. Paul I., Pr. Edward Is., Crozet Is., Kerguelen, Heard Is., C. Leeuwin, Great Australian Bight, Mt. Kosciusko, Bass Strait, Tasmania, New Zealand, North I., South I., Stewart I., Bounty I., Antipodes Is., Macquarie I., Campbell Is., Auckland Is., Bouvet I., ANTARCTIC CIRCLE, Queen Maud Land, Enderby Land, ANTARCTICA, Queen Mary Coast, Wilkes Land, Adélie Land, Victoria Land, Ross Sea, Balleny Is., South Pole, LONGITUDE EAST FROM GREENWICH

Plains

Plains are areas with little relief. They have varying origins. Flood plains, or alluvial plains, derive from alluvial deposits along river valleys, where the river often overflows and spreads out an alluvial sediment over a wide area. Coastal plains are often found between the hills and the sea, and are formed from a combination of fluvial and marine deposits along the coasts.

Deserts

Climatic aridity is a main factor in the formation of deserts – the average amount of rainfall is around 200 millimetres annually. The largest desert is the Sahara, running through North Africa. This is a part sandy, part stony wasteland, covering about 8.4 million square kilometres. Even though daytime temperatures are high, the temperature can fall extremely low at night.

Coasts

Tides, currents and above all waves are the main factors influencing the shape of coastlines. Waves sculpt rocky coastlines, cliffs, bays and caves. The pounding of the waves against the coast breaks off the rock and gradually the coastline recedes. These fragments of rock are then deposited in low-lying sandy beaches. The beaches gradually accumulate more material.

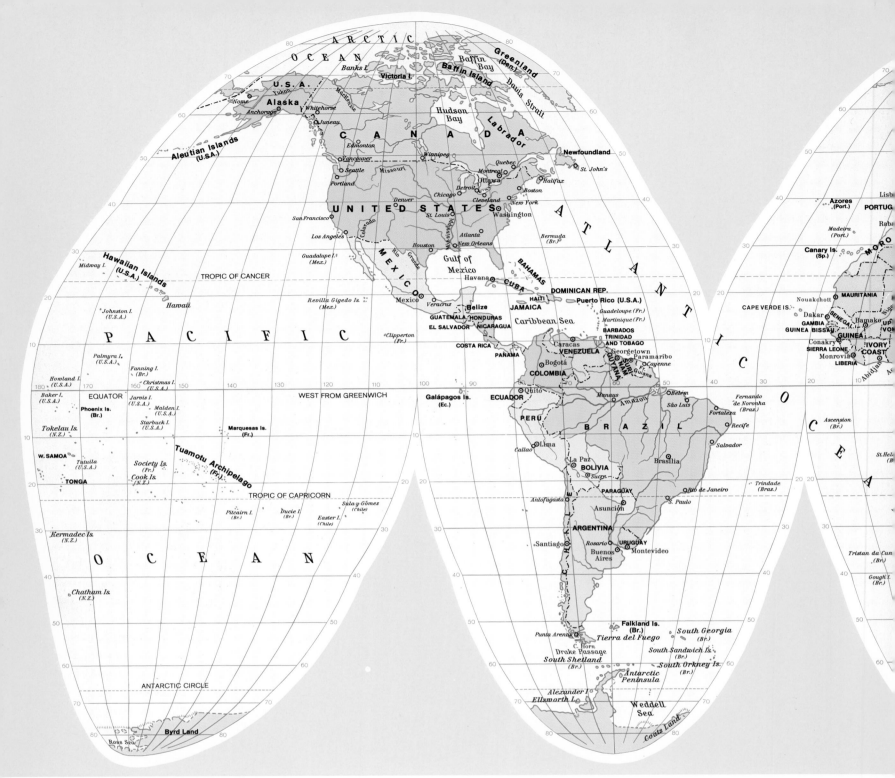

North America
A country of widely contrasting climates, North America has both polar and tropical zones. Its vast open spaces (more than 24 million square kilometres) and enormous agricultural and mineral resources are enjoyed in the central northern area by a population largely of European origin, which has reached an advanced stage of industrial development and prosperity.

South America
Traversed lengthwise by the majestic mountain range of the Andes, South America also has considerable variations in climate. The population (more than 230 million inhabitants) is greatly influenced by Latin (Portuguese and Spanish) culture. Considerable economic and social inequalities persist. Below, a South American Indian village near Lake Titicaca.

Africa
The Sahara separates white Africa, influenced since ancient times by the economic development of the Mediterranean, and black Africa, where the population is predominantly Negroid. This area was dominated by European colonialism until the Second World War, but most African countries have now gained their independence from the colonial powers. Below, an Egyptian pyramid.

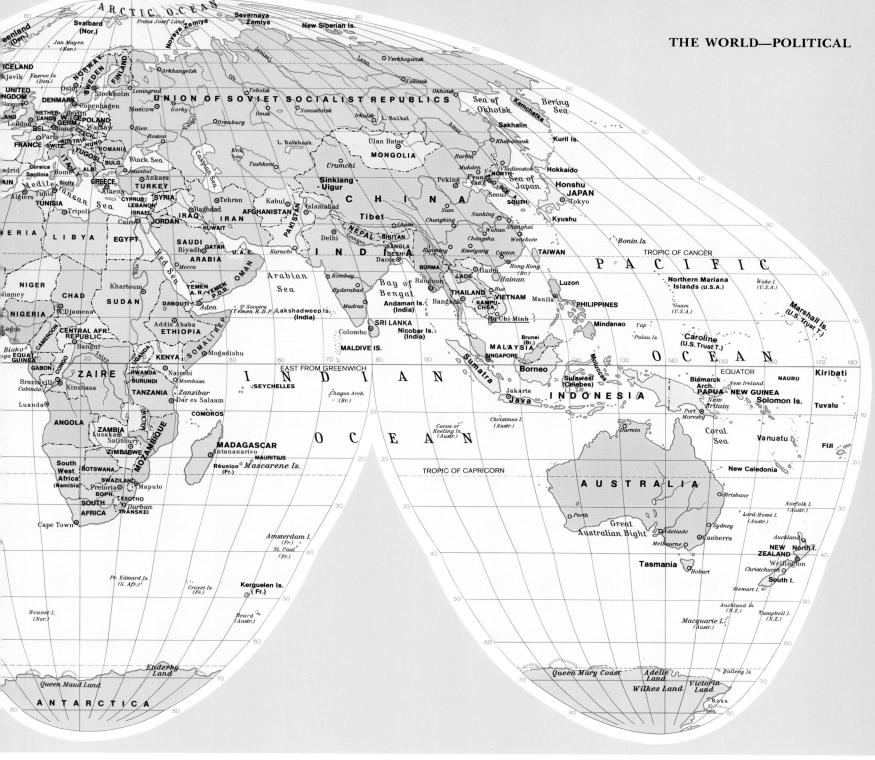

Europe

Although not very extensive (occupying little more than 10.5 million square kilometres) Europe constitutes a vital centre for international trading. It is densely populated (63 inhabitants per square kilometre) and its ancient cultural traditions, linked with the Mediterranean, have given place to the industrial revolution and the age of technology. Below, the Parthenon in Greece.

Asia

Asia is the largest of the continents, covering an area of more than 44 million square kilometres and accounting for about 60 per cent of the world's population. It is the home of ancient civilisations and religions, and much of it was subjected to European colonialism up to the end of the Second World War. Below, the magnificent carvings and statues at a Buddhist temple.

Oceania

The smallest continent in area and, apart from Antarctica, the least densely populated of the continents (with 22 million inhabitants), Oceania was not fully discovered until the 18th century, and its population has been predominantly Anglo-Saxon up to now. Large areas of Australia lie waste, but rapid economic development is now taking place, due to its considerable mineral resources.

The oceans

The Earth's system of seas and oceans is known as the hydrosphere. It covers about 70 per cent of the surface area of the planet. In fact, of the Earth's total area of 510 million square kilometres more than 360 million square kilometres are covered by sea. Although there are notable differences in temperatures and degrees of salinity, the seas and oceans constitute a continuous system, as distinct from the continents, so that it is possible to move from one to another without interruption. It is only through geographical conventions and historical developments that the sea masses have been divided into three oceans, the Atlantic, the Pacific and the Indian, which are enclosed between continental masses, and into numerous seas. The latter fill the inlets and surround the promontories of the continental coastlines, such as the Mediterranean Sea, the Baltic Sea, and the Red Sea; then there are the coastal waters which form the China and Arabian seas, and the island seas, such as the Celebes Sea.

Oceans and seas vary considerably in depth. The continental shelf stretches along almost all the continental coastlines. This is a gently sloping underwater area at a depth ranging from sea level to about 180 metres. The greatest depths have been found to correspond with the oceanic trenches: 11,033 metres in the Marianas Trench and the trenches of Tonga, Curili and the Philippines, all in the Pacific Ocean and all descending to more than 10,000 metres. The deepest Atlantic rift is that of Puerto Rico (9,212 metres), and in the Indian Ocean that of Java (7,450 metres).

One of the most considerable and obvious differences between seas is their degree of salinity. Sea water is in fact a salt solution. The percentage of salt is about 3·5 per cent and consists mainly of sodium chloride. Hence 1 kilogramme of sea water contains about 35 grammes of dissolved elements. Sea water also contains magnesium chloride, calcium sulphate and potassium chloride. The salinity varies according to evaporation (4·2 per cent in the Red Sea) and with the influx of fresh water from the continental rivers.

The temperature of the sea surface also varies in relation to latitude and seasonal heat patterns. In the ocean depths, it is more or less uniform, varying between 2°C in Equatorial areas and −2°C in polar. There are three types of movement in oceanic sea water masses. The waves are determined mainly by wind. The tides are governed by the gravitational pull of the Sun and Moon. Ocean currents are caused by chemical and physical variations in the various water masses.

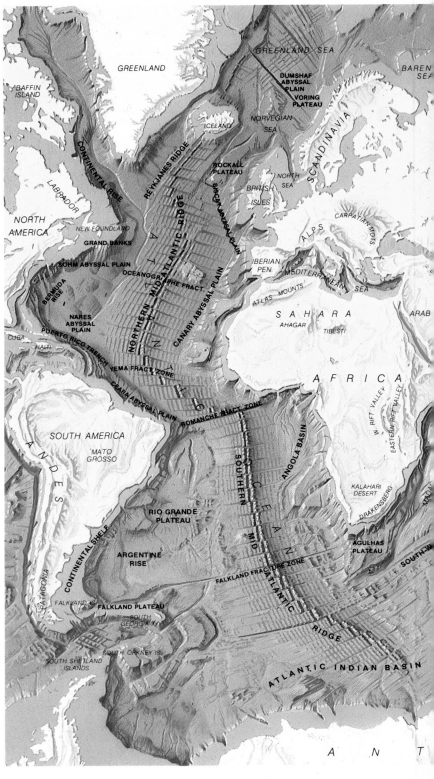

Submarine landscape
Science and modern technology have revealed to us the complex morphology of the ocean depths, where majestic mountain chains (ridges) alternate with the trenches and the continental shelf.

A) Continental (granitic) plate
B) Shallow continental shelf
C) Basaltic crust
D) Oceanic trench
E) Mantle
F) Central ocean ridge
G) Guyot (submarine mountain with flat top)
H) Volcano
I) Oceanic islands

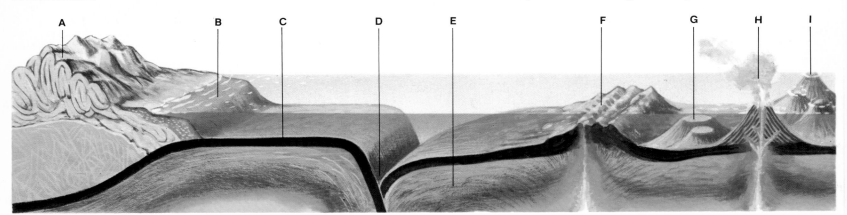

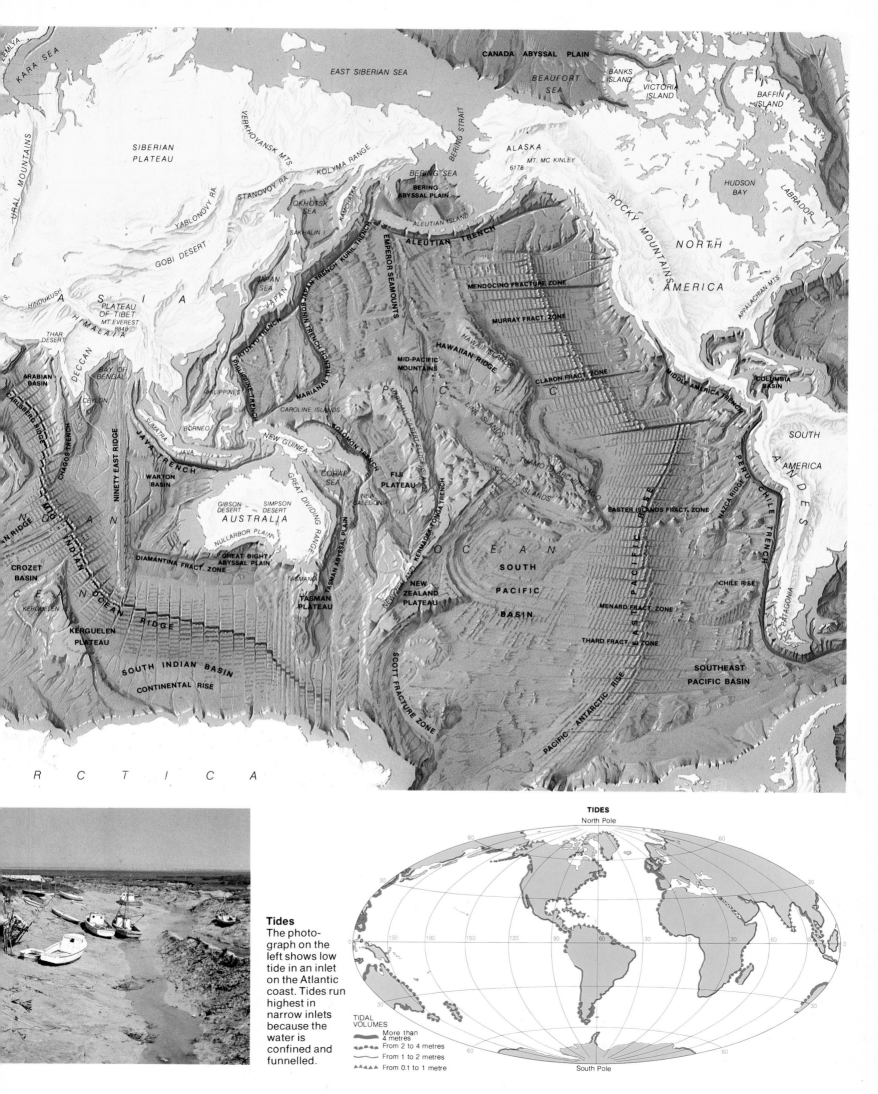

Tides
The photograph on the left shows low tide in an inlet on the Atlantic coast. Tides run highest in narrow inlets because the water is confined and funnelled.

TIDAL VOLUMES
More than 4 metres
From 2 to 4 metres
From 1 to 2 metres
From 0.1 to 1 metre

TROPICAL CLIMATES

Hot and humid

Hot with summer rains

ARID CLIMATES

Steppes

Deserts

The hot and humid (Equatorial) climates and hot climates with summer rains are prevalent in the inter-tropical zones, such as the Amazon and Zaïre basins, the islands of the Indonesian archipelago and New Guinea. The annual rainfall here is about 2,000 millimetres, while daily temperatures may vary widely.

Arid climates prevail in the hot and cold desert zones. It is in the former that the Earth's highest temperatures are recorded (59°C in the Dasht e Lut, a desert in eastern Iran), and in the latter there is a clearly defined cold season, with temperatures below many degrees below zero.

TEMPERATE CLIMATES

Mediterranean

Continental

Oceanic

Temperate climates vary according to latitude and to proximity to the sea, the sea having a moderating effect. Temperate climates are of three kinds, Mediterranean, continental and oceanic, and they have four distinct seasons. Europe has a temperate climate.

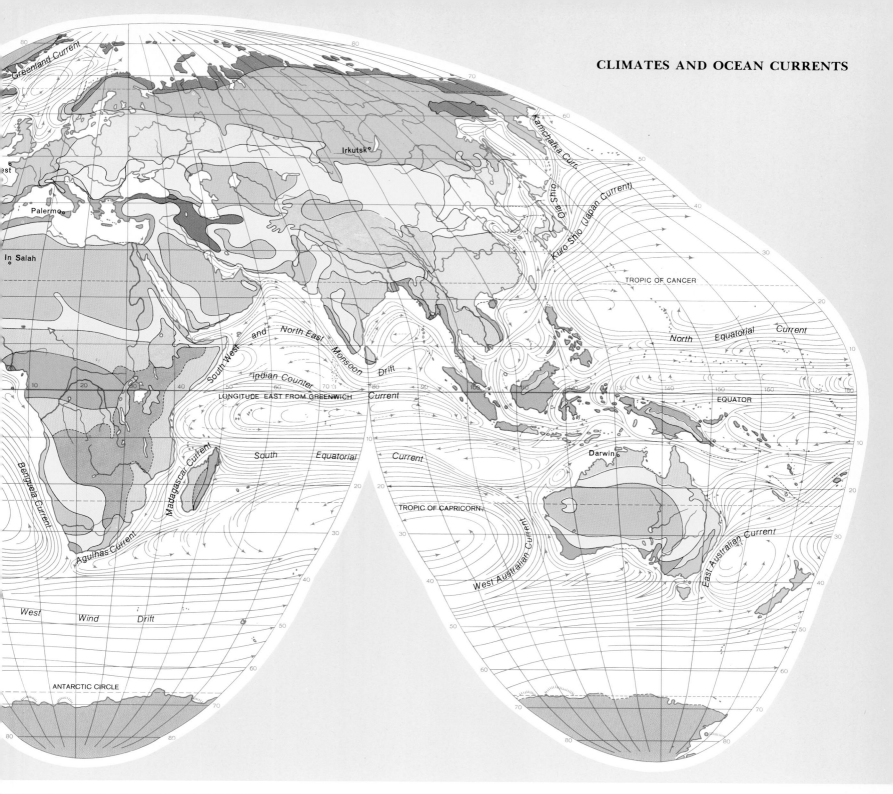

Greenland Current

Irkutsk

Palermo

In Salah

Kamchatka Curr.

Oya Shio

Kuro Shio (Japan Current)

TROPIC OF CANCER

South West and North East Monsoon Drift

Indian Counter Current

LONGITUDE EAST FROM GREENWICH

North Equatorial Current

EQUATOR

Benguela Current

Madagascar Current

South Equatorial Current

Darwin

Agulhas Current

TROPIC OF CAPRICORN

West Australian Current

East Australian Current

West Wind Drift

ANTARCTIC CIRCLE

COLD CLIMATES

Continental (hot summers)

Continental (cool summers)

Sub-arctic

Continental masses also strongly influence cold climates, which may be differentiated from one another on the basis of their average summer temperatures, which are sometimes higher than 20°C.

COLD CLIMATES IN HIGH MOUNTAIN AREAS

Altitude, latitude and exposure are the factors which largely characterise the cold high mountain climates, where in the hottest month the average temperature is less than 10°C. The temperature drops with the altitude, in the Alps by 0.5°C per 100 metres on the north face, and by 0.6°C on the south. Above a certain height there is permanent snow.

POLAR CLIMATES

Tundra

Ice all the year round

Areas of polar climate, with a covering of tundra and constantice, have temperatures in the hottest month between 0 and 10°C, whilst winter temperatures can fall to −30°C or even lower. Very few people live in these areas.

Rainfall

Atmospheric humidity, or the amount of water vapour contained in the air, derives from evaporation from the ocean and lake surfaces. The quantity is not infinite but is a function of the temperature. In fact at 0°C the air can contain a maximum of 4.8 grammes of water vapour per cubic metre, whilst at 25°C, the figure is 32.8 grammes per cubic metre. Rainfall depends on the condensation of water, and has a very varied distribution. Maximum annual rainfall occurs along the Equator, where hot and humid air masses occur. Rainfall is lowest at a latitude of about 30°, due to the presence of permanent tropical anticyclones. The highest annual rainfall ever recorded was in Assam (26,401 millimetres) in the monsoon region.

ANNUAL PRECIPITATION

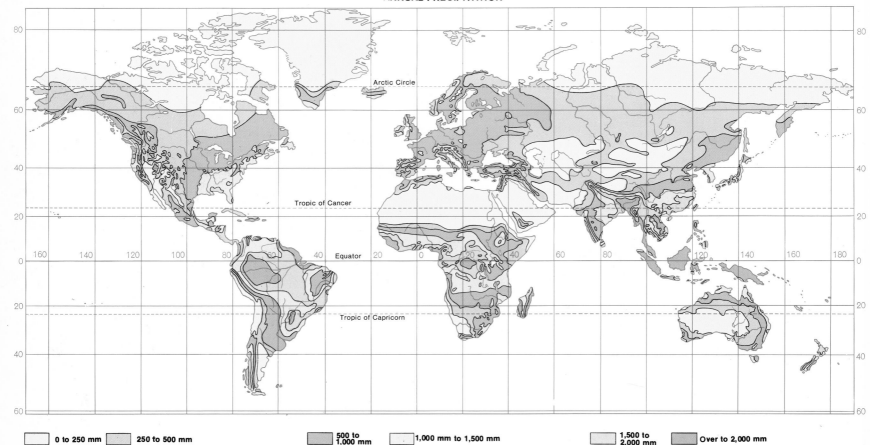

0 to 250 mm	250 to 500 mm
500 to 1,000 mm	1,000 mm to 1,500 mm
1,500 to 2,000 mm	Over to 2,000 mm

Areas of scanty rainfall (between 0 and 500 millimetres) are found in two belts around the tropics. There is also low precipitation in the polar regions, where high pressure prevails as a result of cold air masses containing little moisture.

Areas with annual rainfall between 500 and 1,500 millimetres are found at central latitudes, where tropical and polar air masses converge. The land relief has a considerable influence on the distribution of rainfall.

Areas with the heaviest rainfall (between 1,500 and more than 2,000 millimetres) are found at a latitude of 10° north and 5° south, where intense heating by the sun causes moisture-laden air to rise in fast upward currents, causing heavy rain.

The soil

Soil is formed as rock decomposes through chemical and physical processes, to create a soft topsoil, consisting of mineral particles, decomposed organic materials, water, air and living organisms. The type of soil, and therefore its suitability for farming purposes, depends, apart from the type of climate, upon the type of mother rock. In tropical rainy areas, for example, the soil is heavily leached, that is the rain dissolves various minerals. The red colour of these soils is caused by the presence of iron. Such soils are often infertile. The best types of soil are chernozems (black earths) which occur in steppes and prairies. They are coloured by humus formed from dead grass and are organically rich.

TYPES OF SOIL

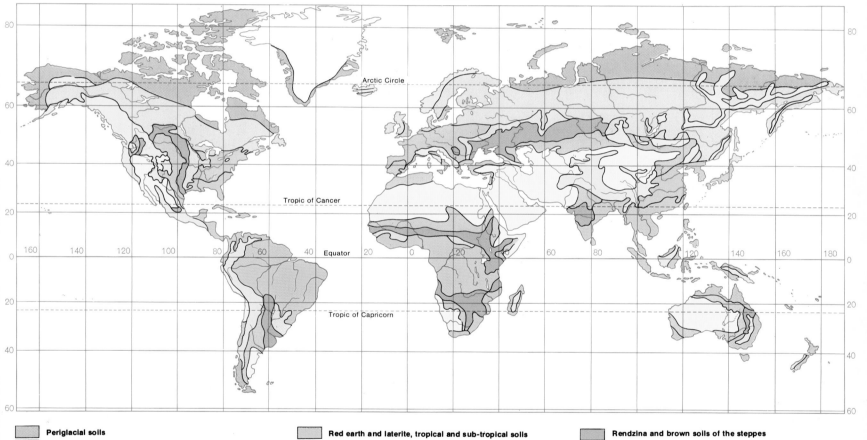

	Periglacial soils		Red earth and laterite, tropical and sub-tropical soils		Rendzina and brown soils of the steppes
	Podsols		Neutral prairie soils		Sandy desert soils
	Greyish-brown podsolic soils		Chernozems		Rendzina and other mountain soils

The grey ash soils of the taiga are known as podsolic soils. Bacterial activity in these soils is very much restricted by the low temperatures.

The red soils of the tropical zones, sometimes called laterites, are high in iron and aluminium. They derive from the leaching of elements in the soil.

The high temperatures and exceptionally low rainfall of deserts render the formation of proper soil almost impossible.

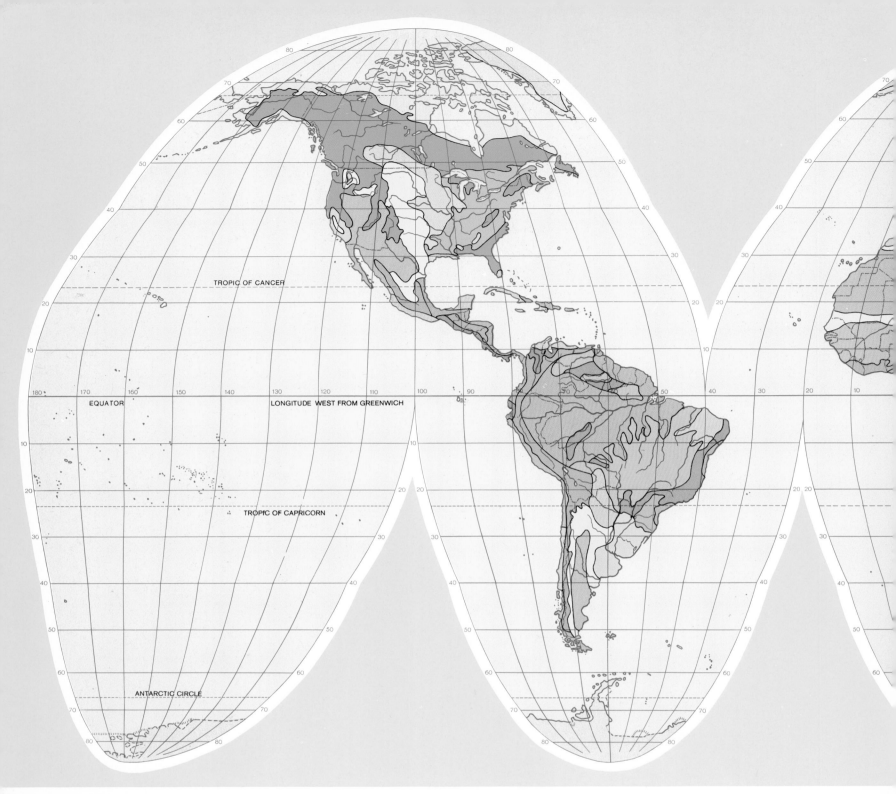

TROPIC OF CANCER

20

EQUATOR

LONGITUDE WEST FROM GREENWICH

TROPIC OF CAPRICORN

ANTARCTIC CIRCLE

Rain forest
Semi-deciduous tropical forest
Woodland

Plentiful rainfall and its even distribution throughout the year give rise in Equatorial regions to an abundance of natural vegetation. These are the rain forests, characterised by the wide variety of plant species, some of which are of high economic value. They include the *Hevea brasiliensis*, providing rubber, and ebony, rosewood, mahogany, oil and coconut palms, and banana plants.

Broad-leaved and mixed forests

Beech, chestnut and oak are the most typical and most widespread species in broad-leaved forests in the temperate regions, where trees are interspersed with undergrowth.

Mediterranean maquis

Maquis is characterised by its low growth – shrubs and drought-resistant bushes, olive trees, umbrella pines and vines are the main species.

Coniferous forests

Coniferous trees with needle-shaped leaves predominate in the coniferous forest zone, or taiga, sometimes along with birch and poplar. The undergrowth is scanty, consisting of herbaceous plants such as bilberries.

Tundra

The tundra vegetation is sparse Only mosses, lichens, some flowering plants and a few stunted trees survive the harsh conditions.

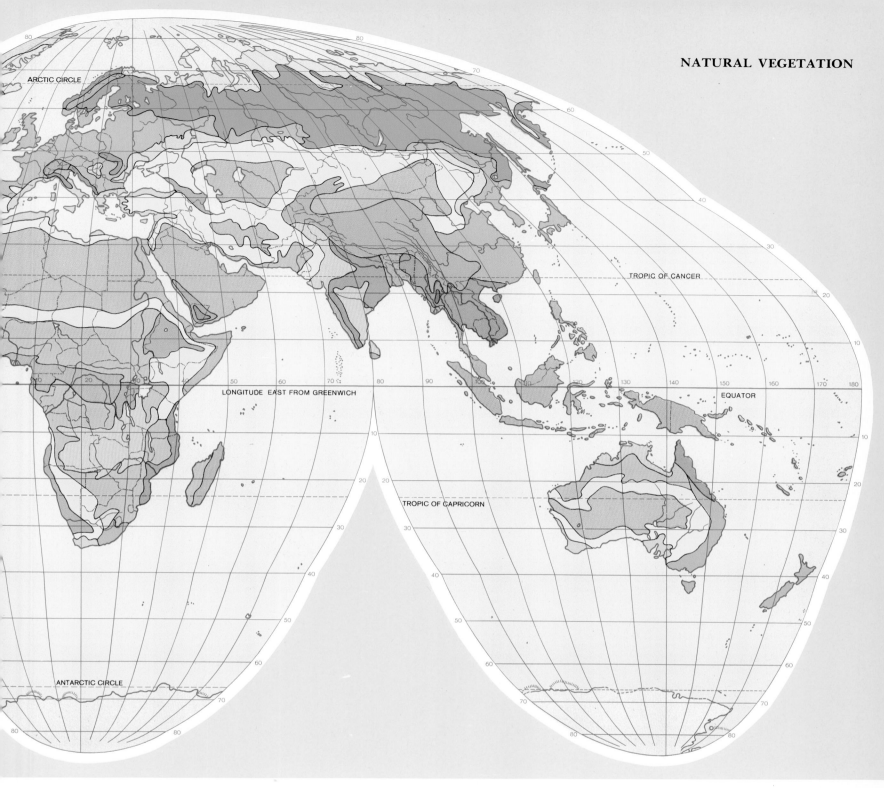

Herbaceous savannah

Prairie

Trees are few and far
between among the
grasses of the prairies.
The moisture is
concentrated in a shallow
layer, and only plants
with roots extending
horizontally can thrive.

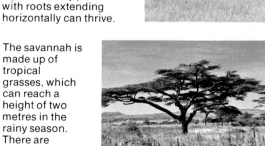

The savannah is
made up of
tropical
grasses, which
can reach a
height of two
metres in the
rainy season.
There are
scattered trees,
such as the
baobab.

Steppes in the tropics
and at central latitudes

The steppes are more
barren than the prairies
and have fewer trees.

Deserts

Only drought-resistant
plants (xerophyles) with
long roots are able to
thrive in desert regions.

High mountain
vegetation

The period of plant
growth in mountain
regions is short.
Broad-leaved trees in the
Alps are found up to
1,700 metres, though
coniferous trees grow up
to over 2,000 metres.
Then there is grass,
mosses and lichens

Ice caps

Obviously plant growth is
not possible where the
land is permanently
covered with ice. Mosses,
lichens and sparse
woody bushes are found
in the small open spaces,
but their growth is
severely limited.

21

| | Uninhabited regions | | 0–1 inhabitants per square kilometre | | 1–10 inhabitants per square kilometre | | 10–25 inhabitants per square kilometre |

Population

About 27 million square kilometres of the Earth's land surface are totally and permanently uninhabited. These are areas where the special climatic conditions are hostile to Man, except where he can create very small microclimates in which to survive, as scientists do in research establishments in Antarctica. Such areas are the polar and circumpolar regions (17 million square kilometres) and, within the habitable world, the deserts, dense forests and high mountains.

The sub-polar regions of Canada, the Amazon forest, the cold deserts of Asia, the hot deserts of Australia and Africa – these are areas of very low population density. Below, desert dwellers in Africa.

The areas which are almost uninhabited are usually surrounded by areas where the population is greater, and where climatic and physical conditions are less harsh. Some of these are the semi-desert, steppe and heathland regions, where there are no more than 10 inhabitants per square kilometre.

Areas where the population density is between 10 and 25 inhabitants per square kilometre are often isolated pockets of land surrounded by less inhabited regions. Some areas of South America, for example, come into this category, as well as large tracts of the eastern USA.

22

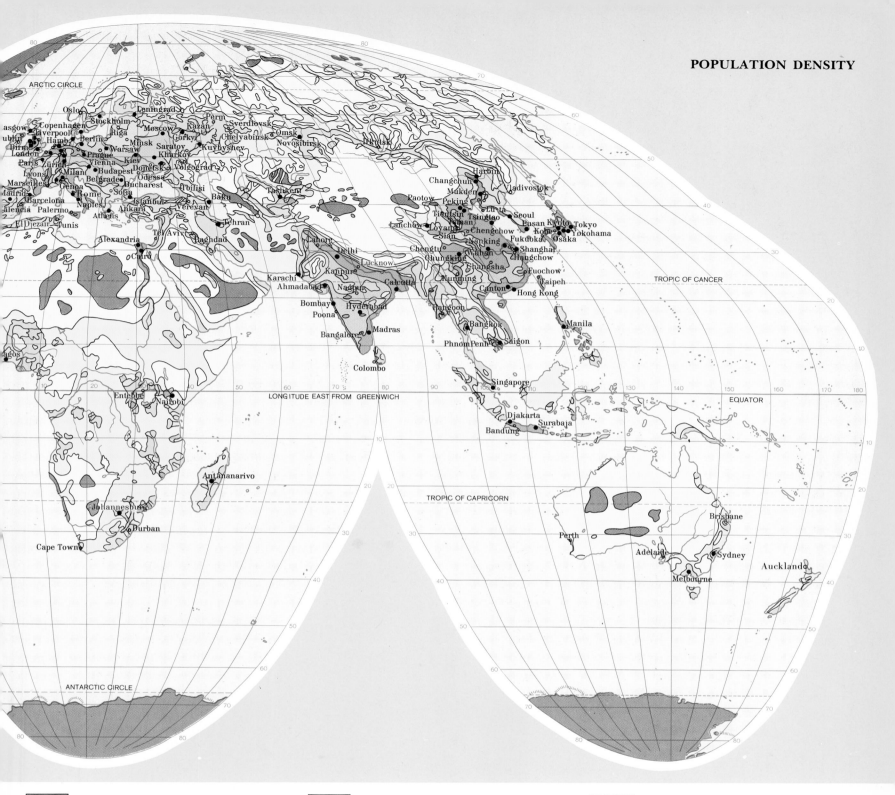

ARCTIC CIRCLE

Oslo Stockholm Leningrad Perm Sverdlovsk
asgow Copenhagen Riga Moscow Kazan
Liverpool Hamb Berlin Minsk Saratov Kuybyshev Chelyabinsk Omsk
ublin Birm Prague Warsaw Kiev Kharkov Volgograd Novosibirsk Irkutsk
London Paris Zürich Vienna Budapest Donetsk Odessa
Lyons Milan Belgrade Bucharest Tbilisi Tashkent
Marseilles Geno Rome Sofia Baku
adrid Barcelona Naples Istanbul Yerevan
alencia Palermo Athens Ankara Tehran
El Djezair Tunis Tel Aviv Baghdad

Changchun Harbin
Mukden Vladivostok
Paotow Peking
Tientsin Lu ta Seoul Kyoto Tokyo
Lanchow Tsinan Tsingtao Busan Kobe Osaka Yokohama
Loyang Fukuoka
Sian Nanking
Chengtu Chungking Wuhan Shanghai
Changsha Hangchow
Kunming Fuochow
Canton Taipeh
Hong Kong

Alexandria
Cairo

Lahore Delhi
Karachi Kanpur Lucknow
Ahmadabad Nagpur Calcutta
Bombay Hyderabad
Poona
Bangalore Madras
Colombo

Rangoon
Bangkok
PhnomPenh Saigon Manila

Singapore

LONGITUDE EAST FROM GREENWICH

Entebbe
Nairobi

Djakarta
Bandung Surabaja

Antananarivo

TROPIC OF CAPRICORN

Brisbane

Johannesburg
Durban

Perth
Adelaide Sydney
Auckland
Melbourne

Cape Town

ANTARCTIC CIRCLE

TROPIC OF CANCER

EQUATOR

| | 25–50 inhabitants per square kilometre | | 50–100 inhabitants per square kilometre | | Over 100 inhabitants per square kilometre |

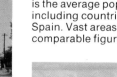

Parts of Europe, mainly in the east, have a population density of between 25 and 50 inhabitants per square kilometre. In other continents, if we exclude some Asian countries such as India and China, a population of this density is rather unusual. Below, horse-drawn transport is still widely used in eastern Europe.

Between 50 and 100 inhabitants per square kilometre is the average population density in most of Europe, including countries such as France, Austria and Spain. Vast areas in India and China also have a comparable figure.

There are a few areas of high population density, in the northern hemisphere and in temperate zones. This high concentration is made possible either by the climatic and land conditions, such as in the fertile delta regions of China and India, or by economic, political and social factors. For example in Europe, the Industrial Revolution, and, in North America, immigration from Europe have created areas of high population density.

The evolution of Man

The origin and development of early Man is a fascinating but problematical area of research. We have only some fragments of bone, mainly jawbones and teeth, on which to base our theories as to the nature and evolution of our forebears.

Their first beginnings are lost in a period which, though geologically quite recent, is historically almost beyond our powers to imagine, millions of years ago. Scientists at present favour the theory that our species and that of the great apes have a common origin, going back between 15 and 20 million years. From fossils discovered in Africa, India and Europe, they believe that these creatures were very different both from the great apes of today and from Man as we know him. It is however highly probable that, from these tree-dwelling hominids, the group emerged which left the forest, started to walk on two legs and looked to the soil for its source of food. They evolved into modern Man.

Early Man
Homo erectus may have descended from *Australopithecus*, which lived in Africa between 4 and 1 million years ago. The remains of *Homo erectus* discovered in the Old World are between 1,000,000 and 5,000,000 years old. *Homo erectus* used tools fashioned from stone, could make fires, and banded into groups which survived by hunting game. He is regarded as the direct ancestor of *Homo sapiens*, of which we know of various forms at various times, thanks to numerous discoveries in Africa, Asia and Europe. *Homo sapiens* is divided into several sub-species, the most notable being *Homo sapiens neanderthalensis*, who lived in the last Ice Age, during which, about 40,000 years ago, *Homo sapiens sapiens*, or modern Man, first appeared.

Discoveries
Pre-hominoid discoveries are restricted almost exclusively to central South America and Africa (*Australopithecus, Ramapithecus*), whilst quantities of remains of the genus *Homo* have been discovered in Europe. Few traces have been found of *Homo erectus*, but remains of various sub-species of *Homo sapiens* (*Homo sapiens steinheimensis, Homo sapiens neanderthalensis, Homo sapiens sapiens*) have been discovered in many places, notably in Tanzania. Fossils of Neanderthal, Steinheim and Cro-Magnon Man have been found in Europe.

■ *Ramapithecus*   ▲ *Homo erectus*
● *Australopithecus*   ★ *Homo sapiens*

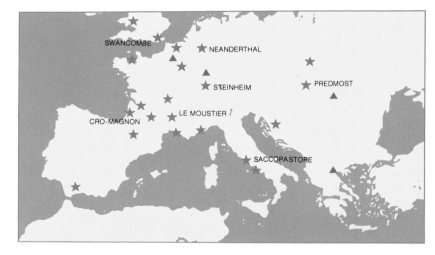

Man the hunter who populates the world
His ability to hunt in groups, and to move around or travel considerable distances permitted *Homo erectus* to move from Central Africa, probably along the valley of the Nile, to the tropical regions of India and south-east Asia, and from there into Europe. During a period of hot climate, about 150,000 to 200,000 years ago, a sub-species of *Homo sapiens*, *Homo sapiens steinheimensis*, populated the plains of northern Europe. After a period of intense cold, accompanied by glaciation, this people was succeeded by another, with different cranial structure, known today by the name Neanderthal. These people occupied western Europe until the final Ice Age, the Pleistocene, and was in its turn replaced by modern Man, about 35,000 to 40,000 years ago. The New World was populated by *Homo sapiens* much later on. The earliest people in North America arrived there around 20,000 years ago. Probably groups of hunters moved into Alaska from Siberia during the final Ice Age, when the two countries were linked by an ice bridge. The population of North and South America was due to the alternation of glaciation and interglacial warmth, causing hunting populations to move in pursuit of migrating fauna and flora, their sources of food.

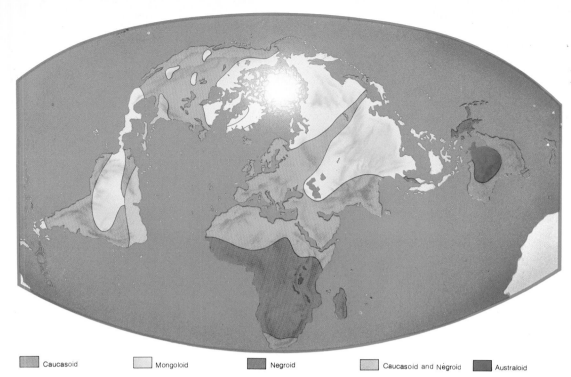

Mongoloids
The classic mongoloids have yellowish skin, straight hair and slanting eyes. They are found throughout Asia (with the exception of part of India and the Middle East) and in the eastern part of Madagascar.

Negroids
Living in central and southern Africa, the western part of Madagascar, Australia, the Philippines and the Indonesian islands, they usually have dark skins and curly hair.

Caucasoids
Found throughout Europe, Arabia, India and northern Africa, the caucasoids have many different outward appearances. For example, the colour of their skin varies from whitish to brown.

| | Caucasoid | | Mongoloid | | Negroid | | Caucasoid and Negroid | | Australoid |

Races

Whilst belonging to the same species *(Homo sapiens)*, human beings differ considerably in their physical characteristics. At one end of the spectrum are the tall Nordic types, with pale eyes and blond hair, at the other the African pygmies, small in stature, with dark skin and black hair. Taking account of the physical and psychological aspects, anthropologists tend to sub-divide the human species into three large groups or races: Caucasoid, Mongoloid and Negroid, whose distribution in the various continents is shown in the map above. This is not, however, a rigid classification. In fact many peoples fall into categories somewhere between these groupings, and there are also considerable variations within the groups themselves.

Migrations

The distribution of groups of human beings has altered considerably over the centuries, and noticeable changes are still taking place. Large movements of populations have taken place on political, economic and religious grounds, and these have sometimes changed the ethnic picture of entire continents. The map on the right shows the main migration patterns from the 16th century to the present day. The European influence is clearly shown. Europeans came several times to settle in North and South America, Africa and Australia. There has also been a great deal of movement within the continent of Europe itself.

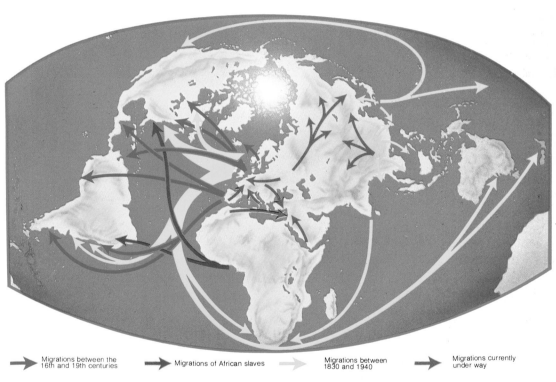

→ Migrations between the 16th and 19th centuries → Migrations of African slaves → Migrations between 1830 and 1940 → Migrations currently under way

LANGUAGES

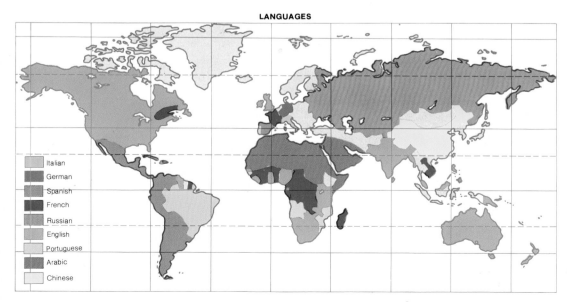

	Italian
	German
	Spanish
	French
	Russian
	English
	Portuguese
	Arabic
	Chinese

Languages

Along with race and religion, there is one other element which distinguishes the inhabitants of Earth from one another – their language. It is hard to say how many languages there are, and not always possible to distinguish between language and dialect. The theory is, however, that more than 2,500 tongues are spoken on Earth; some, like Basque, by only small groups of people, some, like English, by millions every day. Generally, classification may be made on historical grounds – languages of common origin being grouped at various levels. Italian, Spanish, Portuguese and French, for instance, are grouped together as the Romance languages, because all derive from the same Latin root. Historical factors also contribute to the spread of language, this being particularly evident with some European tongues, which have spread to many continents. The most obvious example is that of English, which was taken to North America in the early migrations, and then spread to many parts of the world, such as Africa and Australia, as a result of colonialism.

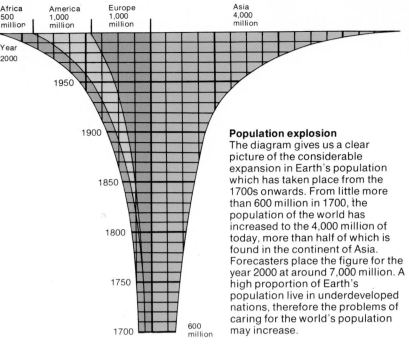

Africa
500
million

America
1,000
million

Europe
1,000
million

Asia
4,000
million

Year
2000

1950

1900

1850

1800

1750

1700

600
million

Population explosion
The diagram gives us a clear picture of the considerable expansion in Earth's population which has taken place from the 1700s onwards. From little more than 600 million in 1700, the population of the world has increased to the 4,000 million of today, more than half of which is found in the continent of Asia. Forecasters place the figure for the year 2000 at around 7,000 million. A high proportion of Earth's population live in underdeveloped nations, therefore the problems of caring for the world's population may increase.

Population

The world's total population, its distribution into areas and its numerical and geographical evolution provide us with data indispensable to the analysis of our major political and economic problems of present-day life. In only a few centuries, the Earth's population has increased dramatically, from about 500 million in 1650 to more than 4,000 million today, and according to the forecasts, there will be no reversal of this trend in the short term.

At first sight, population increase is linked with shifts in the balance of natural and social development. National populations are, in fact, determined by the relative difference between birth and death rates, and are sometimes also influenced by emigration and immigration figures. Clearly such variations depend in their turn upon economic, social and political factors. The recent population explosion on a worldwide scale, for instance, is largely linked with technical and scientific progress, which has improved the standard of living, caused a drop in the infant and child mortality rates, and an increased life expectancy.

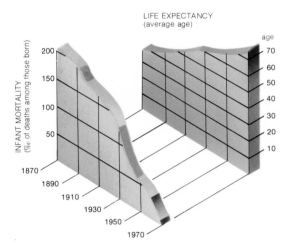

LIFE EXPECTANCY
(average age)

Infant mortality and life expectancy
The graph above contrasts the figures for infant mortality with those for life expectancy over the last hundred years. On a world level, the rate of infant mortality, which was about 200 per 1,000 births in 1870, has shown a marked reduction. Life expectancy, and thus the average age obtained, is now more than 70 years in Western Europe. These figures vary considerably, however, according to geographical location. In southern Africa, the average life expectancy is only 40 years.

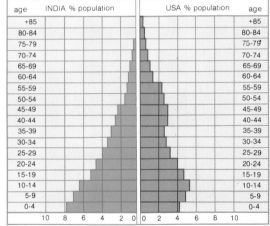

Distribution of populations by age
The graph above compares the percentage distribution of the population by age in a country of advanced economic development (United States) and in an underdeveloped country (India). It is obvious that in India the percentage drops steadily with advancing age, and the people do not generally live beyond 80. In the USA, the variations are more marked. Numbers are declining at the lower age levels, due to the drop in the birth rate which is a feature in all industrialised countries today.

Rate of population increase
In the industrialised countries which already have a high population density (large areas of Europe and the United States), the annual rate of population increase has shown a marked reduction and is currently less than 1 per cent. Major increases (between 2 and 3 per cent and over) are recorded in underdeveloped areas, where the economy is in a period of transition. This is true in particular of large areas of Africa, Asia, and South and Central America, where a limited improvement in living conditions has brought about a drop in the mortality rate, especially among new-born babies.

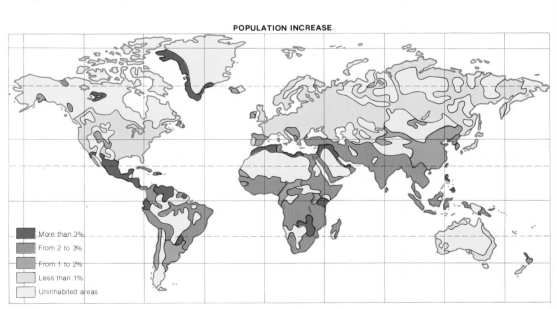

POPULATION INCREASE

More than 3%
From 2 to 3%
From 1 to 2%
Less than 1%
Uninhabited areas

Urbanisation

Urbanisation is not a development exclusive to the twentieth century, nor is it confined to the more advanced countries. The first urban development took place in Sumeria, in the 4th century before Christ, whilst at the height of its splendour, the city of Rome had more than half a million inhabitants. However, it is certainly only since the Industrial Revolution, which began in the late 18th century, that urbanisation has assumed its present form – perhaps the most representative feature of twentieth-century society.

The development of the city, and the attraction is exerts, on people in surrounding districts, is in porportion to its industrial development, the facilities it provides, and the importance of the city itself. In some areas of Europe, such as Belgium, Holland and France, the urban population currently exceeds 70 per cent. In areas of lesser economic development, the percentages are lower (Egypt 44 per cent, India 21 per cent), but the exodus from the country to the city continues. However, the problems created by rapid urbanisation, which have emerged in recent times, appear common to cities both in industrialised and also in under-developed regions.

The city
In many countries, Italy for example (above, a photograph of Florence), cities have grown up around small pockets of habitation whose history is lost in the mists of antiquity. The impact of an industrial civilisation upon urban structures which go back to the Middle Ages and beyond, naturally poses some serious problems. Access is one, pollution another, along with high population density and lack of free space. These problems also affect the suburbs. Right, an aerial photograph of the suburbs of Milan.

The megalopolis
In some countries, towns keep on growing until they join up with other towns, forming an almost uninterrupted urban sprawl, heavily built upon and with high population density. An area of this type is designated a megalopolis, the largest of which is on the east coast of America and extends from Boston to Washington, taking in New York City.

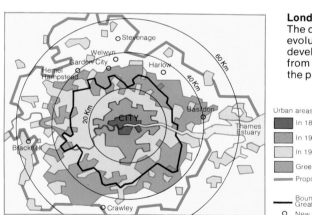

London
The diagram shows the evolution and urban development of London, from the mid 1800s up to the present day (left).

Urban areas
- In 1850
- In 1914
- In 1960
- Green Belt
- Proposed Green Belt extension
- Boundaries of the Greater London area
- ○ New centres

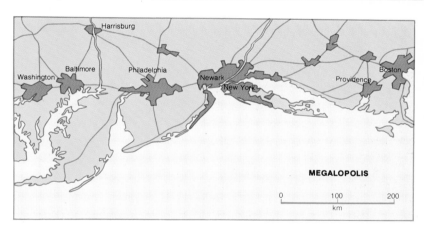

MEGALOPOLIS

0   100   200
km

DENSELY POPULATED CITIES

EUROPE		AFRICA	
Moscow	7,172,000	Cairo	5,300,000
London	6,918,000	Alexandria	2,032,000
Leningrad	4,133,000	Kinshasa	2,500,000
Madrid	3,150,000	Lagos	1,000,000
Rome	2,843,000	AMERICA	
Paris	2,590,000	New York	
Athens	2,540,000	City	11,570,000
Budapest	1,959,000	Mexico City	9,618,000
Vienna	1,615,000	Buenos	
ASIA		Aires	8,353,000
Tokyo	11,600,000	Rio de	
Shanghai	10,820,000	Janeiro	7,094,000
Peking	7,570,000	Los Angeles	7,032,000
Calcutta	7,030,000	Chicago	6,979,000
Bombay	5,970,000	Philadelphia	4,818,000
Seoul	6,879,000	Detroit	4,430,000
Djarkarta	6,000,000	Lima	3,600,000
Teheran	4,496,000	OCEANIA	
Delhi	4,070,000	Sydney	2,874,000
Tientsin	3,600,000	Melbourne	2,584,000

MAJOR URBAN AREAS

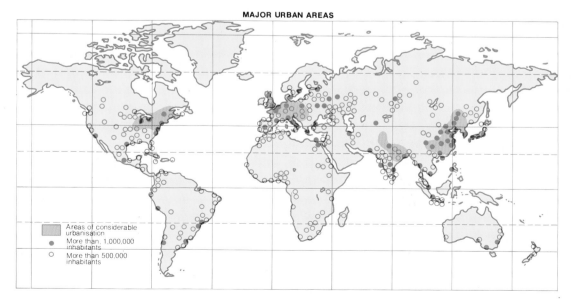

Areas of considerable urbanisation
- ● More than 1,000,000 inhabitants
- ○ More than 500,000 inhabitants

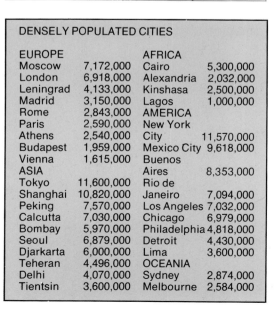

TROPIC OF CANCER

EQUATOR
LONGITUDE WEST FROM GREENWICH

TROPIC OF CAPRICORN

ANTARCTIC CIRCLE

Coastal fishing areas

More than 70 million tonnes of fish are taken from these waters annually, mainly along the continental shelf.

Mining areas

These are found both in areas with a high standard of living and in the underdeveloped regions, where minerals form valuable natural resources.

Areas without an organised economy

These are the areas where there are no stable centres of settlement.

Nomadic pastoralists

The numbers of nomadic pastoralists are dwindling all the time, though they were formerly characteristic features of the vast desert areas and steppe heathlands of Africa and Asia. Some such peoples are the Tuareg in the Sahara, the Bedouins of Arabia and the Mongols of Central Asia, and they move periodically in search of fresh pasture land and water for their flocks. Urban development and industry, followed by oil extraction in desert areas of this type, are now causing people to stay much more in one place.

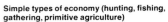

Simple types of economy (hunting, fishing, gathering, primitive agriculture)

Areas where the population engages in hunting, fishing, simple harvesting and very primitive agriculture are those which are sparsely inhabited, such as the Amazon Forest, the Zaire Basin and New Guinea. Small groups of people in these types of areas continue to live at bare subsistence level. The pygmies, for example, are hunters, and also collect fruit, roots and other things which they have not cultivated.

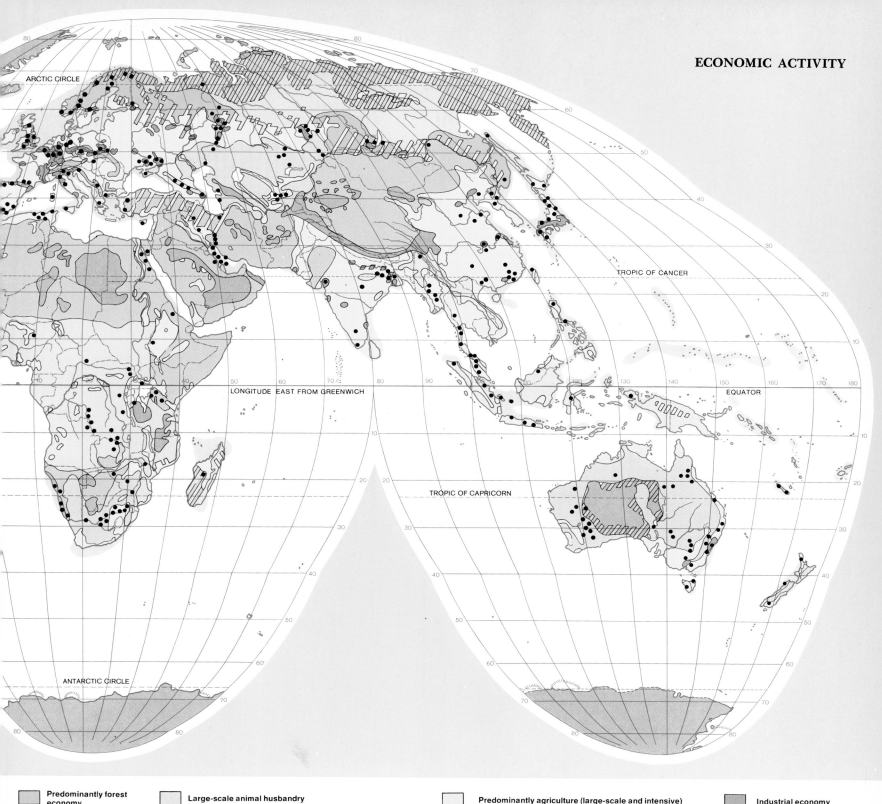

ARCTIC CIRCLE

80

70

60

50

40

TROPIC OF CANCER

30

20

10

LONGITUDE EAST FROM GREENWICH

EQUATOR

10

TROPIC OF CAPRICORN

20

30

40

50

60

ANTARCTIC CIRCLE

70

80

| | Predominantly forest economy | | Large-scale animal husbandry | | Predominantly agriculture (large-scale and intensive) | | Industrial economy |

Traditional animal husbandry is practised on a large scale in vast tracts of central Asia, the Americas and Africa, although the methods are often technically and economically backward.

A predominantly forest economy occurs only in the central northern belt of the temperate zone, where use is made of coniferous timber (pine, conifer and larch) and of birchwood. There is no forest belt in the southern hemisphere.

There are two main kinds of agricultural activity. The type practised in Europe, part of the United States and other countries of high economic development involves the use of modern techniques and a high yield is obtained with low manpower. The other type, using traditional methods, is expensive in terms of labour and productivity is comparatively low.

Many countries now have a highly developed economy based primarily on industry as in Europe, North America and Japan. A high degree of industrial development is accompanied by complex financial and commercial activity.

29

Energy

For centuries the muscle power of man and beast was the type of energy most commonly in use, along with the forces of wind and water. It was from the 18th century onwards that, thanks to technical and scientific developments, coal began to be used on a large scale to provide mechanical power and heat. Then electrical energy came to the fore, produced either in power stations or in hydroelectric installations, opening the way to industrial development for many countries which did not have their own raw materials. Then it was the turn of hydrocarbons, especially oil. This was easy to extract and, until recently, was relatively cheap, so that it became the source of energy most widely used.

Continued expansion of industry, the increased use of motor vehicles, political tensions, and the danger that the hydrocarbon resources will soon be exhausted have encouraged research and development into other energy sources, such as nuclear energy and solar energy.

Energy consumption
The amount of energy consumed annually per head of population can be a good indication of the level of any country's development. As we see from the map the highest consumption of energy is found in mainly industrialised areas, where income per capita is high (the USA, for example).

The same applies to almost all the countries of Europe, and to the USSR and Canada, where consumption is only slightly less. Industry, especially the metal and chemical industries, along with the domestic consumption, account for this accentuated energy use. Consumption is considerably lower in most other regions, but is increasing all the time.

CONSUMPTION OF ENERGY

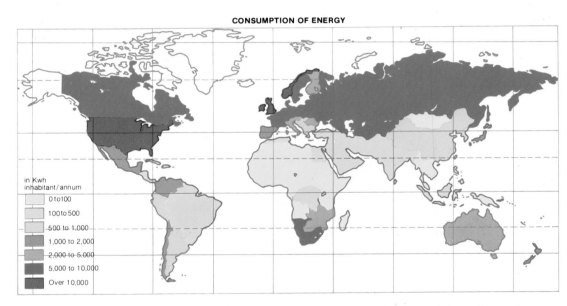

in Kwh
inhabitant/annum
- 0 to 100
- 100 to 500
- 500 to 1,000
- 1,000 to 2,000
- 2,000 to 5,000
- 5,000 to 10,000
- Over 10,000

Producer and consumer countries (below)
The map illustrates the fact that, throughout the world, oil-producer and oil-consumer countries are rarely one and the same. The most striking instance is that of the Arab countries, which produce almost one third of the world's total oil supplies, and export the entire amount. The USSR is a special case, there being a balance between production and consumption. The USA, although it has abundant reserves, consumes more oil than it produces.

WORLD ENERGY CONSUMPTION

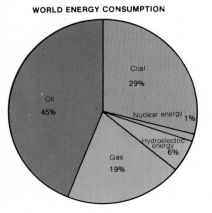

Coal 29%
Oil 45%
Nuclear energy 1%
Hydroelectric energy 6%
Gas 19%

Categories of world energy consumption
As we see from the illustration on the left, more than half the energy now consumed in the world is obtained from hydrocarbons (oil and natural gas). The percentage increase in the use of these energy sources goes back to the early decades of the twentieth century. Coal, which up to about 1910 accounted for almost 70 per cent of total consumption, is now reduced to less than 33 per cent. The percentage of nuclear energy in use is at the moment quite small, as its production involves high costs and an advanced technology.

WORLD OIL PRODUCTION AND CONSUMPTION

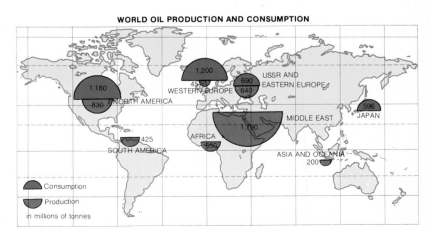

1.200
WESTERN EUROPE 45
1.160
NORTH AMERICA 830
690
USSR AND EASTERN EUROPE 640
596
JAPAN
425
SOUTH AMERICA
AFRICA 556
1.790 MIDDLE EAST
ASIA AND OCEANIA 200

- Consumption
- Production
in millions of tonnes

Economy and society

The size and development of population, increased urbanisation and industrialisation, technical and scientific development, the distribution of lines of communication, the efficiency of methods of transport and availability of resources – these are some of the many factors which condition to some degree our economic development, and thus also the standard of living of the peoples of the world.

There is a stark contrast today between those few countries with an abundance of natural resources which are sometimes wasted, and the many countries whose populations struggle for survival. The disparities between countries are enormous, as is illustrated by the map showing the per capita gross national product in 1974-75. The disparities are only partly attributable to the presence of natural resources. It is easy to see that many countries in the process of development have an abundance of resources (minerals and foodstuffs) but that their exploitation has only limited advantages for the producer countries.

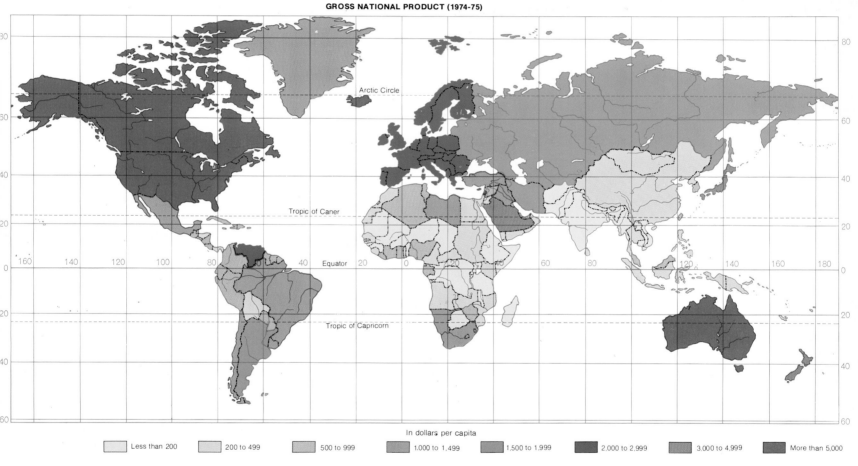

GROSS NATIONAL PRODUCT (1974-75)

In dollars per capita

Less than 200	200 to 499	500 to 999	1,000 to 1,499	1,500 to 1,999	2,000 to 2,999	3,000 to 4,999	More than 5,000

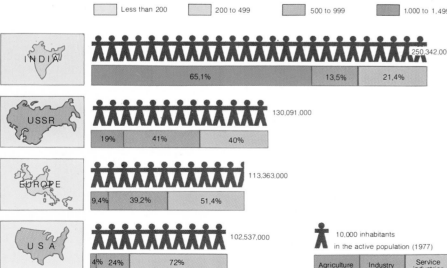

INDIA — 250,342,000 — 65,1% | 13,5% | 21,4%

USSR — 130,091,000 — 19% | 41% | 40%

EUROPE — 113,363,000 — 9,4% | 39,2% | 51,4%

USA — 102,537,000 — 4% | 24% | 72%

10,000 inhabitants in the active population (1977)

| Agriculture | Industry | Service industries |

Occupations

The diagram on the left compares the various sectors of economic activity in four geographical areas of varying standards of living and with different social, economic and political structures. These areas are India, the USSR, the European Economic Community and the United States. It is clear how the percentage of those engaged in agriculture falls as economic prosperity increases. At the two extremes there is India, where more than half the active population is employed in agriculture, and the United States where the percentage is very small. The countries have diametrically opposite agricultural systems. On the one hand traditional subsistence agriculture in India employs a large number of people, is very much affected by natural conditions (above all by the climate and the soil) and is characterised by a very low level of productivity. On the other hand modern agriculture in the USA is characterised by intense mechanisation, high returns and a limited labour force. In the industrial sector the highest percentages of active employees are found at the intermediate levels (USSR and EEC), whilst the service industries are most developed in countries with the most advanced economies, where the metropolitan facilities and services (sanitation, education, transport) are most plentiful and advanced.

Food and nourishment

A useful indication of a population's living standard is found in the type and quantity of food it consumes, and inadequate nourishment is in fact a fundamental characteristic of many of the developing countries of the so-called Third World. It is linked, by cause and effect, to numerous other factors. Developing countries have a higher percentage of their population involved in agriculture, but yields are low and there is limited industrialisation. The fast increase in population also tends to nullify efforts to reduce the food shortage. Rates of population increase are higher in the Third World. Economic growth is slow as there is little or no money for development, and countries frequently become dependent on foreign aid and investment.

Recent studies have shown that today almost 2,000 million people do not have enough to eat, and that there is always a connection between food consumption and level of income. It has in fact been established that both total protein consumption and total calorie consumption increase with increasing income. The developing countries not only have a lower protein consumption in terms of quantity but also in terms of quality. Their diet is rarely varied, as is the diet of people in more developed countries. It often consists mainly of staple foods, rice perhaps, or cereals. Yields are usually low as fields are poorly irrigated and agricultural machinery and methods are out-dated. Reliance on one crop can also be dangerous, as a drought, for example, can ruin the crop and even cause famine.

Daily calorie consumption per inhabitant
The map on the right shows the amount of food available daily to each inhabitant of the countries of the world. It should be noted that, according to the Food and Agriculture Organisation's estimates, an intake of 1,600 calories per day is required in order to sustain a minimum amount of physical activity, whilst about 3,000 are required for a medium-intensity occupation. It is clear from the map that the regions of greatest food shortage coincide with the underdeveloped or developing areas, which are often densely populated. This applies to large areas of Africa and Asia, and many of the Andean countries of South America. The daily calorie consumption is quite adequate in the greater part of the northern hemisphere, and also in Australia and Argentina in the southern hemisphere. Canada, the United States, Australia and Argentina are also great exporters of foodstuffs, cereals in particular. In tropical countries, calorie consumption is markedly lower, and is frequently inadequate to the needs of the population.

PER CAPITA CALORIE CONSUMPTION

More than 2,900
2,500 to 2,899
2,100 to 2,499
Less than 2,100

Different foodstuffs available
The diagrams (below and left) serve to illustrate the quantity and quality of the food available daily to an American labourer and to an Indian peasant respectively. In the American diet, the food, apart from being plentiful, is varied, with fruit, milk and vegetables predominating; in the Indian diet, however, the staple ingredient is rice.

Fats
Eggs
Cereals
Sugar
Meat or fish
Milk
Fruit and vegetables

American labourer's diet
2,110 grammes a day

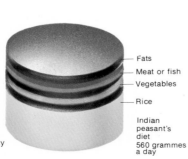

Fats
Meat or fish
Vegetables
Rice

Indian peasant's diet
560 grammes a day

Malnutrition
The effects of malnutrition and starvation, constituted by a prolonged reduction in diet to a point below the minimum required to sustain life, are evident amongst large populations and in vast tracts of our Earth. Many people among the populations of India, numerous African countries, Latin America and the Far East display such symptoms as loss of weight, hypertension, swellings caused by starvation and, particularly in children, retarded growth and conditions such as rickets.

Transport

The economic evolution of a country is fundamentally dependent upon its means of transport and lines of communication. The same is even truer on a world-wide scale today, where the requirements of trade, not only in the economic sector but also in the social and cultural sectors, can be met only if methods of transport and lines of communication develop more rapidly and interconnect more effectively with one another.

For ease of analysis, methods of transport are divided into: continental (road, rail), sea and air. However, obviously there are innumerable combinations of the three types, and for a system of communication to be complete and satisfactory, all transport sectors must develop in parallel with one another.

The range of means of transport, and the layout and density of various lines of communication, are frequently conditioned by natural factors (for instance relief, rivers, and geological and climatic conditions), though these are sometimes overcome by way of very expensive construction work such as bridges or tunnels. Other factors also have their influence – distance, costs, and the kind of goods to be transported.

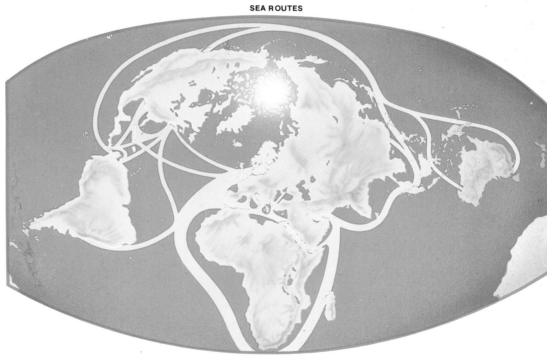

SEA ROUTES

Sea transport
There has been a continuous increase in the amount of goods carried by sea in the course of the 20th century. This is due to the moderate cost of sea transport, making it commerically viable for all goods which do not need to be carried quickly, such as raw materials and fuel. Although little used for passenger transport (ferries excepted), and for the carriage of goods over short distances, ships have increased their useful tonnage appreciably. The main sea routes are shown on the map on the right. Oil accounts for more than half (about 1.5 thousand million tonnes) of the goods carried overall.

Road transport
This ranks foremost in continental transport, above all for passengers and certain types of goods. Motorised transport is often quicker and more comfortable than rail although this is not necessarily true. It is also facilitated by the dense network of roads of various types – trunk roads, main roads and motorways – the development of which has accompanied and promoted the development of motorised transport in general, and the private car in particular. It is estimated that there are almost 34 million vehicles in use on our roads today.

Air transport
In less than 100 years air travel, the last on the scene of all intercontinental means of transport, has revolutionised our concept of distance. It is possible in only a few hours to reach almost any part of the Earth (the Atlantic is crossed in little more than three hours), thanks to the speed of our aircraft. There has been massive development from the 60s over the principal airline routes. Negative factors are the high costs not only of the planes themselves but also of airports, to which has recently been added the rise in the cost of aviation fuel.

Rail transport
The railways are in close competition with road transport and there has been much development in recent years of advanced passenger and freight trains to improve services. One of the most important areas for rail transport is long-distance passenger travel. For many types of goods, the train has to compete with the lorry, wihich can carry goods from door to door and therefore does not involve transfer of the goods from factory to station, for example. Rail transport has remained supreme in very large countries with a small and scattered population.

33

THE BRITISH ISLES

For many centuries, the British Isles took little part in commercial and cultural exchanges with other nations. In particular when the Mediterranean was the centre of west European civilisation, it was forced into a position of isolation.

During the 15th century, Britain became less insular and began to develop as a powerful sea-going nation. The south-coast and Atlantic-facing ports developed, and Englishmen explored and traded throughout the known world and Britain became a great commercial sea power.

With the Industrial Revolution of the 18th century, helped by the country's natural resources, particularly coal and iron, Great Britain became the world's major power in both political and economic terms. This changed following the two World Wars, and the growing influence and industrialisation of the United States and the USSR, which became the two superpowers. The British Empire was broken up and the United Kingdom began to strengthen its links with the European continent. In 1973 it became part of the EEC.

Tower Bridge
Tower Bridge was opened in 1894 and is London's most famous bridge. It stands more than 50 metres above water level, and opens to allow vessels with large tonnages to pass along the River Thames.

The great invasions
Britain was invaded many times between the 1st and the 11th centuries, and this influenced its language, customs and the civilisation of its peoples. The Romans were the first to conquer the island in 55 and 54 BC under the leadership of Julius Caesar. The Romans later penetrated as far as Hadrian's Wall. The Romans were followed in succession by Saxons, Jutes, Vikings, Danes and Normans.

THE MANY INVASIONS OF BRITAIN

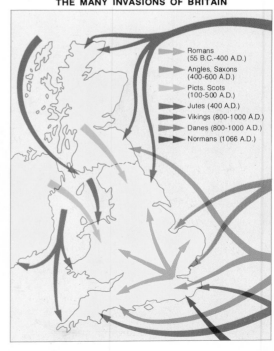

Romans (55 B.C.-400 A.D.)
Angles, Saxons (400-600 A.D.)
Picts, Scots (100-500 A.D.)
Jutes (400 A.D.)
Vikings (800-1000 A.D.)
Danes (800-1000 A.D.)
Normans (1066 A.D.)

Stonehenge
When the sea level rose with the melting of the great Pleistocene ice cap, it transformed Britain into an island. Britain's few inhabitants were hunters, using weapons of stone and bone. Stonehenge was erected in about 2000 BC, during the early Bronze Age. It is one of the major examples of primitive architecture in Great Britain, and consists of concentric circles of colossal stones, often forming a three-stoned arch. Stonehenge may have been a temple for sun-worshippers.

THE GREAT VOYAGES OF DISCOVERY

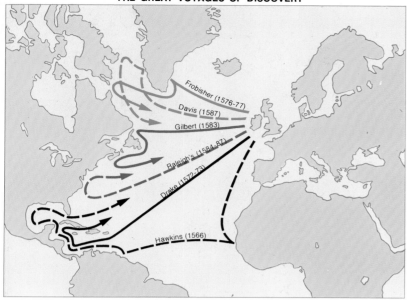

Frobisher (1576-77)
Davis (1587)
Gilbert (1583)
Raleigh's (1584-87)
Drake (1572-73)
Hawkins (1566)

Conquests and discoveries

For Great Britain, the 16th century meant the splendour of the Elizabethan era. Elizabeth I understood that the destiny of her country was indissolubly linked with the sea. She therefore did all she could to promote the development of her fleet and to encourage explorations and maritime trading, triumphantly keeping pace in this with the other great sea power of the period, Spain. Elizabeth made use in her service of the most able navigators of the time, Sir Walter Raleigh, Sir Francis Drake, Sir Martin Frobisher, and others who were pirates. Frobisher made many voyages in the northern Atlantic, looking for the North-West Passage, which it was hoped would be an alternative trade route to the East; however he got no farther than Baffin Island. John Davis also looked for the North-West Passage; he was stopped by the ice floes off the coast of Greenland, close to the strait which bears his name and which is the entry to the passage he was looking for. Richard Chancellor sought the North-East Passage, which was supposed to link Europe with East Asia.

Sir Francis Drake

Sir Francis Drake was a bold and daring navigator who sank many Spanish vessels. Between 1577 and 1580 he led an expedition around the world. He was knighted by Elizabeth I and took part as vice-admiral in the battle which routed the supposedly invincible Spanish Armada.

Castle and fortifications

The civil and religious architecture of Great Britain reflects the styles and tastes not only of the native Saxons, but also of the numerous peoples who came to settle in succession in the island, right up to the end of the Middle Ages, such as Normans, Vikings and Danes. One area which has particularly diverse architecture is south-east England, the region most frequented by the invaders because it led them to the heart of the country and to London. Romans, Vikings and Normans all passed through it. Each of these peoples left behind them a number of fortifications to add to the castles erected for defence purposes in successive eras. There are also many castles in Wales and Scotland. The photograph above right shows Caernarvon Castle in Wales, which was begun by Edward I. The present Prince of Wales was invested there in 1969.

The British Empire

The British Empire reached its greatest extent following the First World War. Its bases had already been established during the reign of Queen Victoria, however, and it was at the height of its power in the second half of the 19th century, during which period the Empire had been extended into various other continents. In Africa, Britain colonised Egypt, Nigeria, Kenya, Uganda and the Sudan, in an effort to establish a continuous route linking the Mediterranean to South Africa. Links with the colonies frequently took on the character of dominions, allowing a greater degree of autonomy to the native peoples. Examples of this are Canada, Australia, New Zealand and South Africa.

THE BRITISH EMPIRE 1919

Great Britain
New Foundland
Gibraltar
Bahamas Is.
British Honduras
Jamaica
West Indies
British Guiana
Sierra Leone
Gambia
Gold Coast
Nigeria
Uganda
Sudan
Aden
Somaliland
Kenya
Bechuanaland
Tanganika
Zanzibar
Nyassa
Rhodesia
South West Africa
South Africa
Swaziland
Basutoland
Tristan da Cunha
Falkland Is.
South Georgia
India
Ceylon
Andaman Is.
Seychelles
Mauritius
Burma
Malaya
Borneo
Cocos Is.
New Guinea
Australia
New Zealand

The British Empire

Abbeys and monasteries

Many cathedrals were built in Great Britain following the Norman conquest. Some of the most famous are those of Canterbury, St Albans, Winchester and Lincoln, built in the Romanesque/Norman style and in the Gothic style which followed it. Lincoln cathedral (the west facade of which is shown in the photograph on the right) was originally built between 1075 and 1090. It was restored 1922-32 and is one of the finest cathedrals in Britain and, with its light stone, dominates the centre of the city.

The British Constitution

The British Constitution has seen many changes down the centuries. The sovereign, for example, enjoyed absolute powers for some time, whereas today the United Kingdom, is in fact ruled by its government in the Queen's name, the monarch acting on the government's advice. It is a constitutional monarchy. Legislative power rests in the hands of the Sovereign and Parliament. The Parliament is divided into two houses: the House of Lords (below right) and the House of Commons. The former is made up of hereditary and life peers and peeresses; the second consists of 635 members of parliament, elected by popular vote at least once every five years. Executive power is exercised by the government, through its prime minister.

The Victorian era

The Victorian era had a profound effect on the history of Great Britain. Queen Victoria (right) reigned from 1837 to 1901. She was a great monarch, although her powers were restricted by her prime ministers, Palmerston, Disraeli and Gladstone. One of the things that made her popular was the effect she had on the spread of education.

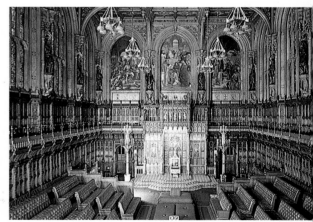

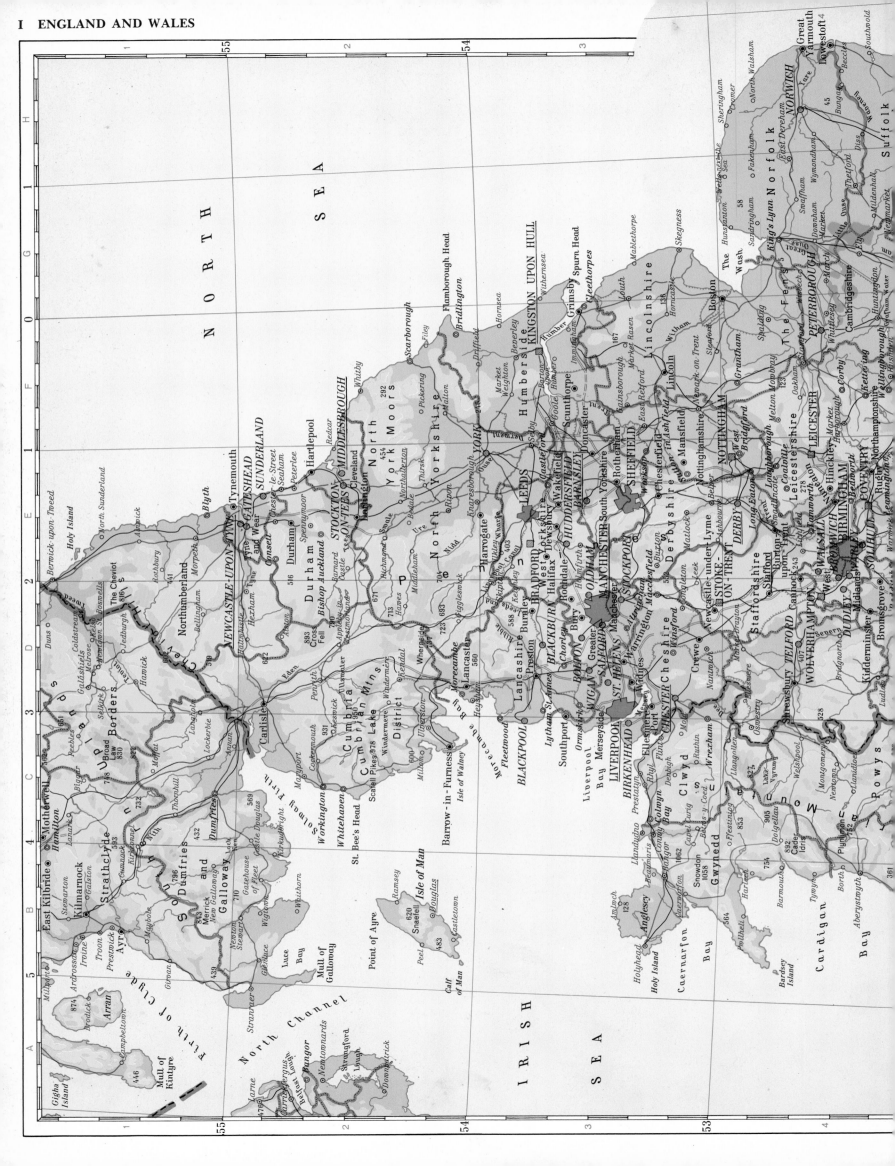

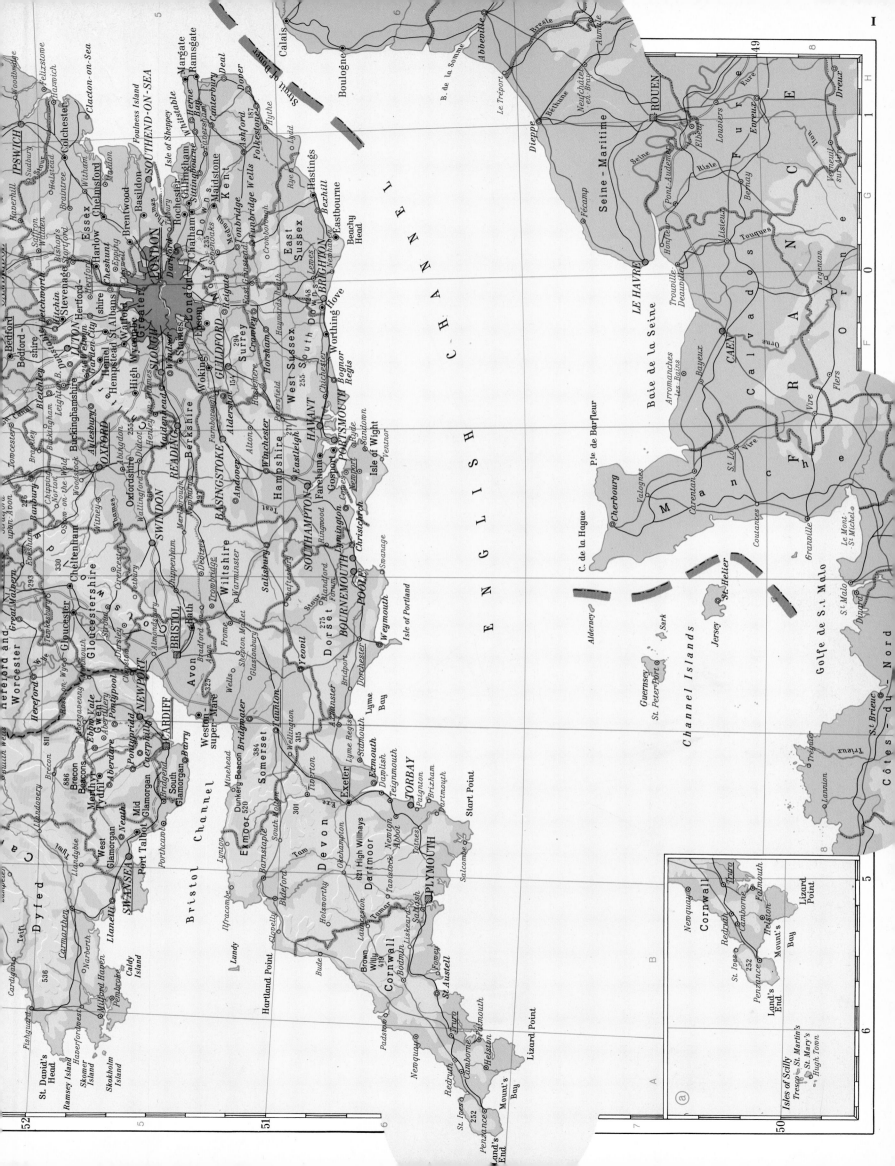

(a) Shetland Isles

Baltasound
Unst
Mid Yell
Yell
Fetlar
Ronas Hill 450
Hillswick
Brae
Whalsay
Mainland
Shetland Isles
Walls
Scalloway
Lerwick
293
Hoswick
Sumburgh Head

Orkney Islands

Westray
Oberbister
Eday
Sanday
Rousay
Stronsay
Mainland
Shapinsay
Stromness
Kirkwall
477
Hoy
South Ronaldsay
Cleat
Pentland Firth
Dunnet Head
Duncansby Head
John o' Groats

Outer Hebrides / Western Isles

Butt of Lewis
Barvas
Carloway
291
Stornoway
Lewis
Clisham 799
571
Tarbert
Harris
Lochmaddy
North Uist
Clachan
347
Benbecula
Gramisdale
488
South Uist
620
Lochboisdale
Barra
Castlebay 384

Highlands / Mainland

Cape Wrath
Durness
Strathy Point
Thurso
Castletown 49
Melvich
Tongue
Halkirk
Wick
Ben Hope 927
763
Scourie 721
908
Altnaharra
Forsinard
Lybster
Inchnadamph
961
705
Lochinver
847
Ben More Assynt 998
Loch Shin
628
Helmsdale
Lairg
Brora
Golspie
Brora
Ullapool
Bonarbridge
Dornoch Firth
Portmahomack
Gairloch
Ben Dearg 1081
692
Tain
Alness
Moray Firth
Loch Maree
981
Achnasheen
1045
Dingwall
Burghead
Lossiemouth
Kinnairds Head
Rosehearty
1109
Fortrose
Cromarty
Elgin
Buckie
Portsoy
Banff
Macduff
Fraserburgh
Torridon
1053
Caledonian Canal
Inverness
Nairn
Forres
Rothes
Aberchirder
Turriff
Peterhead
719
1083
Beauly
Spey
Keith
95
1052
Cannich
Grantown-on-Spey
Huntly
Insch
Inverurie
Ellon
1150
Carn Eige 1182
696
659
840
Don
722
Scalpay
Kyle of Lochalsh
Fort Augustus
Aviemore
803
Grampian
Broadford 1009
1120
Invergarry
Monadhliath Mountains 841
Kingussie
Cairngorm Mountains
1245
1171
Ballater
97
Aberdeen
Ardvasar
1019
Nethybridge
1311 Ben Macdhui
Dee
Banchory
1040
1128
Braemar
1154
Laurencekirk
Inverbervie
Stonehaven
Arisaig
983
Grampian Mountains
1008
1067 Glas Maol
882
Fort William
1148
1121
Blair Atholl
Brechin
Montrose
Ben Nevis 1347
Loch Rannoch
Pitlochry
Kirriemuir
Forfar
North Ballachulish
888
1081
Aberfeldy
Blairgowrie
Arbroath
Kinlochleven
1098
Dunkeld
Tay
Coupar Angus
Carnoustie
Lochaline
1079
Ben Lawers Loch Tay
Dundee
966
1124
Killin
930
Crieff
Perth
Newport-on-Tay
Oban
Dalmally
1130
Crianlarich
Lochearnhead
Earn
Auchtermuchty
Cupar
St Andrews
1174 Ben More
983 Loch Earn
Auchterarder
Fife
208
Fife Ness
Inveraray
Loch Katrine
Callander
Kinross
Glenrothes
974
Dunblane
720
Loch Leven
Kirkcaldy
Tarbert
779
Forth
Stirling
Alloa
Cowdenbeath
Buckhaven
Lochgilphead
Loch Lomond
Dunfermline
Central
Firth of Forth

Western areas / Islands

Point of Ardnamurchan
Coll
527
Tobermory
Tiree
Scarinish
Mull
Craignure
Firth of Lorn
Colonsay
Jura
Sound of Jura
561
784
Islay
Port Askaig
Craighouse
490
Port Ellen
Gigha Island
Strathclyde
Helensburgh
578
Dunoon
Dumbarton
Greenock
Port Glasgow
Kirkintilloch
Cumbernauld
Glasgow 522
Airdrie
Coatbridge
Johnstone
Paisley
Barrhead
Motherwell
Rothesay
Largs
East Kilbride
Hamilton
Bute
Millport
Lanark
Stewarton
Arran
874
Ardrossan
Irvine
Kilmarnock
Brodick
Troon
Galston
Prestwick
Cumnock
593
Ayr
Kirkconnel
732
Maybole
Campbeltown
446
Mull of Kintyre
Girvan
Nith
Thornhill
796
Dalmellington 843
New Galloway
432
Dumfries and Galloway
439
Loch Ken
Lockerbie
Dumfries
Annan
Newton Stewart
710
Castle Douglas 569
Gatehouse of Fleet
Stranraer
Glenluce
Kirkcudbright
Wigtown
Solway Firth
Luce Bay
Whithorn
Mull of Galloway

Borders / Southern Uplands

Biggar
Peebles
Galashiels
Coldstream
Berwick-upon-Tweed
535
Broad Law 830
651
Duns
Selkirk
Melrose
Newtown St Boswells
Tweed
Holy Island
562
Southern Uplands
Borders
Kelso
748
Jedburgh
The Cheviot 816
North Sunderland
Moffat
822
Hawick
Teviot
Alnwick
Langholm
519
Cheviot Hills
Bellingham
Northumberland
602
Rathbury
441
Morpeth
893 Cross Fell
Langholm
Newcastle Upon Tyne
Gateshead
Hexham
Haltwhistle
Tyne
Consett
Durham
516
Carlisle
Cumbria
Eden
Penrith
622
Alston
Appleby-in-Westmorland
790
Maryport
Cockermouth
931
Keswick
Bishop Auckland
Barnard Castle
Workington
Whitehaven

Central Lowlands / Lothian

Grangemouth
Bo'ness
Bathgate
Falkirk
Musselburgh
Edinburgh
Dunbar
Cumbernauld
Dalkeith
Haddington
North Berwick
Lothian
Bonnybridge
St. Abb's Head
Eyemouth

Northern Ireland (inset)

Malin Head
Cardonagh
Moville
615
Buncrana
Lifford
Strabane
683
Rathlin
Fair Head
Portrush
Ballycastle
517
Coleraine
Portstewart
Lough Foyle
Limavady
Ballymoney
76
Larne
Londonderry
Ballymena
Maghera
Mountains of Antrim
Bann
Atlantic Ocean
Inner Hebrides
Sea of the Hebrides
Little Minch
The Minch
North Channel
Firth of Clyde
North Sea

1. Carrickfergus
2. Newtownabbey
3. Belfast
4. Castlereagh
5. North Down

Climate

The climate of Great Britain is temperate and oceanic. This means that it is strongly influenced by the sea, and in particular by the warm Gulf Stream which flows north past its west coast. There are four distinct seasons, and the winters are mild, especially in the south, and the summers fairly cool. The rainfall is quite high, in some areas it exceeds 2,000 mm a year, and falls frequently at all seasons. Snow falls occasionally in winter, particularly on high ground, although heavy snow falls are infrequent in the southern areas. The weather is extremely variable and may change radically from one day to the next, or from morning to afternoon. Rainfall is usually highest in Scotland (left) and Wales.

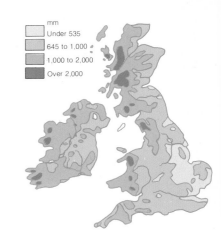

RAINFALL

mm
Under 535
645 to 1,000
1,000 to 2,000
Over 2,000

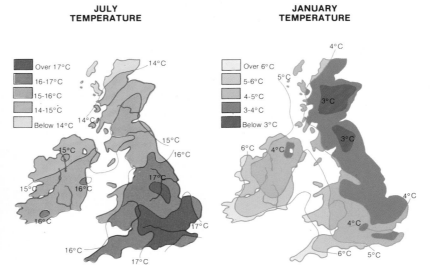

JULY TEMPERATURE

Over 17°C
16-17°C
15-16°C
14-15°C
Below 14°C

JANUARY TEMPERATURE

Over 6°C
5-6°C
4-5°C
3-4°C
Below 3°C

Climate and insularity

There are many factors which influence the special characteristics of the British climate, two of which are its ocean location and its insularity. It is sited between the Eurasian continental land mass and the Atlantic Ocean. It is the latter which creates a blanket of humid air, causing rainfall almost all the year round. A factor which helps to mitigate the English climate is the warm ocean current, the Gulf Stream. Its influence is particularly evident in Cornwall (left).

AGRICULTURE AND ANIMAL HUSBANDRY

Crop farms
Dairy farms
Livestock farms
Moorland and grassland
Built up areas

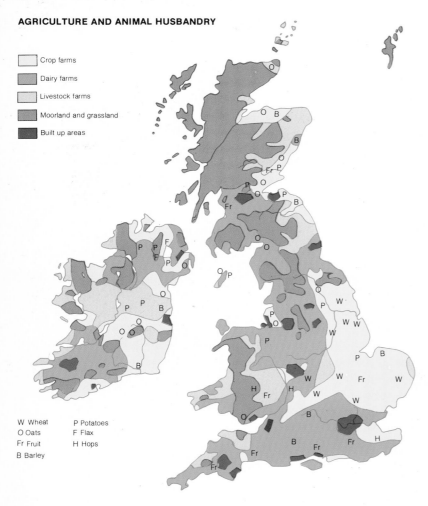

W Wheat   P Potatoes
O Oats   F Flax
Fr Fruit   H Hops
B Barley

Agriculture and animal husbandry

Due to the favourable climate, almost 50 per cent of the land is used for cultivation and permanent grazing. Less than 2 per cent of the active population is employed in agriculture and animal husbandry, but the degree of mechanisation makes for high productivity. Major crops are cereals (above), potatoes and sugar beet. The main farming sector is animal husbandry, cattle (right) and sheep.

Industry

The presence of mineral resources (coal and iron in particular), the influx of raw materials from the colonies, an already existing trading structure, and technical and scientific innovations, all helped to bring about the so-called Industrial Revolution in the second half of the 18th century. Many areas of Great Britain became intensely industrialised, with a consequent increase in population in many centres such as London, Manchester, Liverpool and Birmingham. The 18th and 19th centuries saw a marked development in the textile industry (below, a mechanical loom dating from the end of the 18th century), involving in particular the cotton mills of Lancashire, which processed cotton coming in from the colonies, and the woollen mills of Yorkshire. Steel and engineering works grew up in the areas of coal and iron deposits, contributing to the process of specialisation by area, which for many years has been characteristic of the English industrial structure. The industries of any country are affected by repercussions of the world's economic evolution, and this, as well as internal factors, have caused the decline of some traditional industries. Because of foreign competition, textile industries (particularly the cotton industry) have been restructured, and the mechanical industries have come to the fore, both in the traditional sectors (railway construction, machine tools, shipyards) and above all in the more modern sectors (the car industry, the aeronautical industry and electronics). Considerable progress has also been made in the chemicals sector (petrochemicals).

Iron and steel

This was a major sector in British industry up to a few decades ago (right, a blast furnace), but today the British iron and steel industry is struggling to compete as regards quantity with the production of the great industrial powers such as the United States and the Soviet Union. The industry is centred mainly in Wales, Lincolnshire, Scotland and Lancashire, but it has recently been contracting in order to become more efficient and competitive.

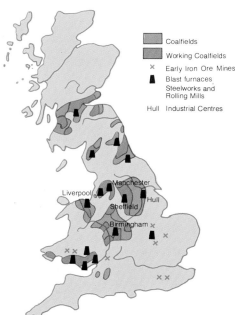

	Coalfields
	Working Coalfields
×	Early Iron Ore Mines
▲	Blast furnaces Steelworks and Rolling Mills
Hull	Industrial Centres

Coal

The principle coal mining areas of Great Britain are situated in Scotland, Northumberland, Yorkshire and Wales, and correspond to the ancient rock strata of the Upper Palaeozoic era. Annual production currently exceeds 120 million tonnes. Below, the pit-head of a coal mine in South Wales.

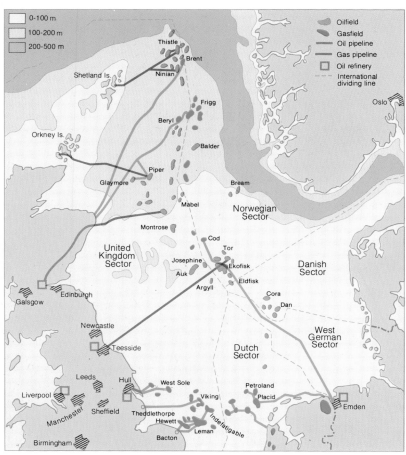

Oil

Dependence on foreign sources for the bulk of her energy needs, accentuated after the Second World War, spurred Great Britain to intensify the search for oil in her own territorial waters. Oil and natural gas deposits discovered in the continental shelf of the North Sea have been exploited since the mid-1970s by both British and American companies. In 1979 crude oil production reached 79 million tonnes.

EUROPE

Concentrated urban development and a predominantly industrial economy, two blocks of countries ideologically and economically opposed to one another, numerous traces of ancient civilisations – these are some of the many and frequently contrasting aspects of the continent of Europe. Its surface area is limited. Even including European Russia, it accounts for about 7 per cent of the world's land areas. This, along with its geographical location, make it no more than an appendage to the continent of Asia, but its historical and economic importance make it a unique and vital region. Europe has about 670 million inhabitants, that is to say 16 per cent of the whole of mankind, and a population density of more than 60 inhabitants per square kilometre. Population was fairly sparse up to the end of the 11th century, but an explosive period of growth occurred in the 1800s. Natural conditions and historical events caused a high population density to develop on the plains. Sometimes these are also the most industrialised areas, but they are also areas of intensive farming activity. The temperate climate, the proximity to the sea of almost all its areas, the abundance of internal water supplies and of raw materials have all promoted settlement and helped to make Europe a focal point in communications and trading. Potential causes for concern in this area today are the differences in economic policy and in standard of living between the capitalist countries and those controlled by socialist governments.

Urban centres
Internal migrations, with movements of people from country to city, are a major feature of European human geography. Baden in Switzerland (above) owes its urban development to its location, which makes it a transit centre and an important railway junction-point.

The Parthenon in Athens
The Mediterranean Sea was the cradle of the great civilisation of ancient Greece, which has left its traces around its shores.

Various aspects of European landscape
Some of the physical characteristics of Europe reflect its economic and cultural vitality: there are vast plains, lofty mountain ranges, although none are sufficiently high to constitute a barrier, and more than 30,000 kilometres of coastline. Left, an agricultural scene in Jutland, Denmark. Below, Sardinia. Right, an Alpine landscape in Bavaria.

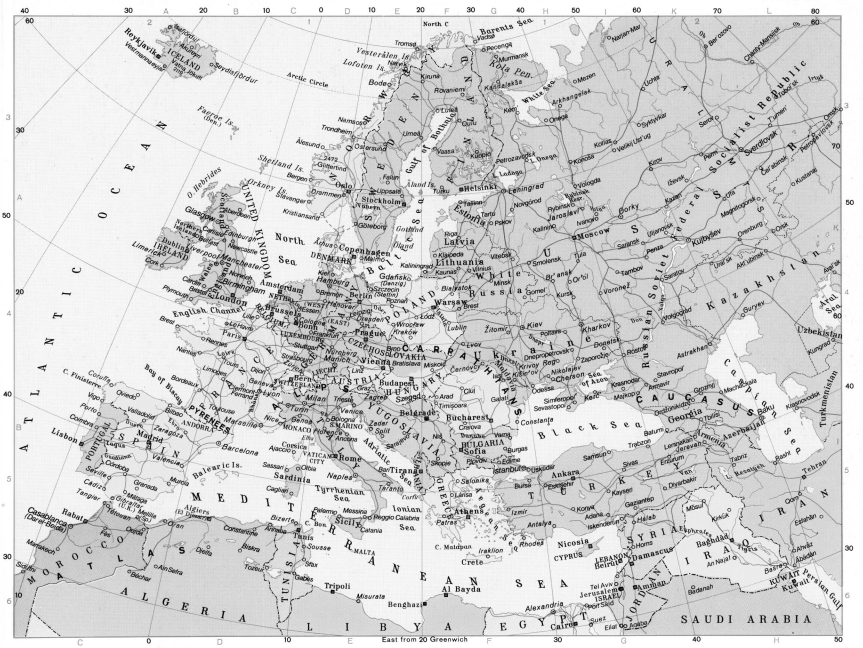

The European Economic Community

The European Economic Community (EEC), was set up in Rome in 1957, and consisted of six west European countries: France, West Germany, Italy, Belgium, the Netherlands and Luxembourg. The United Kingdom, the Republic of Ireland and Denmark joined the Community on 1 January 1973. Above, the British Prime Minister Edward Heath shown signing the document whereby Great Britain became a member. Two other organisations operate at Community level, alongside the EEC: the ECSC (European Coal and Steel Community) which was set up in 1951 and the EURATOM (European Atomic Energy Community). They share common aims, such as co-ordination of the various political economies in order to achieve true economic and political unity. The three Communities have succeeded gradually in integrating their management and administrative departments. However, although successful from the economic point of view, political unity remains a long-term objective.

Overall population of the states of Europe

Europe's population has increased from 100 million inhabitants in the year 1600 to 400 million in 1800, and on to the 670 million of today. The economic evolution of Europe, particularly in the second half of the 1700s, was a factor in promoting this rapid growth, along with improvements in sanitation and nutrition. Today populations are increasing less rapidly, due to a drop in birth rates. This is particularly noticeable in the countries in the central part of western Europe, Great Britain for instance (where the annual increase is 0.1 per cent), West Germany (0.2 per cent), and France (0.6 per cent). The annual rate of increase is higher in the socialist countries (0.9 per cent in the USSR and Poland).

POPULATION OF THE COUNTRIES OF EUROPE

EEC member countries
Countries associated with the EEC
COMECON member countries
Non-aligned countries

Population of the countries of Europe
👤 10 million inhabitants 👤 1 million inhabitants

Scandinavia

The harsh climate caused by high latitude with long bitter winters and very brief summers, is a significant factor in the life of the Scandinavian countries. However, Norway, Sweden, Finland and Denmark have found ways to overcome this negative aspect of their lives, putting to rational use all the natural facilities for development that their countries have to offer. Among the major natural resources of these countries are their vast forests, their iron and hydrocarbon reserves, their inland waters and their sea which, thanks to the influence of the Gulf Stream, keeps their Atlantic ports free of ice even in the winter and brings them fish in abundance.

Each country in this group has developed its own political, cultural and economic structure, linked to its various geographical characteristics. There are in fact considerable differences between the flat landscape of the Danes, formed from the soft sedimentary rocks, and the Scandinavian shield of ancient rock, flattened by the glaciers in Finland, and eroded into rugged mountain scenery in Sweden and Norway. Along with these natural features go, for example, the high level of agricultural productivity found in Denmark, as against the high industrial revenue of the Swedes.

Thanks to shrewd use of their resources, harmonious development of their political institutions and a long period of peace, the Scandinavian countries, particularly Sweden and Denmark, have reached a high standard of living. In Europe, only Switzerland has a higher rate of national income than that of the Swedes.

Norway
Above, the port of Oberdalen in the extreme north of Norway. Below, a Viking ship discovered in a prince's tomb near the bay of Oslo.

The resources of the northern lands
A contributing factor in the economy of the Scandinavian countries is the exploitation of their forest land, which covers more than half the surface area of Sweden and Finland. Timber is conveyed by the rivers (left) towards the industrial centres, there to be transformed into cellulose and pulp for paper. Below, a busy life, reindeer rearing amongst the Lapps who, with a population of about 13,000, inhabit northern Sweden and Finland.

SCANDINAVIA:
LAND USE
- Agricultural/industrial regions
- Agricultural regions
- Forest areas
- Pasture land
- Fishing zones

The Vikings

The Vikings (which means 'warriors') were the antecedents of today's Scandinavian peoples; they were known also as the 'Northmen', or Norsemen, and between the 9th and the 11th centuries they earned a terrible reputation as pirates and predators. They were driven by the impoverishment of their own country, which was little suited to agriculture, towards the sea. Fierce and indomitable fighters, they set out from their coasts in a few slender, highly navigable ships, which hardly seemed capable of withstanding the fury of the sea, but which in fact carried them across the Atlantic Ocean. At the beginning of the 9th century, Swedish Vikings, called Varangians, crossed the Baltic and settled around the eastern Baltic and on the Gulf of Finland, in what is now Russia, subduing the Slavic tribes and setting up the kingdoms of Novgorod and Kiev. They moved along the River Dnepr, and finally reached the Black Sea and Byzantium, the capital of the eastern Roman empire, establishing trading links with the Arab cities. About a century earlier the Vikings had turned westward, landing on the Shetland Islands, where they had built a city, and ports in Ireland, of which Dublin is an example. The period of maximum expansion was in the first few decades of the 11th century. They settled in France, where they were called Normans, and from 1060 onwards in Italy, where they occupied a large part of the south, Calabria, Puglia and the coastal regions of Campania. Their moment of greatest triumph was in 1066 in Hastings, England, where the Norman William the Conqueror routed the last Anglo-Saxon king Harold.

Runic inscriptions

The Vikings used the runic alphabet, some characters of which have been found cut into tombstones. Below, a Viking inscription found at Sigtuna, in Sweden.

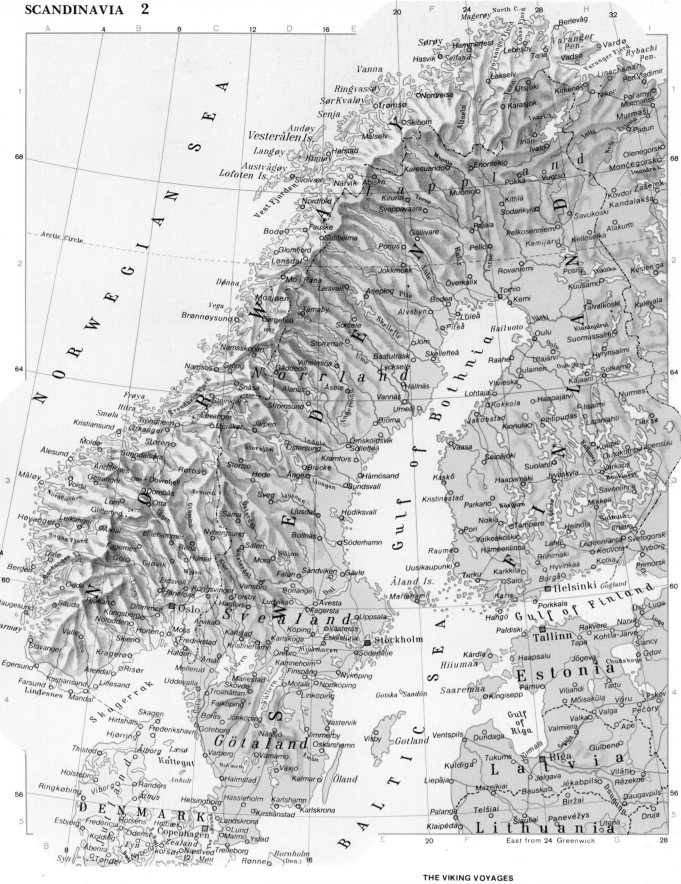

The Viking voyages

Using light vessels equipped with a single mast and square sail (see picture on opposite page), the Vikings demonstrated their remarkable seamanship. Braving the Atlantic Ocean, they reached the 'land of ice', Iceland, in the 10th century. From there, Eric the Red led an expedition to the 'green land', Greenland, and established a number of colonies along its coast. Eric's son, Leif, got as far as the 'land of wine', Vinland. The precise location is not clear but Vinland is possibly situated on the coast of Labrador, or Cape Cod in Massachusetts.

THE VIKING VOYAGES

——— Viking voyages

France and the Benelux countries

To the outward view, there are considerable differences between France and the Benelux countries (Belgium, the Netherlands and Luxembourg). On the one hand, France is the largest country in Europe (the USSR excepted), with great variations in natural landscape and peoples. It stretches from the barren Tertiary mountain chains of the Alps and the Pyrenees to the volcanic landscape of the Massif Central, from the undulating basin of Paris to the vast alluvial plains of the Rhône and of Aquitaine. There are large urban centres such as Paris and Marseilles, which are important both within and beyond Europe, as well as numerous small villages scattered throughout the countryside. This is a land of political unity, acquired and consolidated over many centuries, which has considerable power and influence within the European community. The Benelux countries, on the other hand, are some of the smallest countries in Europe (of the three, the largest is the Netherlands with 40,844 square kilometres surface area). They have less well-defined natural frontiers than other European nations, and a large proportion of the landscape is flat and low, sometimes below sea level. We can find a common bond between France and the Benelux countries in the high standard of living they have achieved and in the stability of their economies, based on their shrewd exploitation of natural advantages.

Abbeys and palaces
The abbey at Saint-Michel (left) and the Maison du Roi in Brussels (above) testify to the importance of the Church and the bourgeoisie in European history.

The solar centre at Odello
France is in the forefront of scientific research. The solar centre at Odello is linked with the tidal-power centre at Rance, in the production of alternative sources of energy.

Vineyards in Champagne
France ranks second in the world to Italy in wine production – more than 70 million hectolitres in 1976. The most highly prized wines, which take the name of their area of production, are mainly exported.

THE HOLY ROMAN EMPIRE

The Holy Roman Empire
The map shows the boundaries of the Holy Roman Empire at the death of Charlemagne (814). This political structure, which was intended to be the Christian continuation of the Roman Empire, did not survive its founder. His successors split up the Empire and destroyed its unity.

Charlemagne
Powerful King Charlemagne, who had already enlarged the eastern boundaries of his kingdom by victories against the Saxons and the Avari, in 773 moved down into Italy and conquered the Lombards. King Charlemagne was crowned Emperor of Rome by Pope Leo III on Christmas Day 800.

FRANCE: VINEYARDS

The polders

A large part of the surface area of the Netherlands (about 50 per cent) consists of polder and fertile reclaimed coastland, often below sea level. It is now dry land, thanks to the many dykes (sea walls), despite the considerable tides and storms of the North Sea. In past ages, the water was pumped off by means of windmills, now a characteristic feature of the Dutch landscape. Modern drainage units have made it possible in recent years to intensify land-reclamation operations, which have to be maintained all the time, as the land has been slowly sinking ever since the Middle Ages. The battle against the sea and the fight to increase the cultivable areas of the country started between the 13th and 14th centuries and is still under way. The major problem facing Dutch agriculture is, in fact, the lack of useful space; the Dutch have to feed a population which has the highest density in Europe (about 340 inhabitants per square kilometre). Dutch agriculture has managed to achieve a high level of efficiency, making it one of the highest producing countries in Europe, thanks to its specialisation and mechanisation, and consequent high yields.

The Zuider Zee

Holland's major reclamation area is the Zuider Zee. The huge bay of the Zuider Zee (more than 2,000 square kilometres), is largely the product of drainage and reclamation.

NETHERLANDS: POLDERS

Waterways

France has a large network of internal waterways (more than 1,500 kilometres), linking up with those of Belgium, Holland and Germany. Most of the inland water collects in five large river basins (Garonne, Loire, Rhône, Rhine and Seine) and a dense network of man-made canals connect up with these.

The canals linking the Rhine with the Rhône and the Saône form a continuous line of communication between the North Sea and the Mediterranean, and are very important and much used. French canals often have out-of-date equipment which restricts their use: this means that less than 7,000 kilometres of the network are actually used to any great extent.

COAL	European production (excluding USSR) 480,000,000 tonnes			
POLAND 39%	U.K. 25%	W. GERM. 19%	OTHER	

LIGNITE	European production (excluding USSR) 646,000,000 tonnes			
E. GERM. 39%	W. GERM. 19%	CZECH 16%	OTHER	

Central Europe

There is no common denominator between the countries of central Europe, so varied are the natural and human landscapes, the languages, the races and the political and economic structures. The south-west is characterised by countries which are typically Alpine in scenery, such as Switzerland and Austria (above), with a high range of mountains, reaching more than 4,000 metres, which has exercised an influence on the history and economy of these areas.

To the north-west is Germany, stretching down from the Alpine chain through the central plateaux, all that is left of the ancient Hercynian mountains, to the northern plain. Here also the landscape was shaped by the Pleistocene glaciers of Scandinavia, which left many moraines, or ridges of glacial debris. The central location of Ger-

many makes it into an axis between the Slavic world, the Anglo-Saxon and the Neo-Latin. It has considerable mineral resources, coal especially, which have made it one of the world's major industrial powers. Following the Second World War it was split into two sections, the Federal Republic in the west and the Democratic Republic in the east. West Germany's economy has made a remarkable recovery in the post-war era, and today it enjoys a high standard of living. East Germany has also developed considerably, and is the most advanced of the communist countries.

All the other countries of east-central Europe (Poland, Czechoslovakia, Hungary) and also Romania to the south-east are linked in various degrees to the political and economic system of the USSR.

CENTRAL EUROPE: LAND USE

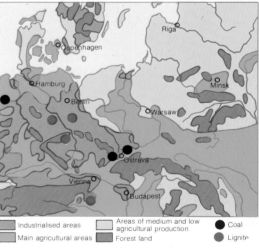

Industrialised areas
Main agricultural areas
Areas of medium and low agricultural production
Forest land
● Coal
● Lignite

Land use
Although heavily industrialised, particularly in the mining districts, the countries of central Europe, Austria and Switzerland excluded, devote about 40 per cent of their land to agriculture.
Below, a farming scene in Czechoslovakia.

The Hanseatic towns
Lübeck and Danzig, the main cities of the Hanseatic League between the 12th and the 14th centuries, are still major ports and industrial centres.
Left, the Holstentor, the fortified gateway which has become the symbol of the city of Lübeck.
Below, the modern Lenin shipyards at Danzig.

The map of Central Europe shows Denmark, Germany, Poland, Czechoslovakia, Austria, Hungary, and surrounding countries with numerous cities labeled.

The first united Germany

Before 1871, there were a number of independent German states, such as Bavaria, Würtemberg, Saxony, Prussia, the cities of Hamburg and Lübeck, and many other small states. Prussia was the prime mover towards unification, under the leadership of Chancellor Otto von Bismarck who, along with Emperor Wilhelm I of Prussia, created the German Empire. Alsace and Lorraine also formed part of this empire, won from the France of Napoleon III in the war of 1870.

Germany following the First World War

After its defeat in the First World War, Germany's lands were reduced by the Treaty of Versailles. Parts of East Prussia and Upper Silesia were allocated to Poland, thus isolating a strip of German territory on the Baltic, whilst Alsace and Lorraine were returned to France, and Northern Schleswig was returned to Denmark after a plebiscite to decide what the people wanted. This territorial structure lasted until 1933, when the Third Reich took the place of the Republic of Germany.

Berlin, the divided capital

With the end of the Third Reich, Germany was split between the powers that had defeated her, and two separate and independent countries were established, linked with the two political and economic blocks which have emerged from the cold war. Berlin, the ancient capital of Germany, was divided into four sectors by the Allies, thus ceasing to be the economic and cultural centre of Germany. In August 1961 the celebrated Wall was built, to isolate the Soviet sector from the western sectors.

GERMANY IN 1871

GERMANY IN 1919

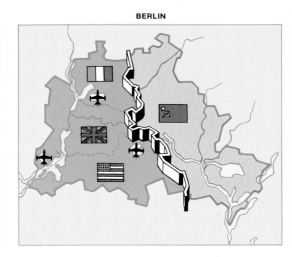

BERLIN

The wall of Castello di Gormaz in Spain

Spain and Portugal

Spain and Portugal, known as the Iberian countries, have no natural frontier between them. Two independent political entities have, however, existed from the time of the Middle Ages.

Both countries have a per capita income and standard of living amongst the lowest in Europe. Both natural and historical factors have helped to create this situation. For example, the peninsula is on the edge of a Europe which absorbed its energy in encouraging expansion into the colonies. This helped to isolate Spain and Portugal. To this can be added the fact that many areas are relatively infertile because of their physical and climatic conditions. Tertiary mountain chains, such as the Cantabrian Mountains in the north, act as a barrier against the moderating effects of the Atlantic Ocean and give the plateaux of the interior (mesetas) a continental character. Landed ownership, which has dominated the agricultural structure of the countries for centuries, lack of industrial development in the late 18th century, and civil wars and dictatorships are also influential factors. It is only in recent times that Spain and Portugal have given up their colonies and established a modern political economy of their own.

The Pyrenees
The Iberian peninsula is linked to Europe by the Pyrenees, a Tertiary mountain chain forming part of the Alpine-Himalayan system. The highest point is Pico de Aneto (only 3,404 metres), but the Pyrenees have always been difficult to cross. The land is rugged and precipitous, the vegetation sparse garrigue and woodland. Left, Maladetta Peak (3,308 metres).

The Rock of Gibraltar
Gibraltar became a British colony in 1704 and dominates access to the Mediterranean. Its strategic importance is now much reduced, owing to shifts in the balance of international strength. It is currently a much frequented port, and it also has a flourishing tourist industry. It achieved administrative autonomy in 1969 but it is claimed by Spain.

Agriculture
The current economic policy of the countries of the Iberian peninsula is geared to the development of their primary industries and of their service industries, especially tourism. This applies in particular to Spain, where vast sums of money have been invested in basic industry and in tourism. Nevertheless, both in Spain and in Portugal agriculture employs a considerable percentage of the labour force (20 and 28 per cent respectively). From the point of view of production, the best areas are the irrigated regions along the coast, areas of production of oranges, grapes and olive oil (right, an olive tree in Andalusia), of which Spain is one of the world's major producers. Non-irrigated crops prevail in the interior, mainly cereal crops.

LAND USE

Olive groves with some vineyards
Mountain regions, uncultivated
Non-irrigated crops: cereals, pasture land, olive groves
Irrigated crops: vegetables, fruit and cereals

The Arab conquest and 'reconquest'

The Iberian peninsula bears many traces of Arab domination. They can be found in its architecture and in its agriculture, its customs and its language. The Arabs, or Moors, began to expand northwards in AD 711 when, fired by the doctrine of Islam, they crossed the Strait of Gibraltar, which took its name from their leader Tarik (Gebel el Tarik, Rock of Tarik). The kingdom of the Visigoths, divided by internal warfare, put up no resistance. Within a short period of time the Arabs occupied the entire peninsula, crossed the Pyrenees and reached the plain of the Loire, where their advance was halted by the Franks led by Charles Martel. However at the beginning of the 9th century, some small northern Spanish kingdoms which had maintained their independence had started the struggle to regain the lands occupied by the Arabs. The 'reconquest', instigated by the king and in the name of Christianity, continued into the 15th century.

The map on the right shows the various phases in the Spanish advance, which took a considerable step forward with the unification of the two Christian kingdoms of Castille and Aragon. At the end of the 15th century there remained of the Spanish Caliphate only the kingdom of Granada which was conquered in 1492. Many of the Moors left Spain, depriving it of a good deal of valuable support and technical expertise. Religious fanaticism led to the expulsion of those who had at first chosen to stay. The periods of greatest splendour during Arab rule were between the 9th and 11th centuries, when Spain had reached a high level of economic and cultural development. The Arabs gained their most considerable successes in agriculture, expanding irrigation and introducing new crops.

Granada

One of the most prosperous centres of civilisation during the Arab rule of Spain, Granada had about 400,000 inhabitants and many libraries and schools. Right, the Alhambra, the royal fortress with its porticos, fountains and Moorish archways. Below, the Court of the Lions in the Alhambra.

THE MOORS IN SPAIN

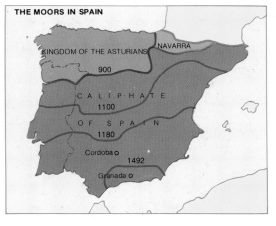

KINGDOM OF THE ASTURIANS NAVARRA

900

CALIPHATE
1100
OF SPAIN
1180
Cordoba
1492
Granada

Italy and the Balkans

The south-eastern countries of Europe may be divided into two groups: the Mediterranean lands of Italy, Yugoslavia, Albania and Greece; and the Danube lands of Romania and Bulgaria. This is a convenient division as there are many differences between these countries from the physical, economic and political points of view. One thing they do have in common is that they all belong to the least developed area in Europe.

Italy occupies a special place in this picture. From the Second World War onwards, the country has developed its industrial sector, altering the traditional structure of the country. Immediately after the unification of the country in 1861 the national product was derived from agriculture to the extent of 60 per cent. This percentage has now dropped to 8 per cent, in favour of primary and service industries. Italy has not developed in any uniform fashion, progress being concentrated mainly in the northern regions, to the detriment of the south. Recently, development has slowed down due to the international oil crisis, which is particularly serious for a country with no coal and few oil resources of its own.

Yugoslavia and Albania are also seaboard states, but both are in closer contact with the eastern Danube regions than with the Mediterranean. The Yugoslavian economy was traditionally based on agriculture, but the industrial sector is being developed.

Greece is traditionally linked to the Mediterranean. Its barren mountainous landscape has always been more hospitable to marine communications than to communications by land, and it has suffered from the fact that it is located on the edge of European areas. Its economy is primarily based on agriculture.

The Danube states are also moving from an agricultural economy to a more modern and industrialised structure, somewhat later than the other socialist states of central Europe because of their isolation from them – a fact which has had a considerable influence on their development for centuries.

Ancient settlements
Dubrovnik (below) was built on an easily defended site, and was a flourishing trading centre for centuries. It is now a tourist centre.
Above, S. Ilario in Campo, on the island of Elba, one of the oldest settlements on the island.
Top, a view of the Dolomites.

Harvesting citrus fruits at the foot of Mount Etna
Citrus fruits are an important sector of Mediterranean agriculture. Italy produces more than 16 million metric quintals of oranges and nearly 8 million metric quintals of lemons per annum, constituting a thriving export business.

Tectonic map of south-east Europe
Earthquakes occur frequently throughout this region, many of them catastrophic; there are also many active volcanoes, such as Etna and Vesuvius. The seismic and volcanic activity indicates considerable instability of the Earth's crust, in relation to the movement of the Earth's plates. The African plate is slightly turned towards the European, and encloses the Mediterranean depths. The line of contact between the two plates runs through southern Italy and Greece and is shown as broken lines on the map.

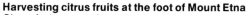 Folds Fissures ● Volcanoes

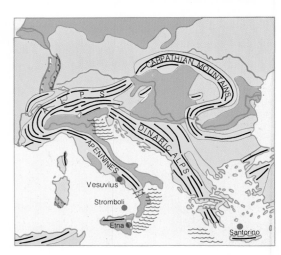

52

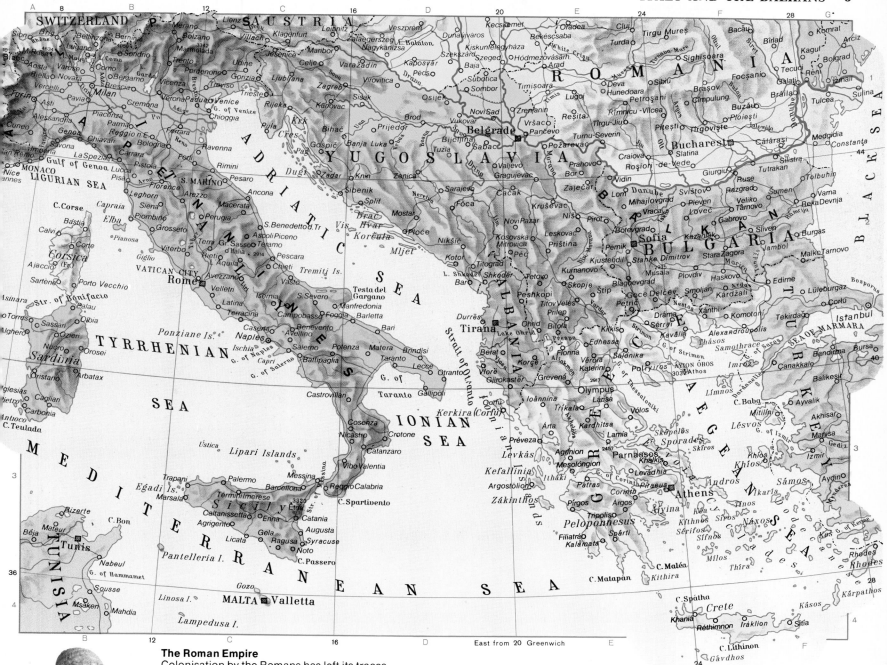

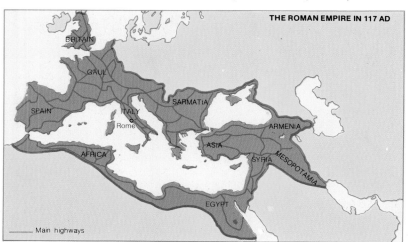

The Roman Empire

Colonisation by the Romans has left its traces clearly, not only on the language of the Latin peoples but also on the culture, art and legal systems of the other European peoples. Roman authority expanded as its own political structure evolved, first as a monarchy, then as a republic, and finally as an empire. It was with Trajan (98-117) that the Empire achieved its maximum expansion, from the Atlantic Ocean to the Caspian Sea and the Persian Gulf. The fall of the Empire was swift, and opened the way to government by the people actually living in the Empire.

Left, a bust of Emperor Hadrian (117-138).

THE ROMAN EMPIRE IN 117 AD

Greek civilisation

The greatest influence in the eastern Mediterranean was that of the Greek civilisation, which laid the foundations of European culture. The Romans themselves were considerably influenced by it, particularly in their literature, their art and their legal system. Greece has never had true political unity. Problems of communications, and the inaccessible mountain chains of the interior have always promoted an individualist policy in Greece, typified in particular by the struggles which took place between the most powerful city-states, such as Athens, Sparta and Thebes. This lack of unity caused Greece to fall to attack by a compact national entity such as Macedonia, and later by the Romans. Independence was not achieved until 1830

The Greek colonies

The infertile soil of their own country, over-population, invasions, and their own seamanship, caused the Greeks to cross the Mediterranean and to settle along its coastlines. Many colonies were established in southern Italy. Some colonies, like Syracuse, Selinunte, Catania and Agrigento, formed independent kingdoms. Right, the temple of Concordia in Agrigento.

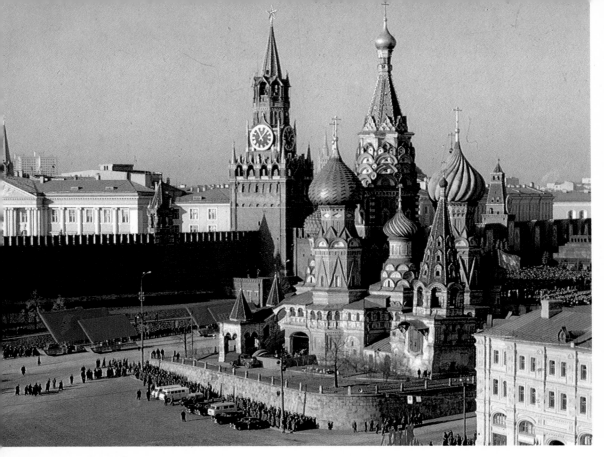

European USSR

The Union of Soviet Socialist Republics, whose territory extends over a large part of Asia, constitutes the largest state in the world. The largest of its republics is that of Russia (Federal Socialist Republic of Soviet Russia) which covers more than 17 million square kilometres to the west and east of the Urals. The capital of this country, Moscow, and the most densely populated and oldest cities such as Leningrad, Kiev and Gorki, are situated in the European zone. The expansion of the Russian state towards Asia did not start until the 13th century.

Following the revolution in 1917 and victory in the Second World War, the Soviet Union developed a foreign policy which was opposed to that of the United States, exercising its own supremacy on the countries of central-eastern Europe.

The European zone of the USSR is a vast plain with slight undulations, the remains of very ancient mountain chains which have been levelled by erosion. The availability of space, the lack of mountain chains imposing a barrier, and the fertility of some of its land, such as the Ukraine's chernozem soils, have encouraged settlement of peoples and commercial trading. Within 60 years the Soviet Union has completely transformed its own economic structure, which was predominantly agricultural, and has become one of the world's major industrial powers.

The Empire of the Tsars
Dominated by the wall of the Kremlin and the Church of St Basil, Red Square in Moscow (above left) is the same today as it was in the 16th century. Peter the Great (above) began the modernisation of the Empire, symbolised by the foundation of St Petersburg (now Leningrad) in 1703.

Russian technical advancement
The USSR was responsible for launching the first man into space: Yuri Gagarin, in the capsule Vostok 1 in 1961.

Political organisation of the USSR
The map below shows the location and dimensions of the 15 autonomous republics which make up the Union of Soviet Socialist Republics.

COMPARATIVE SURFACE AREAS OF THE USSR, USA AND CHINA

USSR	USA	CHINA

STATES OF THE USSR

Grid: A 20 B 24 C 28 D 32 E 36 F 40 G 44 H

SWEDEN

FINLAND
Pori, Uusikaupunki, Åland Is., Marienham, Stockholm, Turku, Salo, Hangö, Karjaa, Porkkala, Paldiski, Valkeakoski, Tampere, Hämeenlinna, Lahti, Heinola, Mikkeli, Kouvola, Kotka, Borgå, Helsinki, Hyvinkää, Svetogorsk, Imatra, Soitavala, Elisenvaara, Pitkäranta, Salmi, Priozersk, Olonec, Petrozavodsk, Vyborg, Primorsk

BALTIC SEA

Gulf of Finland
L. Ladoga, Kronshtadt, Leningrad, Zelenogorsk, Sestrorezk, Ruškin, Gatchina, Lomonosov, Ust'-Luga, Kingisepp, Čudovo, Nazýa, Volchov, S'as'stroj, Lödejnoje Pole, Podporozje, Voznesenje, Vytegra, Kargopol, Vel'sk, Kuloj, Vel. Ust'ug, Kizema, Nikol'sk

Estonia
Tallinn, Haapsalu, Hiiumaa, Saaremaa, Pärnu, Kingisepp, Kärdla, Rakvere, Narva, Tapa, Kohtla-Järve, Jõgeva, Viljandi, Tartu, Moisakula, Võru, Slancy, Gdov, Chudskoye Ozero, Konosha, Vožega, Charovsk, Sokol, Tot'ma, Soligalič

Latvia
Ventspils, Dundaga, Gulf of Riga, Kuldiga, Liepāja, Tukums, Jürmala, Riga, Jelgava, Bauska, Valmiera, Valka, Valga, Apé, Pečory, Pskov, Ostrov, Novoržev, Opočka, Gulbene, Vilāni, Rēzekne, Jēkabpils, Daugavpils

Lithuania
Palanga, Klaipēda, Telšiai, Biržai, Šiauliai, Panevėžys, Mažeikiai, Kalmingrad, Sovetsk, Čern'achovsk, Kaunas, Kėdainiai, Ukmergė, Utena, Postavy, Vilnius, Kapsukas, Alytus, Varena, Molodečno, Vilejca, Pleščenicy

POLAND
Braniewo, Kętrzyn, Olsztyn, Elk, Suwałki, Augustów, Grodno, Skidel, Lida, Mława, Białystok, Łomża, Ostrów, Ciechanów, Warsaw, Siedlce, Biała Podlaska, Brest, Kobrin, Radom, Lublin, Chełm, Kovel, Krasnystaw, Hrubieszów, Zamość, Vladimir-Volynskij, Luck, Stalowa Wola, Rzeszów, Rava-Russkaja, Tarnów, Przemyśl, Jarosław

White Russia
Minsk, Novogrudok, Nesviž, Osipoviči, Baranoviči, Sluck, Bobrujsk, Slonim, Volkovysk, Pružany, Ber'oza, Soligorsk, Žlobin, Luninec, Pinsk, Stolin, Mozyr, Petrikov, Rečica, Gomel, Dobruš

Ukraine
Sarny, Ovruč, Novograd-Volynskij, Korosten', Malin, Irpen', Kiev, Brovary, Borispol', Zdolbunov, Dubno, Slavuta, Žitomir, Rovno, L'vov, Ternopol, Kremenec, Šepetovka, Berdičev, Starokonstantinov, Chmel'nickij, Vinnica, Kazatin, Skvira, Fastov, Kanev, Berdyčev

CZE Užgorod, Ivano-Frankovsk, Nadvornaja, Mukačevo, Chust, Kamenec-Podol'skij, Kolomyja, Bučač, Čortkov, Žmerinka, Gajsin, Tal'noje, Uman', Korsun'-Ševčenkovskij, Špola, Kremenčug, Aleksandrija, Žoltyje Vody, Kirovograd, Krivoy-Rog, Zaporožje, Nikopol

HUNGARY
Nyíregyháza, Debrecen, Satu Mare, Baia Mare, Sighet, Černovcy, Suceava, Botoșani, Soroki, Balta, Pervomajsk, Voznesensk, Snigir'ovka, Nikolajev, Cherson, Skadovsk

ROMANIA
Oradea, Zalău, Cluj, Dej, Bistrița, Vatra-Dornei, Piatra-Neamț, Roman, Iași, Bălcy, Rybnica, Kotovsk, Orgejev, **Moldavia**, Kishinev, Tiraspol', Bendery, Dnestr, Komrat, Kagul, Izmail, Odessa, Deva, Hunedoara, Sibiu, Sighișoara, Tirgu Mureș, Turda, Bacău, Bîrlad, Vaslui, Focșani, Tecuci, Galați, Reni, Brăila, Sulina, Tulcea, Kilia

Lugoj, Rîmnicu-Vîlcea, Tirgu-Jiu, Turnu-Severin, Craiova, Roșiori-de-Vede, Slatina, Pitești, Tîrgoviște, Buzău, Ploiești, **Bucharest**, Călărași, Medgidia, Constanța, Giurgiu, Silistra, Tutrakan, Ruse, Svištov, Mihajlovgrad, Lom, Vidin

RUSSIA (S.S.R.)
Moscow, Podol'sk, Naro-Fominsk, Obninsk, Serpuchov, Kaluga, Aleksin, Tula, Novomoskovsk, Stupino, Kolomna, R'azan, Kašira, Skopin, R'ažsk, Michurinsk, Tambov, Lipeck, Jelec, Livny, Or'ol, Mcensk, Br'ansk, Navl'a, Pocep, Sevsk, Dmitrov, Klin, Zagorsk, Orechovo-Zujevo, Vladimir, Ivanovo, Šuja, Kineшма, Kostroma, Jaroslavl', Rybinsk Resr., Rostov, Pereslavl'-Zalesskij, Kovrov, Murom, Vyksa, Arzamas, Sem'onov, Dzeržinsk, Gorky, Volga, Pavlovo, Vetlužskij, Šarja, Manturovo, Makarjev, Čuchloma, Gr'azovec, Čerepovec, Vologda, Danilov, Buj

Suda, Šeksna, Cagoda, Babajevo, Boksitogorsk, Tichvin, Pestovo, Vesjegonsk, Bežec, Maksaticha, Bologoje, Uglovka, Boroviči, Kalinin, Kimry, Kal'azin, Uglič, Tejkovo, Lichoslavl', Toržok, Kuvšinovo, Vyšnij Voločok, Valdaj, Demjansk, Staraja Russa, Kholm, Andreapol', Ržev, Zubcov, Staica, Sychovka, Gagarin, V'az'ma, Safonovo, Jarcevo, Demidov, Belyj, Veliž, Gorodok, Polock, Vitebsk, Smolensk, Rudn'a, Orša, Mogil'ov, Bychov, Rogačov, Čausy, Mstislavl', Kričev, Kost'ukoviči, Suraž, Uneča, Klincy, Novozybkov, Sem'onovka, Železnogorsk, Ščors, Šostka, Mena, Glučhov, L'gov, Kursk, Oboj an, Belgorod, St. Oskol, Gubkin, Nov. Oskol, Voronež, Georgiu-Dež, Povorino, Uvarovo, Balašov, Rtiščevo, Arkadak, Sasovo, Kirsanov, Kadom, Moršansk, Zemetčino, Niž. Lomov, Krasnoslobodsk

L. Onega, Onega, Vologda, Kashin

Ukraine (cont.)
Černigov, Nežin, Konotop, Ichnya, Romny, Prilúki, Lubny, Poltava, Romny, Sumy, Lebedin, Krasnograd, Lozovaja, L'ubotin, Kharkov, Volčansk, Kup'ansk, Iz'um, Slav'ansk, Kramatorsk, Gorlovka, Vorošilovgrad, Donetsk, Novočerkassk, Šachty, Novošachtinsk, Kr. Luč, Debal'cevo, Lisičansk, Starobel'sk, Svatovo, Bogučar, Serafimovič, Millerovo, Morozovsk, Rossoš, Valujki, Nov. Oskol, Michajlovka, Novoanninskij, Ur'upinsk, Žerdevka

Dnepropetrovsk, Aleksandrija, Melitopol', Berd'ansk, Ždanov, Taganrog, Azov, Rostov-n-D., Bataisk, Sal'sk, Zimovniki, Orlovskij, Bašanta, Volgodonsk

Crimea
Džankoj, Jevpatorija, Simferopol', Sevastopol', Jalta, Feodosija, Kerc, Temr'uk, Primorsko-Achtarsk, Tichoreck, Kropotkin, Kavkazskaja, Krasnodar, Slav'ansk-n-K., Novorossijsk, Gelendžik, Belorečensk, Armavir, Majkop, Stavropol', Tuapse, Kuban'

SEA OF AZOV

BLACK SEA

Junks and modern merchant ships in the port of Shanghai.

ASIA

Stretching between the frozen polar cap and the humid monsoon regions is Asia which covers more than 44 million square kilometres. It is the largest continent on our planet, and more than half the Earth's entire population live there.

Because of its vast size, it has widely differing climates, rock formations, peoples and economies. Broadly speaking its climates and types of landscape can be divided into four bands, roughly following the lines of latitude. To the north there are the Arctic regions of Siberia, which are mainly covered with tundra and coniferous forests (taiga). Further south, there is a strip of desert which is hot in the west (in the Arabian Peninsula, Iran and part of India), and cold and continental in the east, as in the Gobi Desert. Further south again there are the massive mountain ranges of recent origin which form a compact chain winding from the Anatolian Peninsula to Pamir, the Himalayas and Tibet. There the chain divides, one section leading north-west into Manchuria, and the other south-west into Indo-China. The southernmost section of the Asian continent is characterised by rain forests and large deltas, where the monsoons blow in from the south-west in the summer, bringing wet weather with them.

Obviously very different peoples inhabit such varied climates and surroundings.

Alongside the almost uninhabited areas where the concentration of population is small – desert and sub-desert areas like Mongolia, for example, where there is less than one person per square kilometre – there are areas of very dense population, several thousand per square kilometre, as in Singapore (with more than 3,900 inhabitants per square kilometre).

From the social and economic points of view, Asia is made up mainly of so-called developing areas. While some countries have progressed to a high degree of technology and wealth, Japan for example, others, despite vast resources of oil, still have social and economic problems to solve.

Traditional life in Asia
In a large part of the continent of Asia, the traditional methods of agriculture and trading still prevail.
Left, a team of pluckers harvesting tea in a plantation in China.
Below, a caravan of yak in the mountains of northern Nepal.
Right, a food market in Kampuchea.

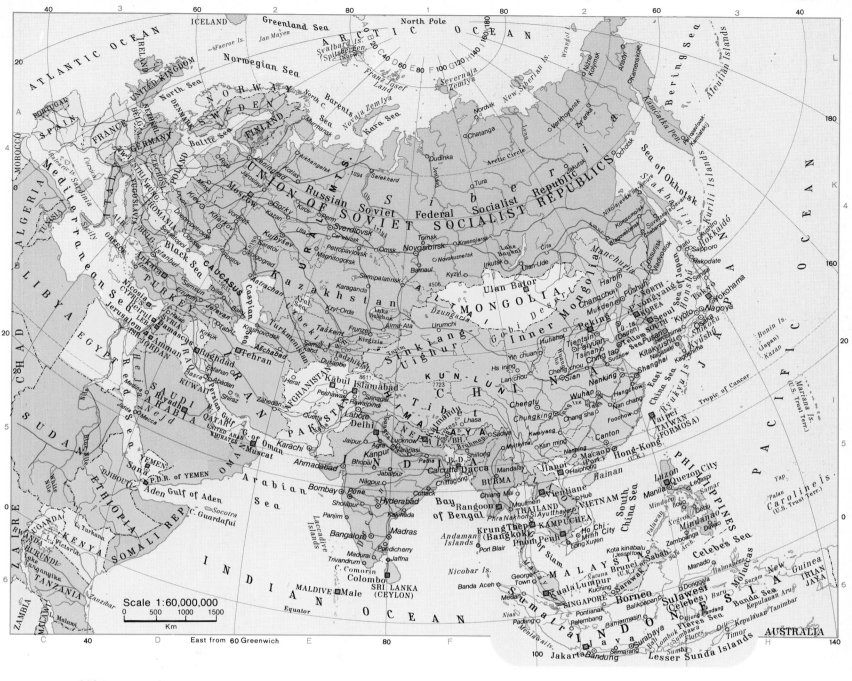

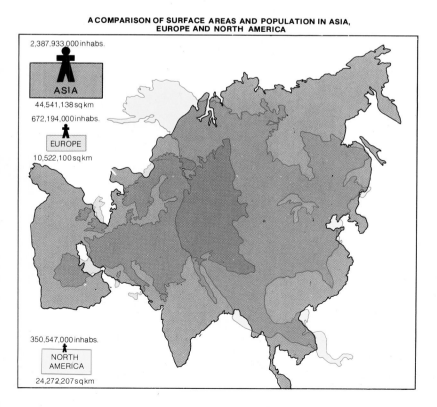

A COMPARISON OF SURFACE AREAS AND POPULATION IN ASIA, EUROPE AND NORTH AMERICA

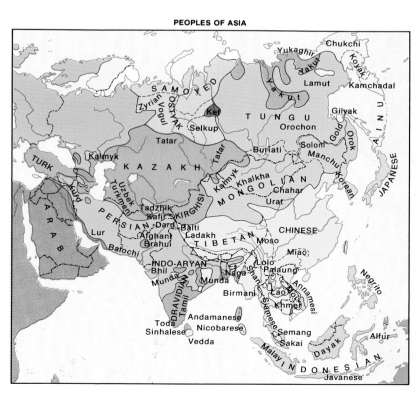

PEOPLES OF ASIA

Asian USSR

The Asian part of the USSR occupies a very special place in the continent of Asia. Almost one third of the total surface area of Asia is Soviet territory, though historically and geographically the Soviet Union has always considered itself part of Europe. In fact, west of the low Ural Mountains is European USSR which covers only about one-quarter of the country but contains more than 70 per cent of the USSR's people. For a territory as vast as Asian USSR, the population is rather sparse (less than 70 million inhabitants, a density of 4 per square kilometre), and has only recently begun to increase to any appreciable extent. Many areas of Siberia, which has vast resources of raw materials, are now industrialised; irrigation has come to Kazakhstan, and new cities have sprung up, to swell the local populations.

Samarkand (above)
The tomb of Schah-i-Zinga in Samarkand recalls the splendours of the empire of Tamburlaine. There are many Muslim buildings.

Siberia
Largely covered in taiga (top), Siberia is traversed by the longest railway in the world, the Trans-Siberian railway (left), which links Moscow with Vladivostok, a distance of over 9,300 kilometres. Right, a family of Yakut, one of the largest ethnic groups in Siberia.

Novosibirsk
Novosibirsk (below) can be considered the capital of Siberia. It lies on the route of the Trans-Siberian railway, at the point where other railways from the south converge. In just a few decades, it has developed into a large industrial and trading centre.
Left, a busy Siberian river port.

Agriculture
Only 10 per cent of the USSR is used for arable farming and cultivation.
As you will see from the map on the far right, agriculture is almost impossible over large areas of the USSR. In the extreme north, the tundra predominates. There it is always cold, with both soil and subsoil permanently frozen over. Further south in the taiga, the podzolic soil is not suitable for cultivation. In the south-west it is more fertile, and here there is intensive cultivation of cereal crops.

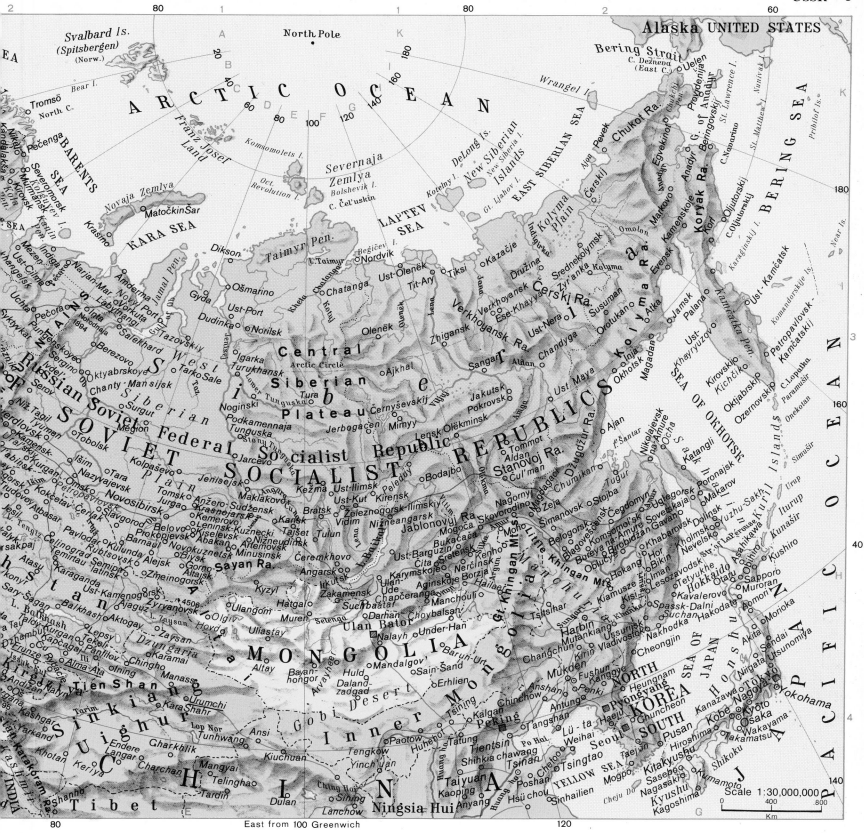

Forests and woods

Tundra with summer pasture land

Intensive crop growing

More than 41 per cent of Soviet territory is forested. The majority of the trees are conifers (pines and firs) and birches.

Only moss and lichen grow in the tundra in the extreme north, and the only profitable farming is the rearing of reindeer.

The most important cereal crops in the USSR are wheat, barley, maize and oats, as well as some oil-bearing plants, and vegetables.

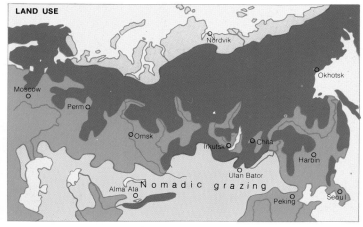

LAND USE

Burning off oil in Saudi Arabia.

The Middle East

The vast area of western Asia, which we know as the Middle East, extends from the Anatolian Peninsula of Turkey to India. It is dominated by deserts and vast barren plains. Its climate is arid, and rainfall is often less than 100 millimetres a year. The most common culture and religion is Islam, with the notable exception of Israel, but even between neighbouring Islamic states there are often sharp differences.

Throughout much of the region there is a sub-stratum rich in oil. The resources of oil and natural gas in the Middle East provide one third of the world's total production, and reserves are estimated at 60 per cent of the world's total, making this one of the 'hottest' areas on the planet. It is in this arena that the interests of the industrialised nations often seem to collide head on with the wishes of the local people.

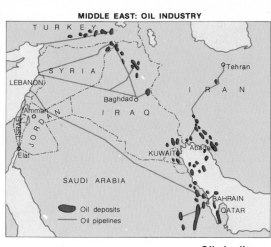

MIDDLE EAST: OIL INDUSTRY

Oil deposits
Oil pipelines

Oil pipelines
A network of pipelines carries some of the crude oil from the production areas to the ports of the eastern Mediterranean.

SAUDI ARABIA 13,6%
IRAN 8,7%
KUWAIT 3,5%
IRAQ 4,3%
OTHER MIDDLE-EASTERN COUNTRIES 6,8%
LIBYA 5,7%

Oil production
The Middle East states produce about one third of the world's oil. Saudi Arabia is the single largest producer, with more than 500 million tonnes in 1979. Only the USSR produced more in that year.

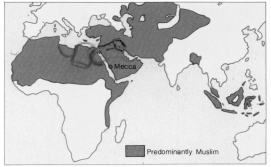

CURRENT DISTRIBUTION OF MUSLIMS

Predominantly Muslim

The ruins at Petra
The palace at Petra in Jordan (left), bears witness to the wealth of the Nabataean kingdom, which flourished from the 4th to the 1st century BC, and extended from the Red Sea to the Gulf of Aqaba. Petra lay on the trade routes running from the Arabian Peninsula to Syria. It remained important until the Nabataean kingdom was annexed by the Roman Empire in 106 BC.

Mosques in Samarra
This Iraqi city on the Tigris river is dominated by its golden cupola and minarets. Founded in ancient times, Samarra was an important trading centre at the time of the Mesopotamian civilisation, until it was swallowed up in the 7th century by the growing Muslim world.

Agriculture and animal husbandry
Despite the many changes brought about by the 'black gold', agriculture and animal husbandry are still the main activities in the Middle East. Left, a peasant in Afghanistan, where more than four-fifths of the population is engaged in agricultural work. Above, tents of nomadic shepherds in the same country.

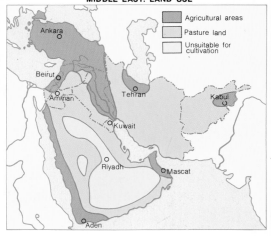

MIDDLE EAST: LAND USE

Agricultural areas
Pasture land
Unsuitable for cultivation

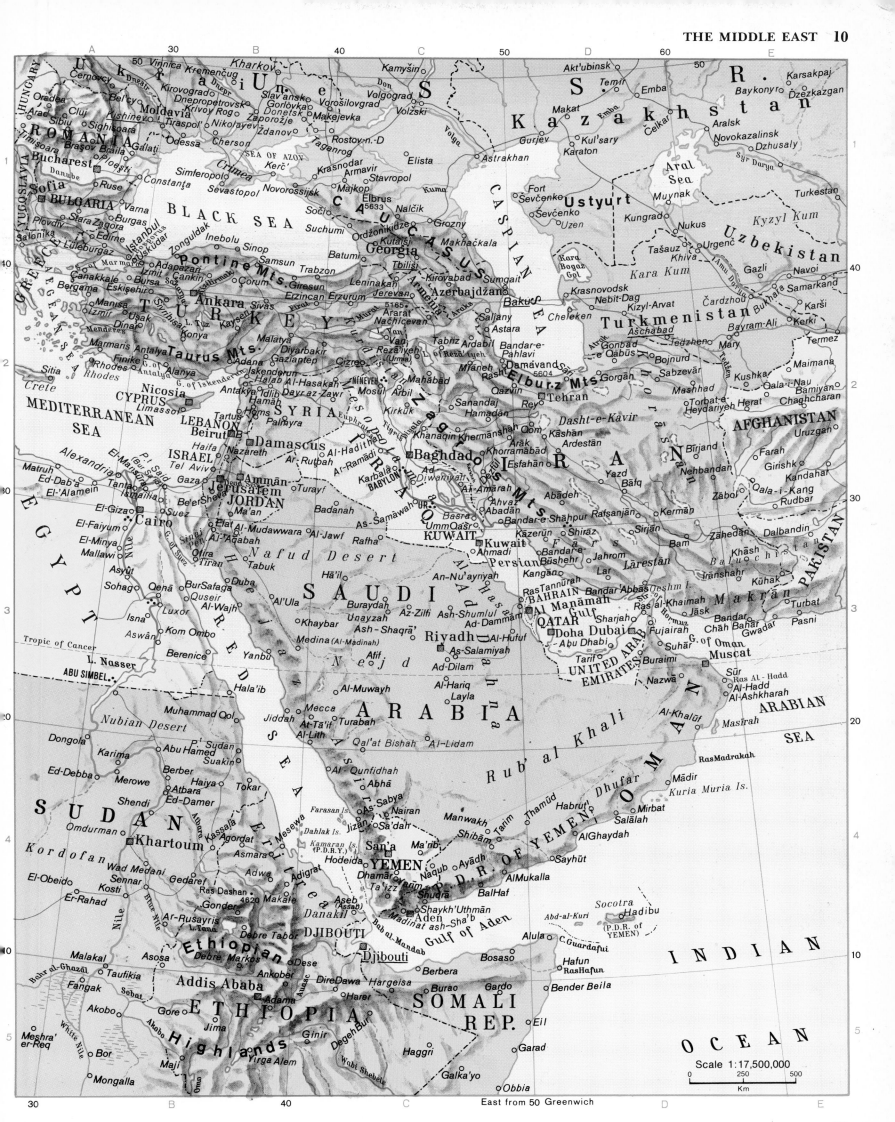

Southern Asia

Southern Asia is often referred to as the 'Indian sub-continent', and this encompasses the area which extends from the island of Sri Lanka to the Himalayas. This vast area, despite its political differences, is largely uniform from the point of view of landscape and peoples. In terms of surface area and population, it is a world on its own. It covers over 4 million square kilometres, and has 800 million inhabitants.

The sub-continent of India is separated from the rest of Asia by the gigantic Karakoram range and by the Himalayas, home of the highest peaks in the world. This vast mountain chain is joined to the Deccan Peninsula by the broad Indo-Ganges plain, formed from the deposits of the Ganges, Brahmaputra and Indus rivers and the network of their tributaries. The Indo-Ganges plain, which is subject at intervals to disastrous floods, is ideal for agriculture, and more than 70 per cent of the working population is engaged on the land.

Hinduism
The sacred cows wandering freely through the city (above) and the purifying bathing in the Ganges at Varanasi, formerly Benares (below), are two symbols of India's Hindu faith.

The massif of Annapurna, in Nepal (above)
For centuries the Himalayan border countries, Nepal and Bhutan, have been isolated from areas of modern economic development. Their economy has remained exclusively agricultural and is based on primitive techniques.

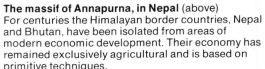

Overpopulation
India has a density of population of 190 inhabitants per square kilometre, and of more than 300 in the coastal regions. With an annual rate of population growth of 2.2 per cent, the population will exceed 1,000,000,000 by the year 2000.

Agriculture
India's agriculture does not always produce sufficient food to support a population which is increasing all the time. Overpopulation is, in fact, one of India's major problems. The farmers are completely dependent on climatic conditions and in particular on the monsoons which bring the rains. Apart from the tea, rubber and sugar cane plantations, most Indian farmland suffers from lack of irrigation, a lack of manure and from backward land tenure systems.
Left, paddy fields in the Deccan Peninsula.

INDIA: LAND USE

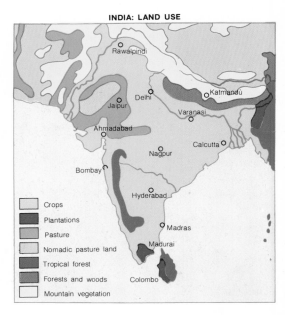

- Crops
- Plantations
- Pasture
- Nomadic pasture land
- Tropical forest
- Forests and woods
- Mountain vegetation

Rawalpindi · Katmandu · Delhi · Jaipur · Varanasi · Ahmadabad · Calcutta · Nagpur · Bombay · Hyderabad · Madras · Madurai · Colombo

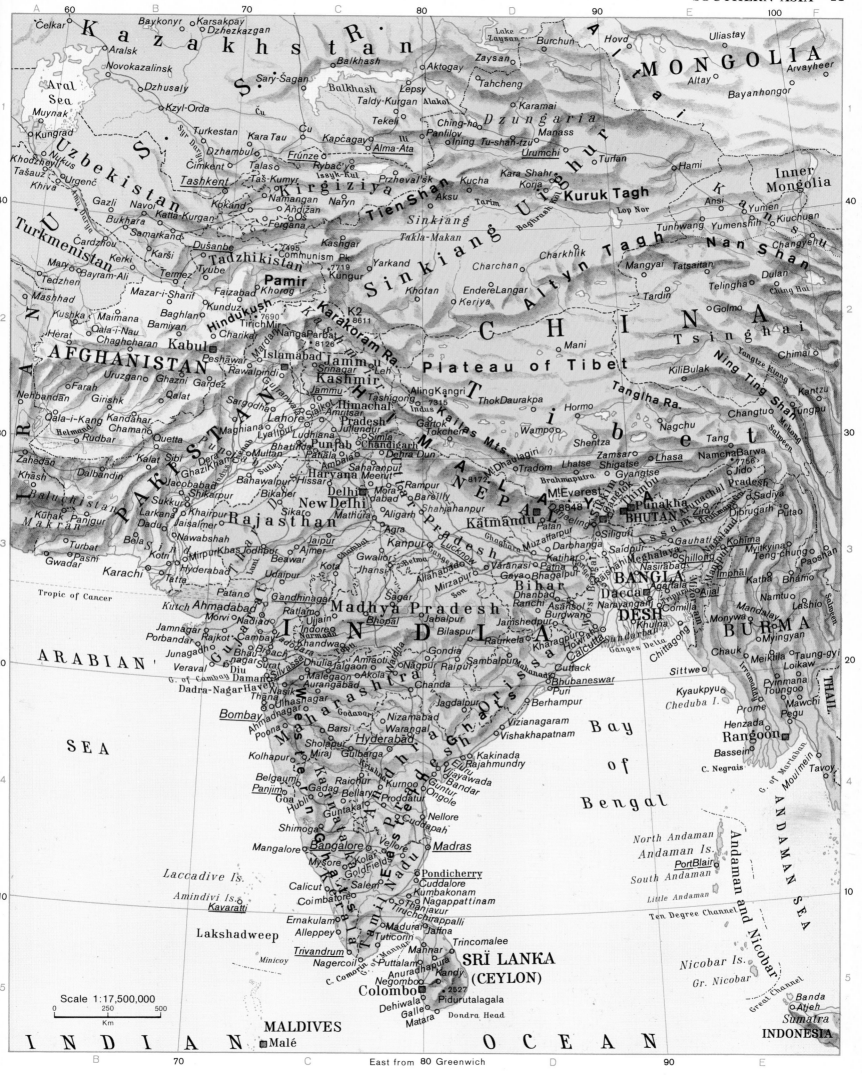

East Asia

The political entities most symbolic of East Asia are probably China and Japan. These countries are, however, very different, and at times totally at variance with one another.

On the one hand there is China, extending over more than 9 million square kilometres, second only to the USSR and Canada in terms of total surface area. China is a vast country with a huge population of about 890 million people. Socially and economically the country is geared to agriculture, and this has not been profoundly affected by the necessary processes of industrialisation, which have served to develop a country that is only slowly emerging from its time-honoured seclusion.

Japan, on the other hand, with an area of only 370 square kilometres and a population of 118 million, is a highly industrialised nation, with a revenue comparable to those of larger countries.

Maoism (above)
The figure of Mao Tse-tung has had a profound effect on the history of the Chinese people, from the time of the 'Long March'.

The great rivers
Top and left, ships on the Si Kiang river in the Kwangsi region. The great rivers and the canals have always been the most important lines of communication and transport.

Canton (right)
A trading centre with a population of almost two million, Canton has grown up on the delta of the Si Kiang, the 'River of Pearls'.

Rice
With a production of over 120 million tonnes a year, rice is China's main crop. A revolution transformed the traditional agricultural structure of the country, and now almost all the land is divided into collective farms. Efforts are being made to expand the areas used for cultivation, and to increase production by using artificial fertilisers.

CHINA: PRODUCTION OF RICE

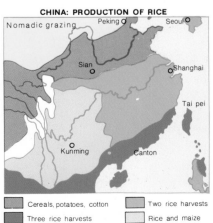

Nomadic grazing · Peking · Seoul
Sian
Shanghai
Tai pei
Kunming · Canton

- Cereals, potatoes, cotton
- Two rice harvests
- Three rice harvests
- Rice and maize

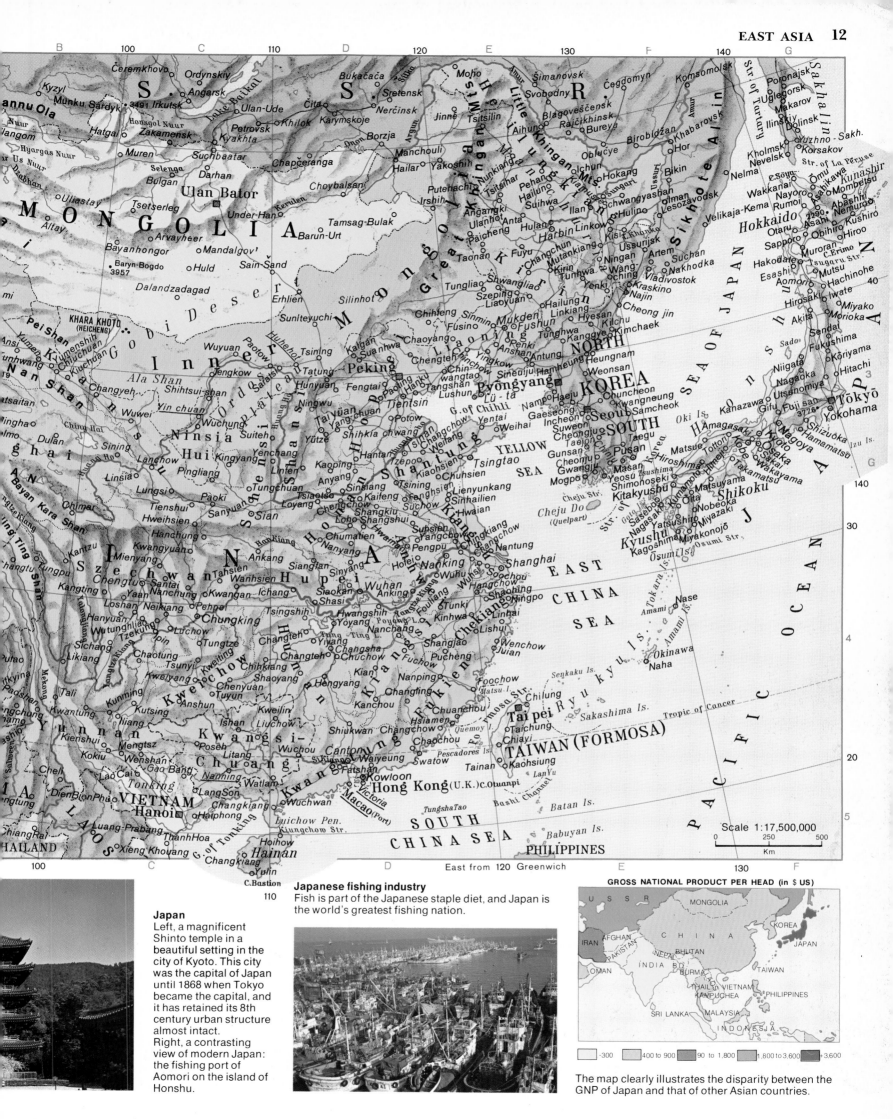

Japan
Left, a magnificent Shinto temple in a beautiful setting in the city of Kyoto. This city was the capital of Japan until 1868 when Tokyo became the capital, and it has retained its 8th century urban structure almost intact.
Right, a contrasting view of modern Japan: the fishing port of Aomori on the island of Honshu.

Japanese fishing industry
Fish is part of the Japanese staple diet, and Japan is the world's greatest fishing nation.

GROSS NATIONAL PRODUCT PER HEAD (in $ US)

-300 | 400 to 900 | 90 to 1,800 | 1,800 to 3,600 | +3,600

The map clearly illustrates the disparity between the GNP of Japan and that of other Asian countries.

Cultivation of rice in the Philippines.

South-east Asia

South-east Asia includes the whole of Indo-China, and the islands that lie east of the Indian sub-continent and south of China. It may be seen as bridging the gap between Asia and the continent of Australia. The Strait of Malacca, always the busiest line of communication between the Pacific and the Indian Oceans, is still a fundamental lifeline for Japanese industry, which is fuelled with oil from the Middle East.

This is a highly fragmented area from both geographical and historical points of view. A unify-ing geographical factor is the monsoon climate, with heavy rainfall to feed the great rivers of Indo-China. The islands are subject to constant seismic and volcanic activity brought about by contact between two slowly moving plates in the Earth's crust. From the economic point of view there are considerable inequalities in the region, which have been exacerbated by recent wars. The underdevel-oped countries are usually agricultural. There is little industrial development, and the movement of populations makes the situation hard to improve.

The temples of Rangoon (left)
Rangoon, the capital of Burma, is a major economic and cultural centre in south-east Asia. The centre of this vast Asiatic city has a European flavour, although this is offset by the scores of Buddhist pagodas, parks and gardens which can be found throughout the city. The constantly shifting population has increased from 400,000 in 1945 to more than 3 million in 1980.

Vietnam (above)
South-east Asia has not known a period of lasting peace since the end of the Second World War, and there has been conflict and warfare in one area or another ever since the lengthy war in Vietnam ended.

Peoples of Indonesia
Indonesia is made up of more than 2,000 islands and has an extremely varied population. In the interiors live the old Malay people, such as the Dyaks in Borneo, the Batak in Sumatra and the Toradja in Celebes. They have retained their traditional customs and ancient beliefs in spite of the influences of western civilisation. Left, a Toradja village in Celebes.

A water market in Bangkok, Thailand (left)
Thai waterways, or klongs, are important for bringing in agricultural products from the surrounding countryside. In Bangkok, as in many other cities in Indo-China, boats are the precarious dwelling or rather sleeping places for tens of thousands of people.
Within the south-east Asian economic structure (see map far right) subsistence farmers grow food crops like rice, maize and manioc. Plantations produce tea, cacao, coffee, sugar cane and rubber.

B · 110 · C · 120 · TAIWAN (FORMOSA) · D · 130 · E

Kokiu Mengtsz Litang Canton Chaochou Tainan
LaoCai Gao Bang Wuchou Swatow
Nanning Fatshan Hifung Kaohsiung Tropic of Cancer
Hoppo Chiangmen Waiyeung Kowloon C.Oluanpi
Liangyang Wuchwan Victoria Hong Kong (U.K.) Bashi Channel
HoaBinh Pakhoi Changkiang Macao(Port.)
enBienPhu Tonking Kiungchow Str. Batan Is.
HoaBinh NamDinh Haiphong Haikow Str. of Luzon
XiengKhouang Vinh Hainan Babuyan Is.
Yulin Changkiang
Thakhek QuangTri C.Bastion Laoag Aparri
NakhonPhanom Hué Luzon Cagayan Ilagan
DaNang Pulog PHILIPPINES
NgocLinh QuangNgai Paracel Is. 2928 Baguio PACIFIC
Kontum Pleiku S.Fernando Dagupan Cabanatuan
StungTreng QuiNhon Lingayen Masinloc Tarlac Daet OCEAN
BanMe Thuot Masinloc QuezonCity
Kratié DaLat Manila S.Pablo Catanduanes
PhanRang Cavite City Naga
Ho Chi Minh City Batangas Legazpi
VungTau Mindoro Sibuyan Sea Yap Is.
LongXuyen Calamian Is. Masbate Roxas
CanTho Nansha Is. (China) Panay Ormoc Samar
VinhLoi Taytay Iloilo Tacloban
Bai Bung Pt ConSon Palawan Bacolod Cebu Leyte
Puerto Princesa S.Carlos Dinagat
Negros Surigao
KotaBaharu Balabac Bohol Butuan
Kuala Trengganu Str. of Balabac Kudat Zamboanga Iligan Gingoog
Bandar Seri Begawan Kinabalu Ozamiz Cagayan de Oro
Brunei (U.K.) 4102 Sandakan Pagadian Mindanao
Kota Kinabalu Serai Basilan Apo Davao
Sabah Jolo G.of Moro 2954 DatuPiang
Kuantan Lutong Tawau Sulu Arch. Tinaca Pt.
Miri Tawitawi Palau Is.
Murud Caroline Is.
Bunguran 2438 Tarakan CELEBES SEA Talaud Is. Sonsorol Is.
Sarawak Sangihe Arch. PuloAnna Merir
Bunguran Is. (Indonesia) Sibu Rajang Morotai Tobi
Anambas Is. C.Api Kuching Kapuas Ra. Manado Klabat 2022
Kuala Lumpur Borneo C.Mangkalihat Gorontalo Ternate Halmahera
SINGAPORE Singkawang (Kalimantan) Tomini Minahassa Pen. Soasiu Waigeo Equator
Tambelan Is. Pontianak Schwaner Ra. Samarinda G. of Tomini Togian Is. Batjan Halmahera
Riau Is. 2278 Mahakam Donggala Peleng Sea Sorong Manokwari Biak
Lingga Is. Sintang Balikpapan Poso Taliabu Mangole Misool Tjendrawasih Serui
Djambi Ketapang Tandjung Celebes Banggai Is. Sula Salawati Japen
Pangkalpinang Karimata Is. Palangka Raya (Sulawesi) Rantekombola Arch. Buru Seram Fakfak West Irian
Palembang Sampit Kotabaru Palopo Kendari Sula Arch. Sanana SERAM SEA Kaimana 5029
Muaraenim Belitung C.Puting Bandjarmasin Madjene 3455 Ambon Pk.Djaja
Martapura C.Selatan Parepare Butung Kai Is.
Tandjungkarang Laut Watampone Agats
Telukbetung JAVA SEA Makasar Kabaena BANDA SEA Aru Is.
Serang Bawean Kabia Tukangbesi Is. Barat Daja Is. Jamdena
Djakarta Tjirebon Kangean Is. Damar Tanimbar Is. Kolepom
C.Lajar Bogor Pekalongan FLORES SEA Wetar Leti Is. Babar Selaru
Sukabumi Bandung Semarang Surakarta Madura Lomblen Alor Ocussi Dili
3428 Slamet Magelang Surabaja Singaradja Flores Ende SAWU SEA Timor
Madiun Kediri Semeru Mataram Sumbawa-Besar Sumba Waingapu Kupang
Jogjakarta Malang 3676 Bali Lombok Sumbawa Sawu Roti TIMOR SEA

Christmas (Austr.)

B · 110 · C · East from 120 Greenwich · D · 130 · E

Intensive cultivation
Rice is the main crop of south-east Asia, their backward methods making the yield per hectare comparatively low.

Plantations
The Hevea brasiliensis tree from which rubber is obtained.

INDONESIA: LAND USE

Manila · Hué · Bangkok · Ho Chi Minh City · Davao · Brunei · Kuala Lumpur · Medan · Palembang · Djakarta · Dili

Tropical forest with sporadic cultivation
Intensive cultivation for food crops
Plantations

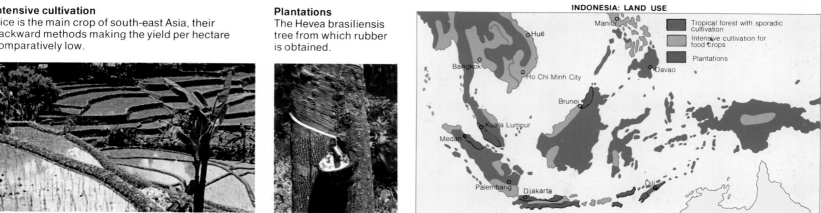

AFRICA

Africa can be divided into Mediterranean Africa and black Africa, with the vast Sahara constituting a dividing line between the two contrasting worlds.

Mediterranean Africa lies to the north and was the birthplace of the Egyptian civilisation. The Egyptians were succeeded by the Greeks and the Romans, but it was left to the Arab peoples to place their stamp on the area and to bring its peoples together. Black Africa to the south is populated by Negroid peoples, who belong to one of more than a thousand language or dialect groups.

The physical characteristics of Africa itself have contributed to the isolation of some groups. It is a vast continent, so large areas of the interior are a long way from the sea, in fact more than 50 per cent of the continent is an average distance of over 500 kilometres from the coast. Also, the shores are not easily accessible as the rivers are often difficult to navigate, and some, such as the Zaire and the Niger, have falls and rapids near their mouths. The Equator lies at the heart of the continent, and sets the pattern for its climatic conditions and natural vegetation. The main climatic bands are Equatorial and tropical, so deserts, rain forests and savannah prevail.

Black Africa
Two typical scenes in black Africa.
Above, animals of the savannah in a national park.
Below, a crowded market in the Ivory Coast.

Mountains and deserts
The peaks of the Ruwenzori (left) lie a little north of the Equator, and are always capped by snow and ice. The highest peaks in Africa are close to the Rift Valley, the great tectonic trench running generally north-south for many kilometres through eastern Africa.
Below, a typical scene in the Sahara, the largest desert on Earth, with a surface area of more than 8 million square kilometres.

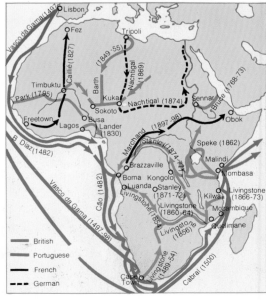

EUROPEAN EXPLORATION IN AFRICA

The discovery of Africa

In all probability, Africa was the birthplace of mankind. Prehistoric human remains more than a million years old have been found in the Olduvai Gorge, in what is now Tanzania. It is from here that early man might have migrated, forming himself into different groups of peoples. In Africa these divide into white peoples, such as the Berbers of the north, and black peoples, such as the many Bantu-speaking peoples of south-central Africa. It is often said that the Europeans brought civilisation to Africa, but, aside from the great Egyptian civilisation, Nigeria and East Africa had civilisations of their own before the birth of Christ. Wealthy towns such as Zimbabwe grew up in the 15th century. Slave-trading continued into the 19th century, and more than 30 million Negroes were shipped to the plantations of America. This was the most tragic chapter in the history of black Africa. In the last century, the African interior was explored by Europeans, in anticipation of the conquest and colonisation officially sanctioned by the Berlin Congress in 1884. By 1914 only Liberia and Ethiopia remained independent. Decolonisation started after the Second World War, accelerating in the 1960s. Many of the new states are facing considerable difficulties, however, such as lack of financial resources and technology, inadequate urban development, and internal political warfare. In some cases, these have been exacerbated by foreign interference.

Stanley and Livingstone

Henry M. Stanley met the celebrated explorer at Ujiji on Lake Tanganyika, on 28 October 1871.

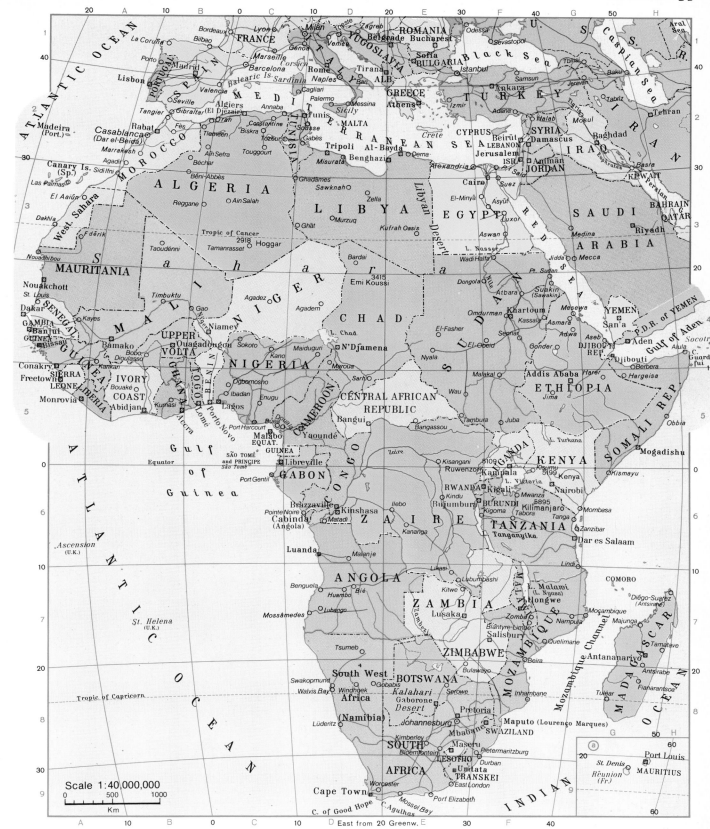

Scale 1:40,000,000

0   500   1000

Km

The African peoples

Whilst in the north the peoples are mainly of white Caucasoid origin, almost all the African population south of the Sahara is Negroid.
Below, Sudanese Negroes in Senegal.

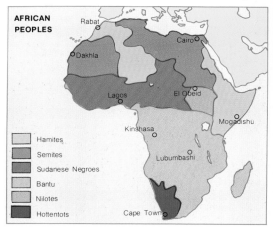

AFRICAN PEOPLES

- Hamites
- Semites
- Sudanese Negroes
- Bantu
- Nilotes
- Hottentots

North-west Africa

North-west Africa is a region of great diversity. To the north there are the Atlas Mountains and the countries bordering the Mediterranean. These are closer to the Middle East in their ethnic and religious (Islamic) character than to black Africa. Here we find a struggling agricultural economy, and in recent times the exploitation of mineral resources, particularly oil. In the centre there lies the barren Sahara, with its sand dunes and vast tracks of bare rock, traversed only by the caravan routes. To the south, steppes and savannah gradually give place to Equatorial forest, and to the true black Africa. The one unifying factor has been colonisation by the whites, mostly French-speaking peoples.

The Sahara (above)
Saharan scenery at Taghit, close to the Great East Erg.

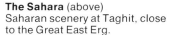

Roman Africa (above)
The theatre of Sabratha in Libya, one of Africa's best-preserved examples of Roman colonial architecture.

High Atlas (left)
A view of the High Atlas in Morocco. Apart from some fold mountains in South Africa, the Atlas Mountains are the only range of Tertiary origin in Africa. The peaks, eroded by glaciers of the Quaternary period, create an Alpine scene.

The Tuareg (right)
One of the Berber group of peoples, the Tuareg are nomadic stock breeders and traders along the Saharan caravan routes.

Agriculture
Left, a market in Ghana, a typical scene in black Africa. Agriculture is the main occupation of the peoples living around the Gulf of Guinea. They grow mainly millet, manioc and maize. There are also plantations producing cocoa, coffee, cotton and groundnuts, crops introduced into the region during the colonial period.

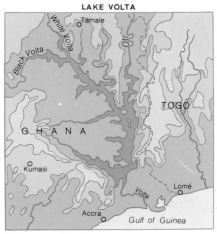

LAKE VOLTA

Tamale · White Volta · Black Volta · GHANA · Kumasi · TOGO · Volta · Lomé · Accra · Gulf of Guinea

Ghana and Lake Volta
Ghana has the largest artificial lake in the world – Lake Volta, with a surface area of nearly 8,500 square kilometres. The river Volta was dammed at Akosombo, about 100 kilometres from its mouth, in order to create the lake to assist the country's development. A hydroelectric plant was built on the bay, and a series of canals cut for irrigation purposes. The construction of the dam was started in 1962 and finished in 1965. It now supplies the greater part of Ghana's hydroelectric energy, a total of more than 4,000 kWh per annum.

Scale 1:17,500,000

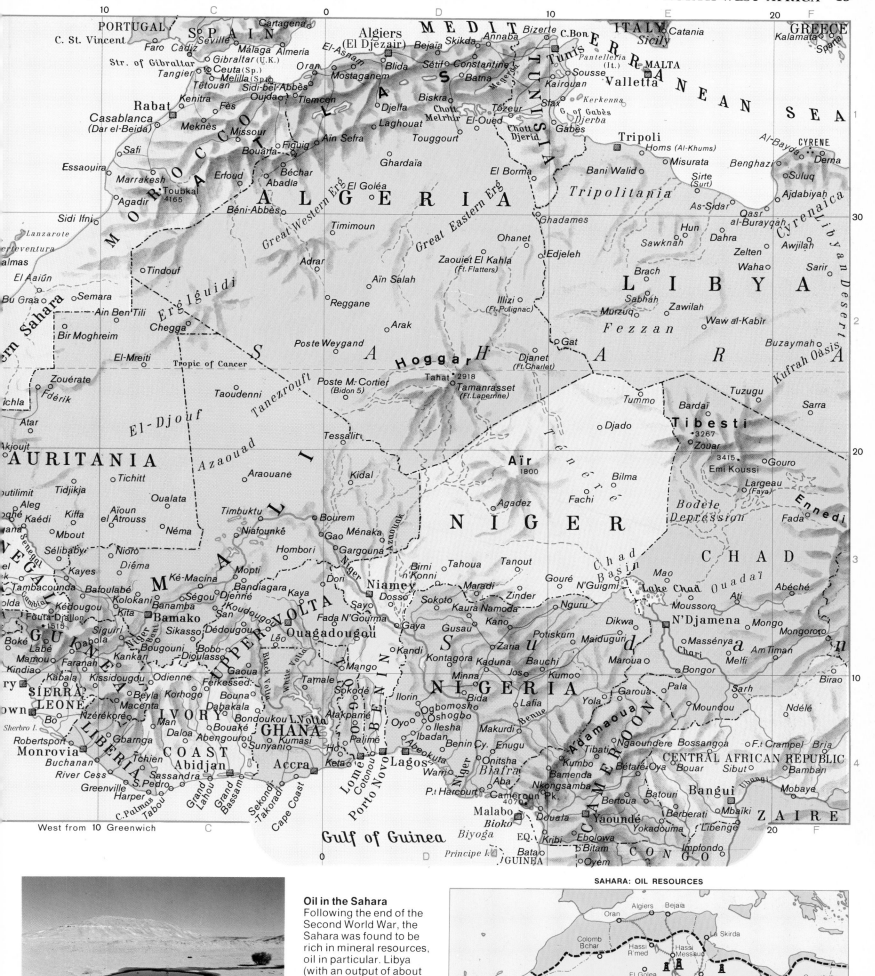

10   C   0   D   10   E   20   F

PORTUGAL   SPAIN   Cartagena   M E D I T   Bizerte   C.Bon   ITALY   Catania   GREECE

C. St. Vincent   Seville   Almeria   Algiers   Skikda   Annaba   Tunis   Sicily   Kalamata

Faro   Cádiz   Málaga   El-Asnam   Bejaïa   Sétif   Constantine   Pantelleria   MALTA   Sparta

Str. of Gibraltar   Gibraltar (U.K.)   Oran   Mostaganem   Blida   Batna   Kairouan   Sousse   Valletta

Tangier   Ceuta (Sp.)   Sidi-bel-Abbès   Tlemcen   Megerda   Sfax   Kerkenna

Tétouan   Melilla (Sp.)   Oujda   Biskra   Tozeur   G. of Gabès   Djerba

Rabat   Kenitra   Fès   Djelfa   Chott   El-Oued   Gabes   Tripoli   Al-Bayda   CYRENE

Casablanca (Dar el-Beida)   Meknès   Missour   Laghouat   Melrhir   Chott Djerid   Homs (Al-Khums)   Derna

Safi   Figuig   Aïn Sefra   Touggourt   Bani Walid   Misurata   Benghazi   Suluq

Essaouira   Marrakesh   Erfoud   Béchar   Abadla   Ghardaïa   El Borma   Sirte (Surt)   Ajdabiyah

Agadir   Toubkal 4165   ALGERIA   El Goléa   Great Eastern Erg   Ghadames   Tripolitania   As-Sidar   Qasr al-Burayqah   30

Sidi Ifni   Béni-Abbès   Ohanet   Edjeleh   Hun   Dahra   Cyrenaica   Libyan Desert

Lanzarote   El Aaiún   Tindouf   Timimoun   Great Western Erg   Zaouiet El Kahla (Ft. Flatters)   Sawknah   Zelten   Waha   Sarir

Fuerteventura   Bu Graa   Semara   Adrar   LIBYA   Brach   Awjilah

Palmas   Ain Ben Tili   Erg Iguidi   Aïn Salah   Illizi (Ft. Polignac)   Sabhah   Zawilah   2

Bir Moghrein   Chegga   Reggane   Murzuq   Waw al-Kabir

El-Mreiti   Poste Weygand   Arak   Fezzan   Buzaymah   Kufrah Oasis

Zouérate   Tropic of Cancer   S   A   Hoggar H   Gat   A   R   A

ichla   Fdérik   Poste M.-Cortier (Bidon 5)   Tahat 2918   Djanet (Ft. Charlet)   Tummo   Tuzugu   Sarra

Atar   Taoudenni   Tanezrouft   Tamanrasset (Ft. Laperrine)   Bardaï

Akjoujt   El-Djouf   Tessalit   Djado   Tibesti 3267   Zouar

MAURITANIA   Azaouad   Araouane   Kidal   Aïr 1800   Bilma   3415 Emi Koussi   Gouro   Ennedi   20

outilimit   Tichitt   Agadez   Fachi   Largeau (Faya)   Fada

Tidjikja   Oualata   Timbuktu   Bodele Depression

Aleg   Kiffa   Aïoun el Atrouss   Bourem   Niafounké   NIGER

Kaédi   Mbout   Néma   Gao   Ménaka   Birni n'Konni   Tahoua   Tanout   Chad Basin   CHAD   Ouadaï   3

Sélibaby   Nioro   Diéma   Hombori   Niger   Gargouna   Maradi   Mao   Abéché

Kayes   Ké-Macina   Mopti   Dori   Niamey   Sokoto   Zinder   Gouré   N'Guigmi   Ati

SENEGAL   Bafoulabé   Bandiagara   Kaya   Dosso   Kaura Namoda   Nguru   Lake Chad   Moussoro   Mongororo

Fouta-Djallon   Diéma   Ségou   Djenné   Sayo   Kano   Dikwa   N'Djamena   Mongo

Kédougou   Kolokani   Banamba   San   Fada N'Gourma   Gaya   Gusau   Zaria   Maiduguri   Massénya   Am Timan

Kita   Bamako   MALI   Sikasso   Dédougou   Koudougou   Kaduna   Potiskum   Chari   Melfi   10

Siguiri   Bougouni   Bobo-Dioulasso   Ouagadougou   Kontagora   Bauchi   Bongor

GUINEA   Kankan   UPPER VOLTA   Léo   Gaoua   Kandi   Minna   Jos   Kumo   Maroua   Birao

Labé   Kissidougou   Odienne   Ferkessé   Tamale   Mango   NIGERIA   Garoua   Pala   Sarh   Ndélé

SIERRA LEONE   Beyla   Korhogo   Bouna   Bida   Ilorin   Minna   Lafia   Makurdi   Yola   Moundou

Bo   Nzérékoré   Macenta   Dabakala   Bondoukou   L.Volta   Atakpamé   Oyo   Oshogbo   Ibadan   Benin Cy.   Enugu   Adamaoua   Ngaoundere   Bossangoa   Ft Crampel   Bria

LIBERIA   Man   Daloa   IVORY COAST   GHANA   Kumasi   Sunyani   BENIN   Ogbomosho   Ilesha   Onitsha   Aba   Tibati   Bouar   Sibut   Bambari

Monrovia   Gbarnga   Tchien   Abengourou   Bouaké   Palimé   Abeokuta   CENTRAL AFRICAN REPUBLIC   4

Buchanan   River Cess   Sassandra   S.Pedro   Sekondi-Takoradi   Ho   Keta   Lagos   Onitsha   Kumbo   Bamenda   Betaré-Oya   Bouar   Bangui

Greenville   Harper   Tabou   Grand Lahou   Grand Bassam   Cape Coast   Lomé   Cotonou   Porto Novo   P.t Harcourt   Nkongsamba   CAMEROON   Bertoua   Berberati   Mbaïki   ZAIRE

C.Palmas   Sherbro I.   Cameroun Pk. 4070   Malabo   Douala   Yaoundé   Yokadouma   Libenge

West from 10 Greenwich   C   Gulf of Guinea   Bioko   Biyoga   EQ.   Kribi   Ebolowa   CONGO   Impfondo   20   F

0   D   Principe I.   Bata   GUINEA   Bitam   Oyem

Oil in the Sahara

Following the end of the Second World War, the Sahara was found to be rich in mineral resources, oil in particular. Libya (with an output of about 100 million tonnes of crude oil per annum) and Algeria are amongst the world's major producers of oil.

Left, a small lake of oil in the Algerian desert.

SAHARA: OIL RESOURCES

Oran   Algiers   Bejaïa   Colomb Bchar   Hassi R'med   Hassi Messaoud   La Skirda   Tindouf   El Golea   Ghadames   Dahra   Guarabub   Reggane   Ain-Salah   Edjeleh   Hun   Zelten   Siwa   Fort Gourand   Gat   Murzuq   Sabhah   Kufra

- - - Approximate boundary of the Sahara   ⛏ Oil   Natural gas   Oil pipelines   Methane pipelines

A Fresco on a tomb in the Valley of Kings, in Egypt

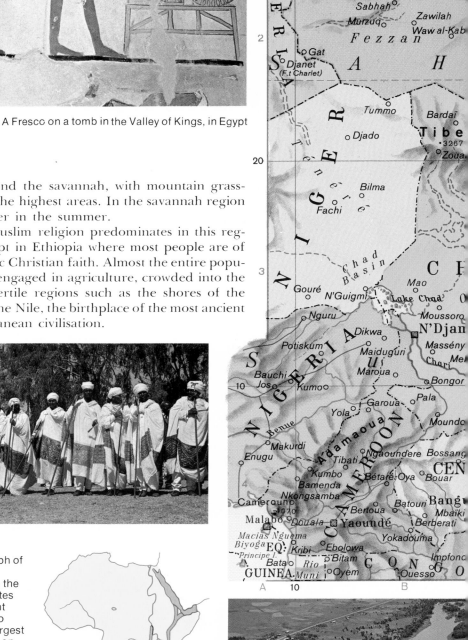

North-east Africa

North-east Africa is a land of deserts and mountains. There are the eastern areas of the Sahara, including the Libyan desert, the Tibesti mountains, and the Ethiopian plateaux more than 4,000 metres in height. The only large river is the Nile, flowing south to north through the Egyptian desert, where its volume is considerably reduced by heavy evaporation, and thence to the Mediterranean Sea. Further south, following exactly the same pattern as in West Africa, there are the steppes and the savannah, with mountain grasslands in the highest areas. In the savannah region it is wetter in the summer.

The Muslim religion predominates in this region, except in Ethiopia where most people are of the Coptic Christian faith. Almost the entire population is engaged in agriculture, crowded into the limited fertile regions such as the shores of the delta of the Nile, the birthplace of the most ancient Mediterranean civilisation.

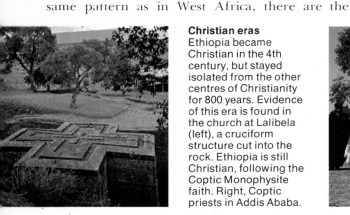

Christian eras
Ethiopia became Christian in the 4th century, but stayed isolated from the other centres of Christianity for 800 years. Evidence of this era is found in the church at Lalibela (left), a cruciform structure cut into the rock. Ethiopia is still Christian, following the Coptic Monophysite faith. Right, Coptic priests in Addis Ababa.

The Horn of Africa
A satellite photograph of the Strait of Bab el Mandab, which with the Gulf of Aden separates the African continent from Asia. These two coasts border the largest series of Rift valleys on Earth, situated in East Africa. The trench follows a broadly north-south direction, from Lake Malawi (Nyasa) in Mozambique up to the Red Sea. The two sides of the Rift Valley, which is recent from the geological point of view, are in a continuous state of change. In fact, the slow drift of Arabia from Africa still continues.

Rift Valley
The map above shows the East African Rift Valley along which there is considerable volcanic and seismic activity.

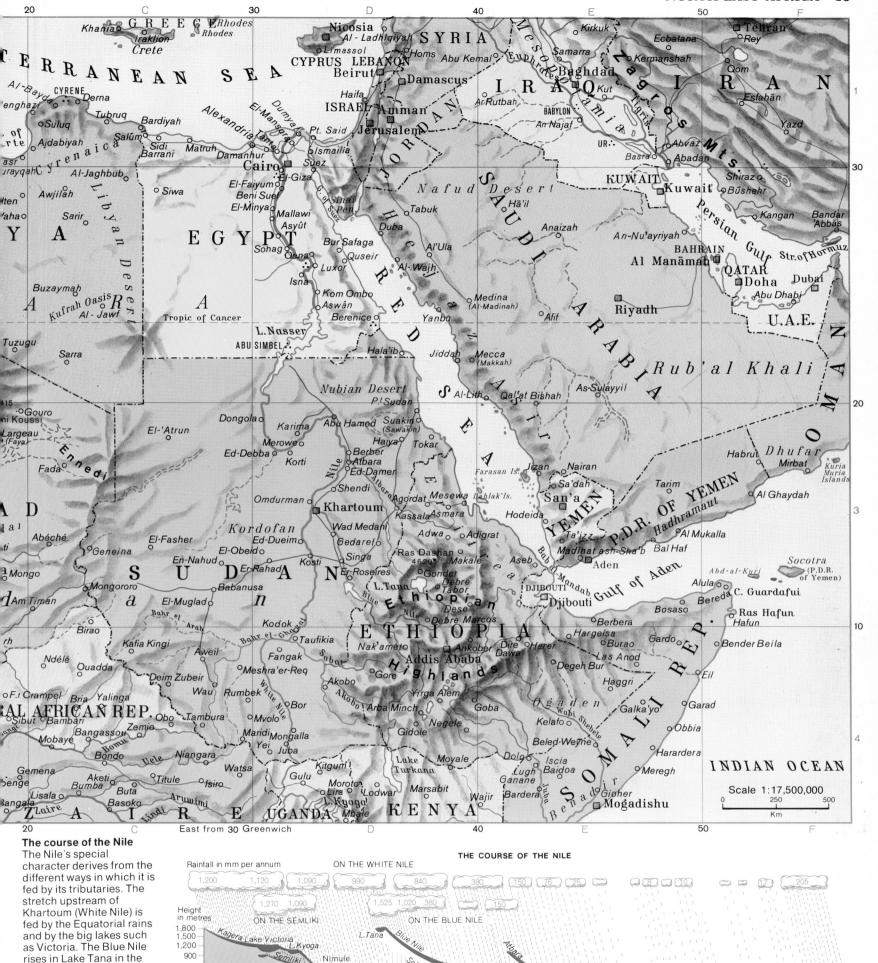

The course of the Nile

The Nile's special character derives from the different ways in which it is fed by its tributaries. The stretch upstream of Khartoum (White Nile) is fed by the Equatorial rains and by the big lakes such as Victoria. The Blue Nile rises in Lake Tana in the Ethiopian Highlands, and there is flooding each summer. When the two Niles converge, they continue for more than 2,000 kilometres and flow out into the Mediterranean. Left, falls on the Blue Nile.

THE COURSE OF THE NILE

Rainfall in mm per annum · ON THE WHITE NILE
1,200 · 1,120 · 1,090 · 990 · 840 · 380 · 150 · 78 · 25 · 17 · 205
1,270 · 1,090 · 1,525 · 1,020 · 380 · 150

Height in metres · ON THE SEMLIKI · ON THE BLUE NILE

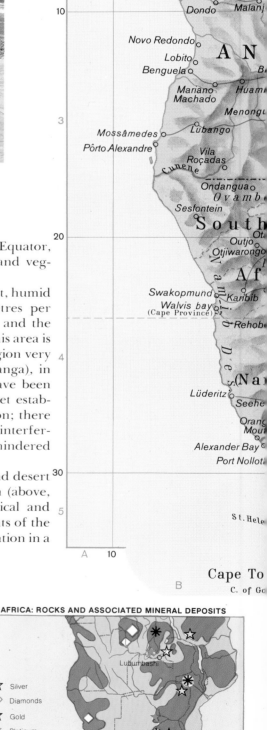

Southern Africa

Primitive tribes
Pygmies (left) inhabit the Equatorial forest, from which they derive their living. They are skilled hunters, and use weapons of bone and wood.
Below, a group of Masai dancers. The Masai are nomadic shepherds in the savannah, and were once powerful warriors, but were devastated in the 1800s by epidemics which wiped out both men and herds.

The central part of southern Africa, south of the Equator, reproduces almost exactly the various climates and vegetations of the north.

Astride the Equator there is rain forest with a hot, humid climate and rainfall in excess of 2,000 millimetres per annum. This is an environment hostile to man, and the density of population is very low. A large part of this area is occupied by the gigantic Zaire Basin. This is a region very rich in mineral resources; Shaba (formerly Katanga), in Zaire, is in the Copper Belt. These countries have been subject to European colonisation and have not yet established a balance between resources and population; there has also been tribal warfare and, in some areas, interference from external foreign sources, which have hindered their development.

Further south, beyond the steppes, savannah and desert (Namibia), there is the Republic of South Africa (above, Cape Town and Table Mountain). Here, political and economic control is still in the hands of descendents of the Dutch and English colonists, with the black population in a markedly subordinate position.

Zimbabwe (left)
The imposing ruins of Zimbabwe are the relics of a civilisation which, in the 15th century, may have stretched from the Kalahari Desert (in modern Botswana) to the Indian Ocean.

Madagascar (right)
The large island of Madagascar has a characteristic flora and fauna arising from its isolated position. The population is part Negroid, part Asiatic.

AFRICA: ROCKS AND ASSOCIATED MINERAL DEPOSITS

☆ Silver
◇ Diamonds
☆ Gold
✦ Platinum
✳ Uranium
Older rocks, often metamorphosed
Younger rocks, mainly sedimentary

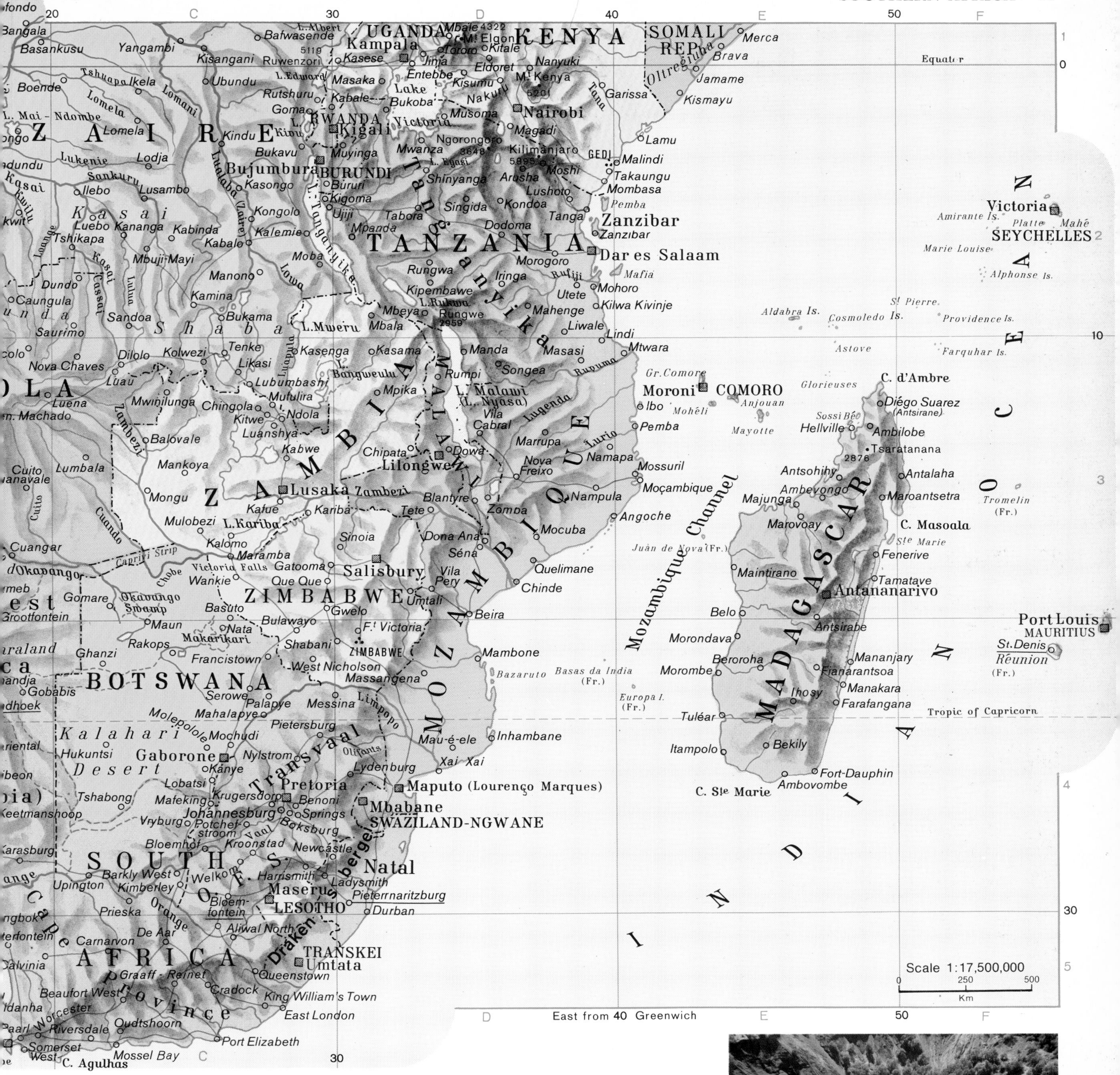
UGANDA
Kampala
KENYA
Nairobi
SOMALI REP.
RWANDA
Kigali
BURUNDI
Bujumbura
ZAIRE
Kisangani
TANZANIA
Dar es Salaam
Zanzibar
L. Tanganyika
L. Victoria
Mombasa
Mt. Kenya
Kilimanjaro
ZAMBIA
Lusaka
MALAWI
Lilongwe
L. Malawi (L. Nyasa)
MOZAMBIQUE
Maputo (Lourenço Marques)
Beira
ZIMBABWE
Salisbury
Bulawayo
BOTSWANA
Gaborone
Kalahari Desert
Pretoria
Johannesburg
SWAZILAND-NGWANE
Mbabane
Natal
Durban
Maseru
LESOTHO
TRANSKEI
Umtata
SOUTH AFRICA
Cape Province
Port Elizabeth
East London
C. Agulhas
MADAGASCAR
Antananarivo
Mozambique Channel
COMORO
Moroni
SEYCHELLES
Victoria
MAURITIUS
Port Louis
Réunion (Fr.)
INDIAN OCEAN
Tropic of Capricorn
Equator
Scale 1:17,500,000
0 250 500
Km
East from 40 Greenwich

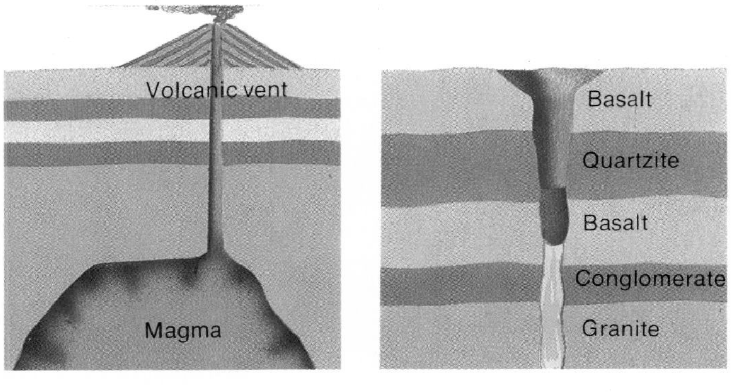
Volcanic vent
Magma
Basalt
Quartzite
Basalt
Conglomerate
Granite

How diamonds are formed
The diagrams on the left illustrate the formation of diamonds and the structure of a mine. Diamonds originate from carbon particles which crystallise in a basin of magma. The magma rises to the surface along a volcanic vent, with an outlet through a fissure in the Earth's crust. Diamonds are mined from the magmatic rock which fills the path.
Right, the vast cavity of a defunct diamond mine in Kimberley in South Africa, one of the world's greatest exporters of diamonds.

NORTH AMERICA

The two continental land masses of America are at first sight very similar – each roughly triangular in outline, with a huge chain of mountains dating from the Tertiary period running along the western borders; climates varying from polar or sub-polar to tropical; populations substantially descended from the European colonists, who imposed themselves, frequently by force, upon the aboriginal peoples. If we look more closely, however, the differences between the two Americas become more apparent. The climates only appear to be alike: the North American continent lies almost entirely north of the Tropic of Cancer, with a length north to south of nearly 6,000 kilometres. The prevailing climates are therefore cold and temperate. There are many peninsulas, making North America less compact in outline than the south, and these facilitate access to the interior, assisted by the Great Lakes, the largest expanses of inland fresh water in the world. However, it is from the human and economic points of view that the two Americas differ most obviously. In the north the inhabitants are mainly Anglo-Saxon in origin and the continent has been brought to a high level of prosperity by intensive industrialisation, though certain problems, such as integration of the black population, remain to be solved. Mexico should be considered in a class of its own; from the social and economic points of view it may be said to belong to Central America.

The New World
The contrast of North American urbanisation and North American landscape. Top, a view of New York at night, its skyscrapers symbolising the economic prosperity of the New World. Below, the natural outcrops of Oak Creek Canyon in Arizona. Above, a fragment of a map drawn by Giovanni Vespucci in 1526.

American Indians

The ancestors of the American Indians first crossed the Bering Strait from Asia around 20,000 years ago. Gradually they overran America, developing their own languages and cultures and adapting themselves to the various geographical and climatic conditions. Some tribes, like the Comanches, the Cheyenne and the Sioux, became hunters of bison in the Great Plains; others settled on the west coast of Florida and on the Great Lakes and became farmers, hunters and fishermen; others, like the Shoshonis, occupied the desert areas and led a difficult life; and others still, settled in the more northern areas, surviving mainly on whale meat, reindeer and seal. When the Europeans arrived, the North American Indians probably numbered more than two million. Contact with the European colonists, spreading westward in search of new territory, proved fatal to the Indians, who put up a desperate struggle. Decimated by European diseases and short of food as the bison became extinct, the Indians lost all form of self-government. Today they number scarcely one million.

Above, Indian braves on the west coast – an engraving by Le Moyne in 1591.
Below, a group of Indians in a reserve in Arizona.

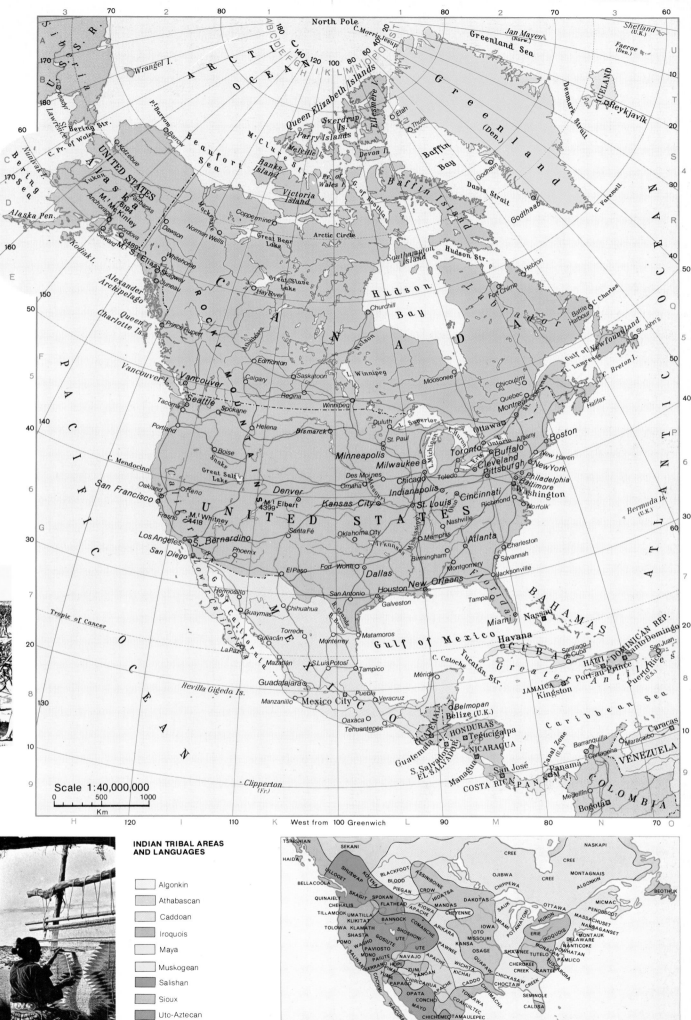

Scale 1:40,000,000
0   500   1000
Km

INDIAN TRIBAL AREAS AND LANGUAGES

- Algonkin
- Athabascan
- Caddoan
- Iroquois
- Maya
- Muskogean
- Salishan
- Sioux
- Uto-Aztecan
- Eskimo
- Other linguistic groups

Scale 1:17,500,000

The extreme north
In the extreme north (above), dense coniferous forests, enclosing lakes of all sizes, give place further north to frozen tundra, the home of the caribou (below) and small lemmings.

Toronto (left)
Toronto, on the shores of Lake Ontario, is a very important industrial and trading centre.

Canada

Canada covers almost 10 million square kilometres, making it the country with the second largest surface area in the world. Its population numbers 23 million, concentrated in the mild southern belt; and the standard of living is high, thanks to the enormous agricultural and mineral resources. These are the main features of this large northern nation.

The more northern areas have an almost impossible climate, with winter temperatures at many tens of degrees below freezing; this is reflected in the density of population: 0.01 inhabitants per square kilometre. However, it is these very areas, ancient in geological terms, that have vast reserves of useful minerals – zinc, uranium, platinum, nickel, iron and copper, not to mention the oil which makes Canada independent as far as energy is concerned. There is also a vast potential for hydroelectric energy.

Canada is a country that can be expected to develop considerably in the future, given the rapid increase in its agricultural and mining techniques, and improved communications.

Greenland
Politically, Greenland is part of Denmark but it became self-governing in 1979. In respect of its geology and climate, however, Greenland may be regarded as forming part of Canada's extreme north. From the point of view of rock formation, its very ancient crystalline rocks tell us that the 'Green Land' originated as part of the Canadian land mass, from which it broke away more than 600 million years ago. The climate is particularly harsh, with average summer temperatures not exceeding 8°C. The salient physical feature is the great ice sheet which covers 80 per cent of the island. The areas of settlement are largely determined by the difficult climatic conditions.
The population is concentrated mainly along the coast, where the ice gives way to tundra. Umanak (the port on the right) is a fishing centre on the east coast.
The population is mainly Eskimo (left).

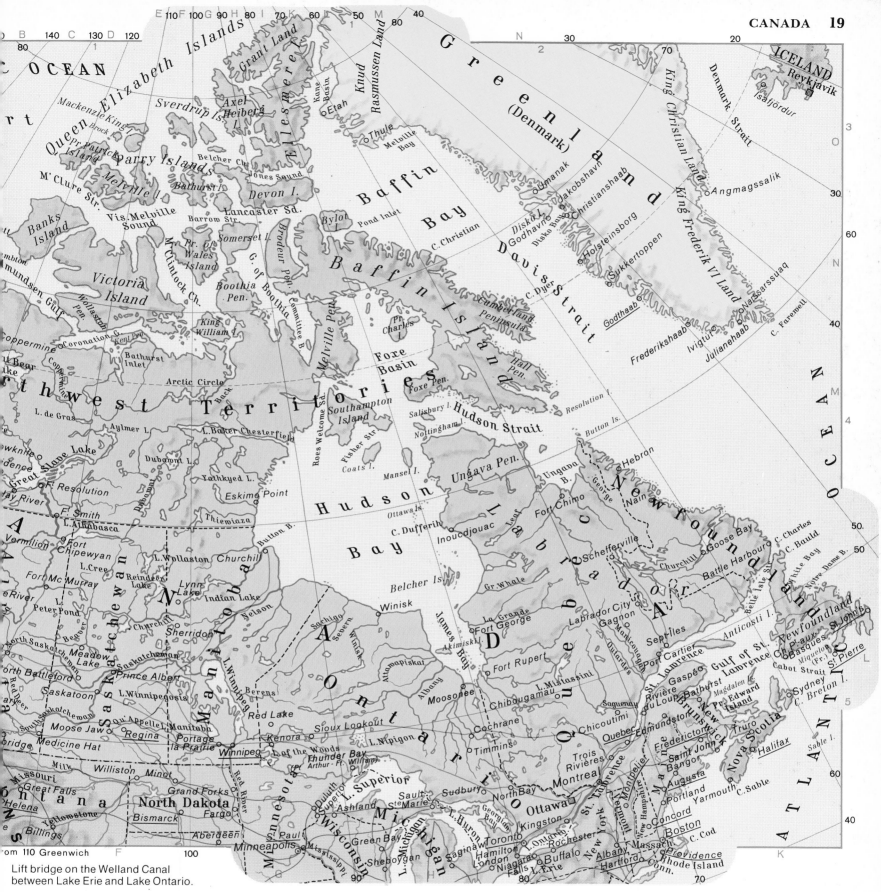

Lift bridge on the Welland Canal between Lake Erie and Lake Ontario.

The Great Lakes

The formation of the Great Lakes, on the borders of Canada and the United States, was caused by glaciation in the Quaternary period. Their basins are vast. Lake Superior has a surface area of more than 84,000 square kilometres, and is the largest freshwater lake on Earth. Their basins trace the courses of former great river beds, subsequently widened and deepened by the ice sheets of the first part of the Quaternary period (the Pleistocene epoch). The gigantic ice sheet of this epoch, known as the Laurentide Ice Sheet, lay more than 2,000 m thick over all this area, passing through various eras of expansion and retreat. The final phase of glaciation, when the lakes began to form at the edge of the ice sheets, goes back almost 14,000 years.

USA

From the point of view of natural advantages, the United States of America may be regarded as a land of privilege. It is situated almost entirely in the temperate zone (excluding Alaska and Hawaii), which means that there are few areas unfit for human habitation. There are vast, fertile plains. The United States has shores on two oceans, and a dense network of rivers, facilitating access to the interior. The rocks are rich in raw materials.

The white colonists, mostly Anglo-Saxon in origin, but with a large percentage of immigrants from other parts of Europe, subjugated the American Indian peoples and turned the country's advantages to good account, developing the United States into the country with the most advanced economy in the world. Its agriculture, in which only 3.5 per cent of the working population is engaged, is without doubt the most advanced in the world, thanks to heavy mechanisation and the extensive use of chemical fertilisers. There are vast mineral resources (especially of coal, oil, iron and uranium) and all sectors of industry are highly developed. The picture is not without its more sombre aspects, however. Wealth is unevenly distributed, and the ethnic minorities, particularly the blacks but also the Puerto Ricans and the Indians, have yet to be fully integrated.

Skyscrapers and natural beauty
Above, New York, a city with almost 10 million inhabitants including its suburbs. Below, a startling landscape in Utah – the Bryce Canyon.

Agriculture
Because of physical and climatic factors, agriculture has tended to develop in latitudinal bands in the eastern United States. To the north there stretches the dairy belt with herds and cattle crops; then comes the corn belt (with a band of cotton), followed by the sub-tropical crops of the extreme south.
Below left, farmland in Pennsylvania. Contour ploughing minimises erosion.

**UNITED STATES:
AGRICULTURAL AREAS**

Predominantly pasture land

Cattle farming

Tobacco

Mixed agriculture and grazing

Cereal crops

Cotton

Forestry products

Fruit crops

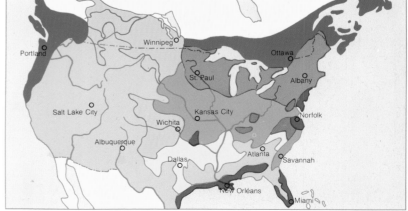

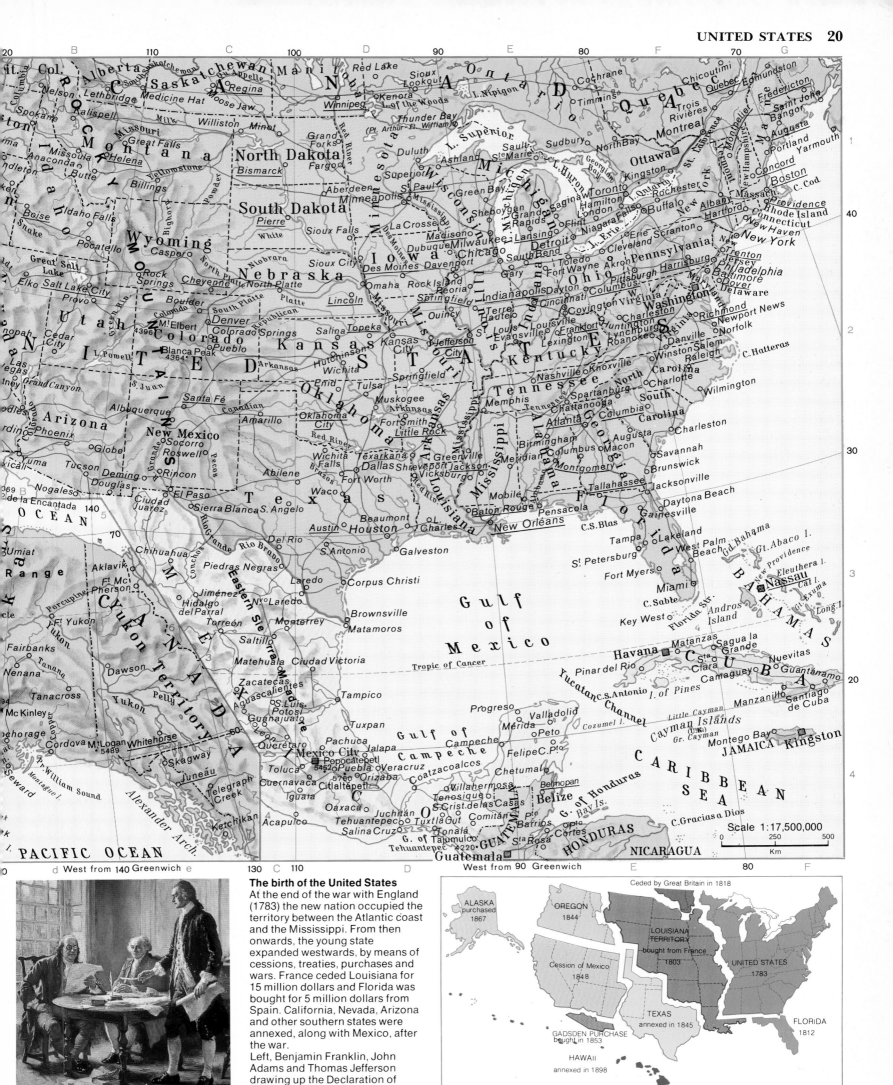

The birth of the United States

At the end of the war with England (1783) the new nation occupied the territory between the Atlantic coast and the Mississippi. From then onwards, the young state expanded westwards, by means of cessions, treaties, purchases and wars. France ceded Louisiana for 15 million dollars and Florida was bought for 5 million dollars from Spain. California, Nevada, Arizona and other southern states were annexed, along with Mexico, after the war.

Left, Benjamin Franklin, John Adams and Thomas Jefferson drawing up the Declaration of Independence (1776).

Scale 1:17,500,000

Ceded by Great Britain in 1818
ALASKA purchased 1867
OREGON 1844
LOUISIANA TERRITORY bought from France 1803
Cession of Mexico 1848
UNITED STATES 1783
GADSDEN PURCHASE bought in 1853
TEXAS annexed in 1845
FLORIDA 1812
HAWAII annexed in 1898

Mexico and Central America

The tropical climate, and such developments as colonisation by the Spanish, along with the present level of social and economic development, make Mexico more a part of Central America, although it is normally included in North America. The territory of Mexico, and above all of Central America and the Antilles, are very young from the geological point of view, as demonstrated by the numerous volcanoes which remain active, and the frequent and disastrous earthquakes. Plate movements in this region may ultimately create a new mountain chain and a new land mass.

The climate, hot and humid or hot and arid, is not very hospitable to man; only in certain restricted areas, such as the 'Temple Lands' of Mexico, is the climate affected by the altitude, becoming more temperate. Almost all these lands are politically unstable and socially and economically undeveloped. The frequently hostile environment and the historical background are compounded by very high levels of population increase (averaging more than 3 per cent), and agriculture blighted by lack of capital and modern technology, very limited industrial development and heavy interference from abroad. Some progress has been made recently, mainly in Mexico, which has substantial mineral and energy resources, notably oil.

Pre-Columbian civilisation
The pyramid at Chichén-Itzá, in Mexico (above), was built in the Maya-Toltec period. The glorious pre-Columbian era saw the flowering of the Toltec, Maya and Aztec peoples.
Below, picturesque market at Chichicastenango in Guatemala.

Scale 1:17,500,000

Mexico – seismic areas
Mexico is under a constant threat of earthquake and volcanic eruptions, because it is situated in an area of seismic instability.
Left, Popocatepetl, one of the active volcanoes.

A REGION OF SEISMIC VIOLENCE

Zone of Moderate Earthquakes
Zone of Intense Earthquakes
Focal Region of Earthquakes
▲ Volcano

Sugar cane
The countries of Central America account for almost 70 per cent of North America's total sugar production.
Above, sugar cane harvest in Vera Cruz, Mexico.

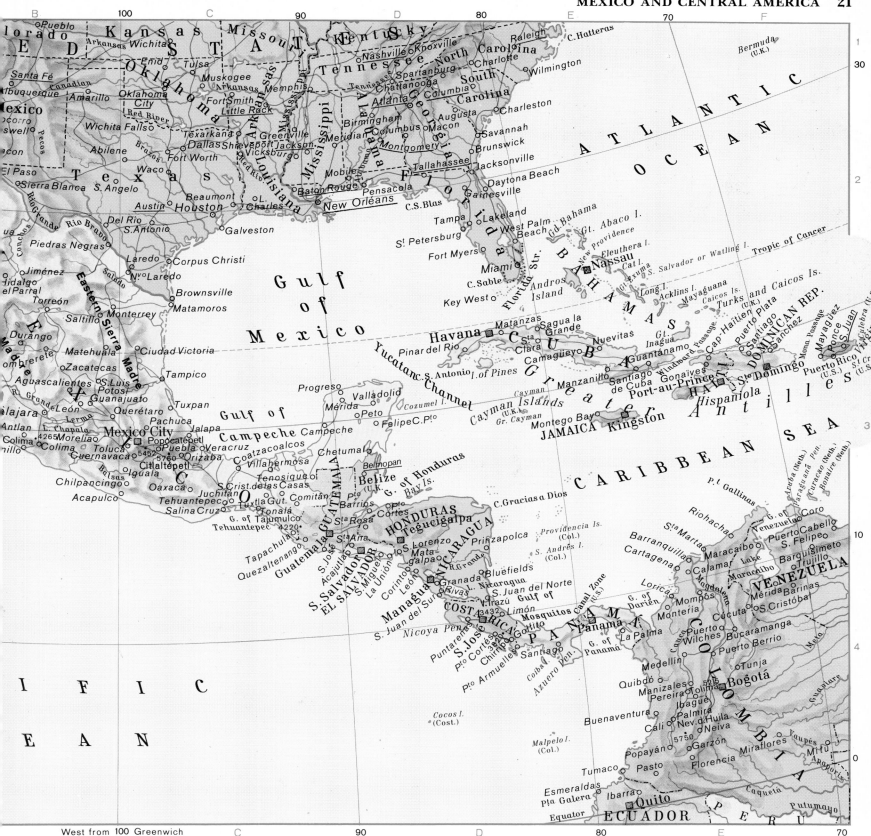

West from 100 Greenwich

Panama

Left, the port of Balboa at the mouth of the Panama Canal. The Canal is Panama's principal economic strength, and provides a vital link for shipping between the Pacific Ocean and the Atlantic. The Canal is controlled by a United States-Panamanian Commission. The former Canal Zone was returned to Panamanian control in 1979.

Mexican Plateau

A large part of Mexico consists of the plateau extending between the Eastern and Western Sierra Madre, at heights between 1,500 and 2,000 metres.

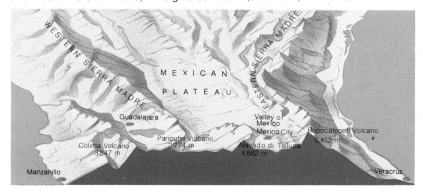

SOUTH AMERICA

More mountainous and compact than the north part of the continent, to which it is linked by the slender isthmus of Central America, the South American continent runs southwards for more than 7,500 kilometres, from the Equatorial belt to the sub-polar. These different latitudes naturally give rise to considerable variations in climate and landscape. One unifying feature is the mountain range of the Andes, running north to south right along the western edge of the continent. This is a young range of mountains, formed in the Tertiary period, and still in the process of settling, as the numerous earthquakes and volcanoes testify. Because of the altitude, climates vary in the Andes and the humidity

and heat which characterise tropical zones are much reduced. Man has been able to settle at high altitudes on the plateaux. La Paz, the administrative capital of Bolivia, is more than 3,000 metres above sea level, Quito, capital of Ecuador, more than 2,800. As the Cordillera is closer to the west coast, there are considerable disparities in the drainage pattern of the slopes on each side. On the western slopes, the rivers are short and plains are narrow. To the east the largest rivers in the world are found, including the Amazon, and an immense lowland region. Many of the South American states, originally colonised by the Iberian people, are in a state of political instability and social and economic crisis.

Machu Picchu (above)
Built by the Incas in the 12th century, and then abandoned, the city of Machu Picchu was not rediscovered until 1911.

Peoples of South America
The ethnic character of Latin America has changed profoundly over the centuries, with the influx of other peoples through colonisation. Only a few areas have retained their original character.
Above, Amazon Indians.
Below, a group of Aymara in Peru.

The Andes (left)
This massive mountain range winds for thousands of kilometres along the western edge of the South American continent. It has characteristic folds going back to the Tertiary period, with imposing rifts of more recent origin. The Andes include the highest peaks of South America, such as Aconcagua (6,960 metres) and Ojos del Salado (6,885 metres).

The Incas

Starting in the 12th century, the Incas built the largest indigenous empire in America, later to be destroyed by the Spanish conquistadors at the beginning of the 16th century. The Incas settled first in the valley of Cuzco, in southern Peru, where a small group of tribes started to take over neighbouring groups. The Incas had many struggles with the Aymara, the Quechua and the Chanca at the start of the 15th century, until, between the end of the 15th and the beginning of the 16th centuries, the empire came to full flower with the conquest of the kingdom of Quito. The Spanish conquest, spearheaded by Francisco Pizarro, began in 1532 and finished at the end of the century, by which time the Incas, after a long struggle had been reduced to semi-slavery. The Incas had created a highly centralised state, governed by a ruling class with a king, known as the 'Inca', as its head. He was regarded as the child of the Sun, and had ultimate political and religious authority. Under him were the dignitaries, each of which had charge of one section of the empire. At the height of its splendour, the empire of the Incas enjoyed a sound economy, based on agriculture and crafts. Part of the land belonged to the Inca himself, and part (one third) to the people. They grew potatoes, beans, maize and tomatoes, and raised animals like the llama and the alpaca. A fine network of roads connected Cuzco with the whole kingdom. The roads, which were straight and paved on the plains, became steep tracks in the mountains. Messengers ran an excellent communications system, covering about 200 kilometres daily. It was thanks to the messengers that it took only three days for the Inca Atahualpa to hear in Cajamarca that Pizarro had landed in Tumbez.

EXPANSION OF THE INCA EMPIRE

Expansion of the empire up to 1525
— Inca roads
▫ Inca cities
Pizarro's expeditions
—— 1526-1528
--- 1531-1533

Scale 1:40,000,000

0   500   1000
Km

The Treasure of the Incas

Like all previous Andean civilisations, the Incas used a great deal of gold and silver for ornamentation and ceremonial purposes. Sadly, the treasures which fell into the hands of the conquistadors were melted down and turned into ingots.
Left, a gold and turquoise ceremonial knife from the kingdom of Chimu (1300-1466).

Cuzco

The Inca capital, Cuzco, grew up right at the heart of the empire, at the precise spot where, according to legend, the golden rod of Manco Capac, child of the Sun, had been driven into the Earth. The city was protected on three sides by the Sacsahuaman fortress (right), a stronghold constructed of enormous blocks of stone, joined together almost invisibly.

Brazil and the north

The mountain range of the Andes, following the line of the coast; numerous chains of mountains with peaks exceeding 6,000 metres; ancient, undulating plains sloping westwards towards the Atlantic; the vast basin of the Amazon at the heart – these are the natural phenomena which characterise the continent's northern sector. A large area of the Amazon basin, divided by the Equator, has a hot, humid climate, with heavy rainfall all the year round. The predominant natural vegetation here is the rain forests, thick and dense, and only recently colonised. A highway, the Trans-Amazon, has now been driven through them. To the north and south of the Amazon, the climate alternates between wet periods and dry ones; these are the areas of grassland, woodland and llanos (savannah), mainly unsuitable for cultivation. In the Andes, it is the altitude which determines the climate – Equatorial on the coast, temperate on the plateaux, and very harsh at higher levels. All the Andean countries share an undeveloped social and economic structure. Only Venezuela seems to have managed to raise its standard of living, thanks to its resources of oil. Brazil is a land of contrasts – poverty and wealth are both in evidence, particularly in the large urban areas, reflecting an imbalance in the exploitation of the country's immense natural resources.

Lake Titicaca (above)
Situated on the frontier between Peru and Bolivia, at an altitude of 3,810 metres, is Titicaca, the largest lake in South America.

Rio de Janeiro (above)
The second largest city in Brazil, Rio de Janeiro illustrates the contradictions of this country. Here you find the most abject poverty, particularly in the slum areas on the edge of the city, rubbing shoulders with ostentatious wealth.

The Amazon
This vast basin covers about seven million square kilometres (see map, right) and the river system has the largest drainage area on Earth. Tributaries of the Amazon rise in Peru, and the river runs eastwards down a gentle gradient, emptying itself into the Atlantic, nearly 6,450 kilometres further on. Most of the basin is covered in rain forest, (left) inhabited by groups of Indians.

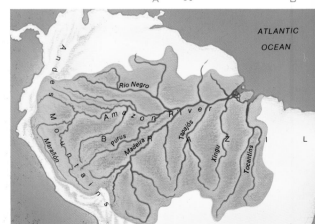

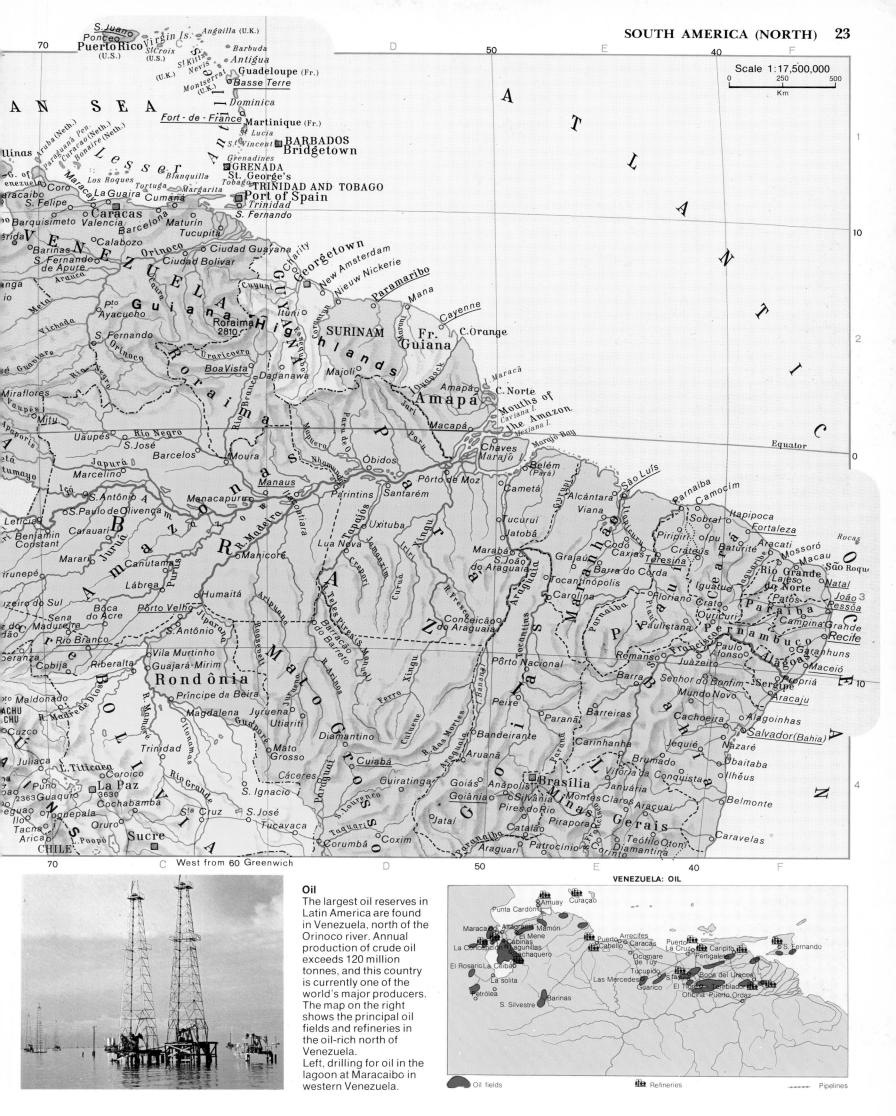

Scale 1:17,500,000

Oil

The largest oil reserves in Latin America are found in Venezuela, north of the Orinoco river. Annual production of crude oil exceeds 120 million tonnes, and this country is currently one of the world's major producers. The map on the right shows the principal oil fields and refineries in the oil-rich north of Venezuela.
Left, drilling for oil in the lagoon at Maracaibo in western Venezuela.

VENEZUELA: OIL

Oil fields   Refineries   Pipelines

Argentina and the south

Chile and Argentina are the two most important political entities in the southern part of the South American continent. Both have grown up mainly in the temperate areas, on the two opposite sides of the Andes. Chile is a narrow land, mostly no more than 200 kilometres wide and more than 4,300 kilometres in length. Argentina on the other hand occupies the vast area running down from the Andes to the Atlantic, consisting partly of extensive plains like the pampas. The physical structure causes problems for both countries. In Chile the amount of flat country suitable for cultivation is very limited, less than 8 per cent of the whole territory in fact, yet most of the population is centred here. The northern area, where the climate is harsh, has vast mineral resources such as copper, of which Chile is one of the world's major producers, and nitrates. The south is cold and uninhabited. The presence of a vast amount of foreign capital has served to upset the economic balance and development of the country, giving rise to the political instability which is common to many Latin American countries. In Argentina also, whole areas of the south are virtually uninhabited. The country's economic centre is situated around Buenos Aires and the surrounding pampas. It is on this endless plain that the main economic activity takes place, including cattle breeding and the cultivation of cereal crops, mainly for export.

The Argentinian Andes (above)
The range of the Andes, seen from the city of Mendoza. Nearby is the highest peak in the Western Hemisphere, Mount Aconcagua.

The gaucho (above)
Both shepherd and farmer, the gaucho of Argentina is accustomed to his solitary way of life and to the vast open spaces of the pampas.

Scale 1:17,500,000

The Antarctic Peninsula (left)
This vast, inhospitable peninsula is situated in the continent of Antarctica, between the Bellinghausen and Weddell Seas. It is claimed partly by Argentina, which has set up a number of scientific bases there, and partly by Chile. At present, however, it is part of the British Antarctic Territory.

Tierra del Fuego (left)
This island is the southern extremity of South America, divided politically between Chile and Argentina. It is an area of harsh rock formations, shaped by the ice. There are many snow- and ice-capped peaks, not more than 2,500 metres in height, and numerous fjords cutting into the coastline, where colonies of penguins make their homes.

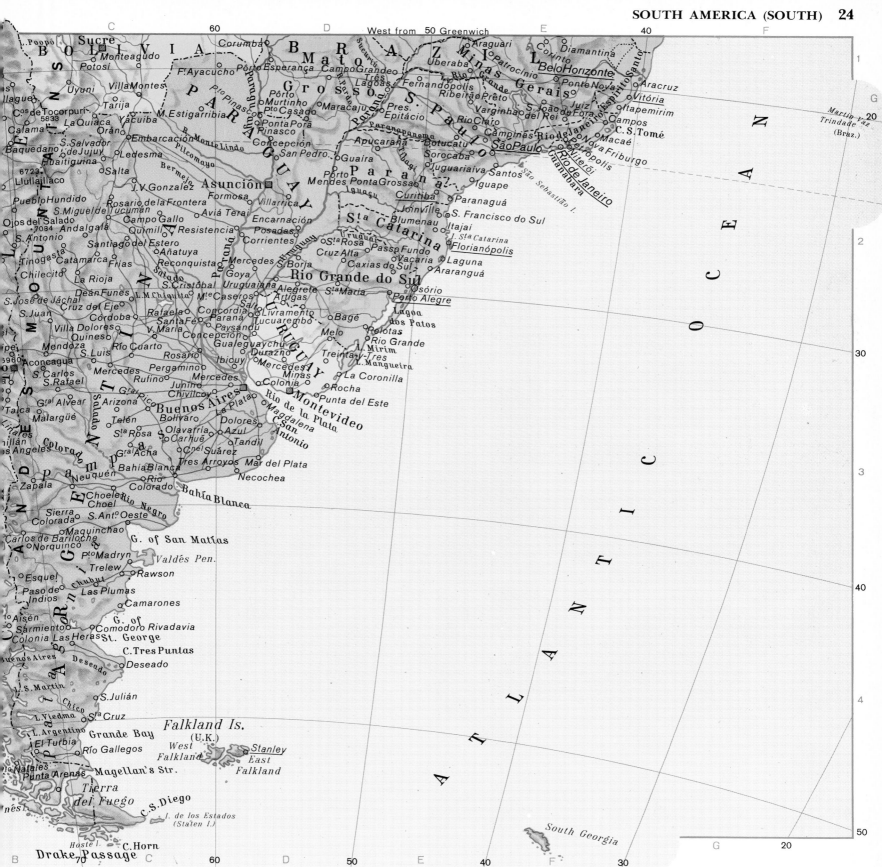

West from 50 Greenwich

ARGENTINA: AGRICULTURE

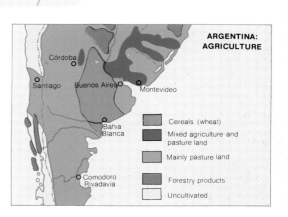

	Cereals (wheat)
	Mixed agriculture and pasture land
	Mainly pasture land
	Forestry products
	Uncultivated

Argentinian agriculture

The Argentinian economy is still largely based on agricultural products and animal husbandry – meat, wool, tobacco and cereals are the main products for export. Wheat is cultivated on the fertile soil of the pampas, a vast plain 600,000 square kilometres in size (Argentina is the largest producer and exporter in South America), along with maize, barley and oats. There are more than 60 million head of cattle and 34 million sheep.
The cattle graze in the open, on vast estates known as 'estancias' (left), where the owner has his own property and there are also houses and stores for his dependents. The cattle are looked after by the gauchos.

OCEANIA

Oceania is the smallest of the continents, and, apart from icy Antarctica, it was the one most recently discovered by the peoples of the west. It is made up of two very different geographical areas. On the one hand there is Australia, which is almost as large as the United States, and on the other, four smaller islands and thousands of tiny ones. There are also considerable geographical and climatic variations over the whole region.

Australia is a very old country, much of it flattened by erosion, whilst the islands of the ocean are of more recent origin. On some of these, New Guinea and New Zealand for instance, are recent mountain chains of the Tertiary period. The smallest islands are volcanic; and many islands were formed as the result of the activity of organisms in the warm seas, namely coral polyps. The majority of the islands of Oceania, if we exclude almost all of Australia, have a hot, humid climate. Only Tasmania and New Zealand are cool and temperate, on account of their latitude.

Apart from Australia, the islands of Oceania are grouped in three areas: Melanesia, comprising the islands from New Guinea to Fiji; Micronesia, which lies north of Melanesia and includes such groups as the Mariana and Caroline Islands; and Polynesia, made up of the eastern archipelagoes enclosed in a triangle formed by New Zealand, Hawaii and Easter Island.

'Tahitians on the beach'
One of Paul Gauguin's earliest pictures of Tahiti. He went to live there in 1891, looking for a simple way of life, unspoiled by civilisation.

The atolls
An atoll is a ring of coral islands surrounding a lagoon. These are only found in the tropical belt, where the temperature of the water is a steady 25°C.
Top, a coral island.
Below, the formation of an atoll, according to Darwin's theory.

New Guinea
New Guinea is the second largest island in the world. A mountain range dating from the Tertiary period, and more than 5,000 metres in height, runs across this territory. Heavy rainfall and high temperatures characteristic of these Equatorial zones have combined to produce dense rain forests, covering the entire island. These physical features have helped extremely primitive groups of peoples to survive in the interior (left, an Okapa warrior). Most of the population of New Guinea is Melanesian, with Papuans predominating, though there are still a few groups of peoples of Negrito origin.

Polynesian peoples
The dugout canoe or pirogue (above) is still the most common method of transport in Polynesia, used both for fishing and for travelling between the islands. It was on board canoes exactly like these that, from the 12th century BC onwards, the earliest Polynesians migrated to the most remote Pacific islands.

Coral forms in shallow water around a volcanic islet which is slowly sinking (or the sea level is rising), producing a coral reef.

The island is almost completely submerged, whilst the coral continues to grow upwards, building on the existing structure.

The island is completely submerged; the coral reef is either circular or elliptical in shape, and covered with vegetation.

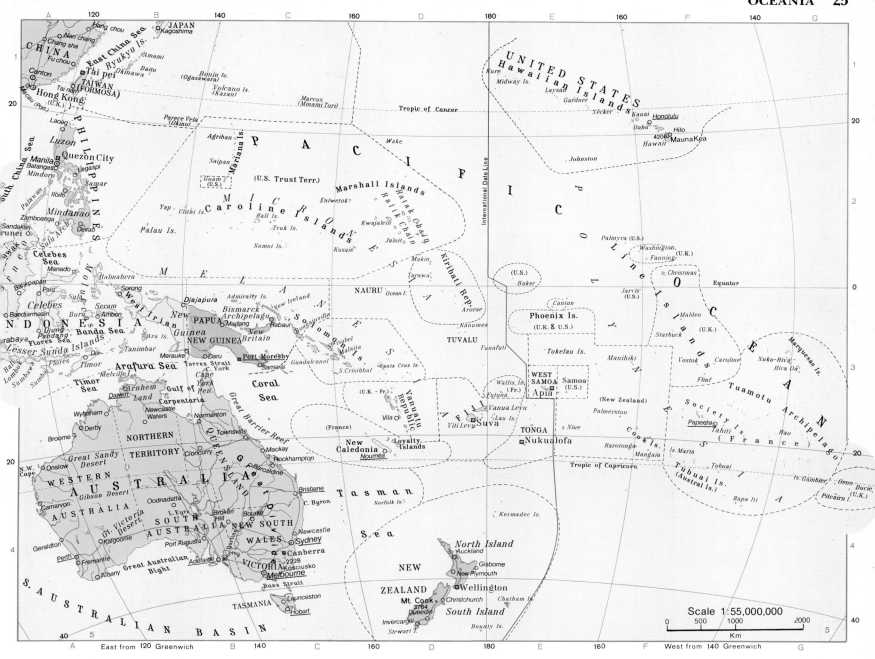

Scale 1:55,000,000

James Cook
The English explorer James Cook led three expeditions to Oceania in the mid-18th century. They conducted a systematic survey of the islands, and did a vast amount of geographical research. On the first voyage, Cook discovered and circumnavigated New Zealand, and then went on to disembark at Botany Bay near Sydney on the east coast of Australia. On the subsequent voyages, he ventured north as far as the Arctic Circle, and south as far as the Antarctic. He died in Hawaii, killed during a fight between his crew and the natives, in 1779.

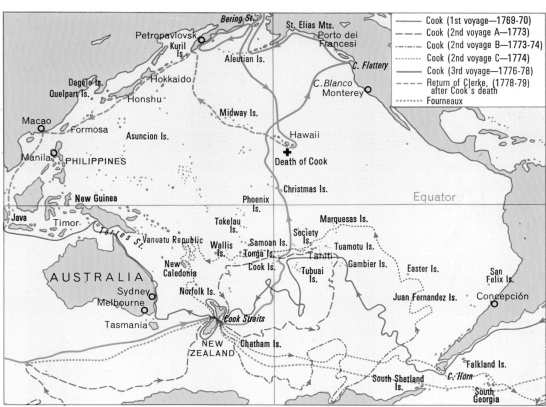

— Cook (1st voyage—1769-70)
-- Cook (2nd voyage A—1773)
-·- Cook (2nd voyage B—1773-74)
···· Cook (2nd voyage C—1774)
— Cook (3rd voyage—1776-78)
-- Return of Clerke, (1778-79)
    after Cook's death
···· Fourneaux

Australia

Australia has a monotonous landscape, much of which has been flattened by erosion. Only on the east coast are there some large mountain peaks, though these are hardly more than 2,000 metres in height. The climate too is uniform. The northern part of the vast Australian tablelands are in the tropical belt, where high pressure prevails, and are therefore covered by deserts and drought-resistant plants and dry scrub. The main feature of the continent is its aridity, and two-fifths of Australia has an average annual rainfall of less than 250 millimetres.

Apart from the Aborigines, people have mostly avoided the interior and settled on the coastlands, where the climate is more humid. For many years, the Australian economy and export trade has been based on cattle breeding and the cultivation of cereal crops. In recent years, however, there has been some industrial development, mainly in mining, and the mineral resources are in fact considerable and varied – gold, iron, coal, zinc and a great deal of oil. The Australian economy is still in the process of development, as shown by the country's ability to absorb vast numbers of immigrants every year.

Ayers Rock
Ayers Rock (right) is a sandstone outcrop, the remains of an ancient mountain chain now almost completely eroded.
The Australian Alps (above) have a similar character; these sandstone formations at Inselberg are the eroded remnants of old land surfaces.

Australian Aborigines
The primitive inhabitants of Australia had a population of about 300,000 when the Europeans arrived, but now number around 100,000. By contrast with their technological backwardness, the Aborigines have a sophisticated social structure and a rich mythology.

Sydney
Founded in 1788, Sydney is the oldest and largest city in Australia.
Above, the modern Sydney Opera House, now a famous Australian landmark.

Animal husbandry and agriculture
About half of Australia is covered by pasture land of varying quality, and most of the country's exports derive from animal husbandry, and especially from sheep farming. In terms of head of sheep, Australia is second only to the USSR in the world. Despite the fact that so much of the country is given over to pasture, about 2 per cent of the land is devoted to crop growing, mainly of wheat and sugar cane.

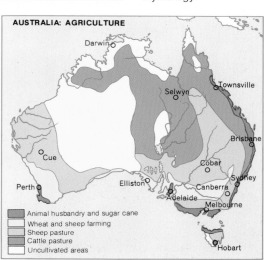

AUSTRALIA: AGRICULTURE

Darwin

Selwyn   Townsville

Cue

Perth   Elliston   Brisbane

Cobar

Sydney

Adelaide   Canberra

Melbourne

Hobart

- Animal husbandry and sugar cane
- Wheat and sheep farming
- Sheep pasture
- Cattle pasture
- Uncultivated areas

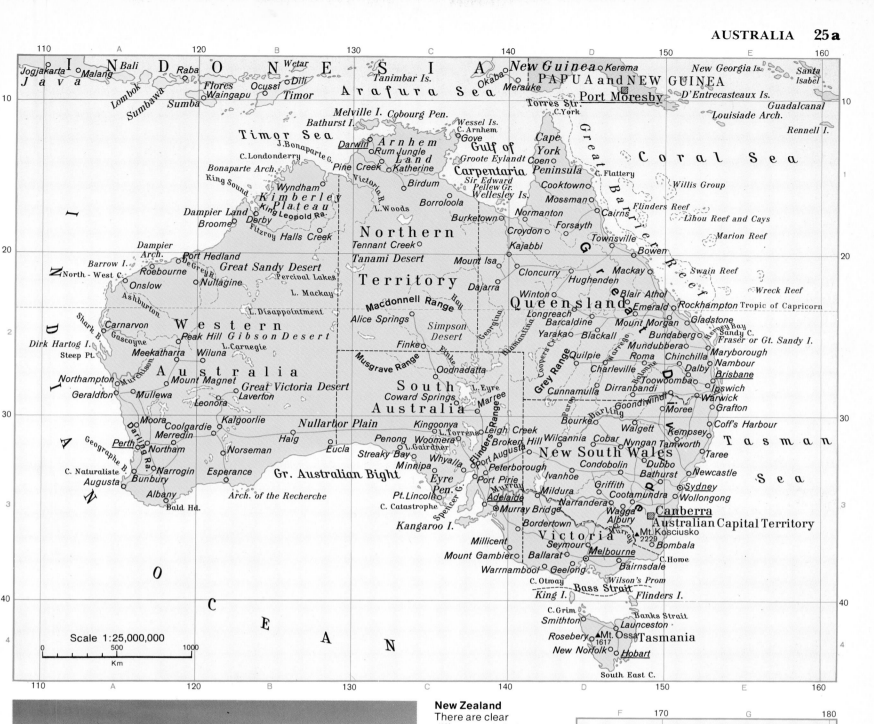

Scale 1:25,000,000

New Zealand Alps

An Alpine landscape on the South Island, New Zealand. This vast chain, called the Southern Alps, was formed in the Tertiary period. It forms the backbone of the country and stretches for 1,500 kilometres, with a height of more than 3,000 metres (the highest peak, Mount Cook, reaching 3,764 metres). The landscape, particularly on the South Island, is reminiscent of the European Alps – jagged rock formations, snow- and ice-capped peaks, some of them quite low. In the Quaternary period, New Zealand was also covered by huge glaciers, stretching down to the sea. When they retreated, this, along with the variations in sea level, gave rise to the numerous fjords which cut into the coastline, particularly in the South Island of New Zealand.

New Zealand

There are clear differences in latitude, climate and morphology between New Zealand and Australia. The New Zealand archipelago is situated in the temperate zone, and characterised by an oceanic climate with heavy rainfall. A mountain chain runs along most of its length. Most of the population is British in origin; the original inhabitants of these islands, the Maoris, almost became extinct in the 19th century, though there are now nearly 300,000 of them. The main economic activity is animal husbandry, principally sheep, whose products (meat, wool and cheese) are exported in large quantities. Half of the surface area of the country is covered with pasture land.

Scale 1:17,500,000

THE ARCTIC

The Arctic and Antarctic areas are similar in geographical location (both being at high latitudes of their respective polar circles) and have constantly low temperatures. However, whilst the Antarctic is a continental land mass covered with ice, the Arctic is mainly made up of a sheet of ice, floating on the surface of the Arctic Sea, plus the northernmost areas of Canada, Alaska, Siberia and the whole of the large island of Greenland.

Temperatures are very low, with variations monthly between +1.5° and −30°C. Even though the sun does not set for days or even months north of the Arctic Circle (66°30′N), the amount of useful heat is limited, because of the considerable angle at which the sun's rays strike the land (in fact it does not rise more than 23°30′ above the horizon.)

In the summer, the sheet of pack ice, with a thickness of as much as 4 metres, breaks up and is reduced in area, forming large floes, which drift away. Their surface is not uniform; the ice is compressed and broken up by wind and currents, forming channels of varying dimensions. A typical tundra vegetation (moss and lichen) covers the more southern areas in summer when the frozen topsoil thaws. The subsoil remains permanently frozen.

Arctic peoples
The population of the Arctic regions is sparse, on account of the low temperatures, and those who live here have to adapt to a particularly hostile environment. The peoples of the polar regions, all Mongol in origin, have settled in Greenland (Eskimoes), Siberia (Samoyeds and Chukchees) and Scandinavia (Lapps). Their economy is based almost exclusively on hunting and fishing. The Eskimoes in particular hunt for seal and walrus, from which they derive meat, fuel oil and clothing.
Left, an Eskimo hunting seal.

Icebergs
Icebergs constitute a grave hazard to shipping. Some of them are immense, and we know that the part which is visible represents only one seventh of the whole. These enormous blocks of ice are not caused by the fragmenting of pack ice, but derive from the glaciers of Greenland, which stretch down to the sea.
Above and left, icebergs along the coast of Greenland.

The riches of the Arctic
Amongst the resources in the Arctic, oil is the most outstanding: rich deposits have been discovered in Alaska, the Canadian Arctic and Siberia. Considerable deposits of iron, nickel and uranium are also starting to be mined. However, the harsh ambient conditions make it difficult to take full advantage of them.

Robert E. Peary
The North Pole was reached on 6 April 1909, by the American explorer Robert Peary (right). He left the island of Ellesmere, and reached the Pole after walking for more than a month, with his assistant, Matt Henson, and four Eskimoes.

The North West Passage
Vessels in the Arctic shown searching for the North West Passage. Taken from an 1850 engraving.

THE ANTARCTIC

As distinct from the Arctic, the ice of the Antarctic rests on a base of solid rock. It is a true continent, larger than Europe, and containing 90 per cent of the world's ice.

The great polar ice sheet, formed from snow which has been deposited here over thousands of years, has an average thickness of 2,000 to 3,800 metres. Vast glaciers flow over hundreds of kilometres from the interior to the ocean. There are hundreds of peaks in the glaciers, some higher than 4,000 metres. The highest is Mount Vinson, 5,139 metres above sea level, in Ellesworth Highland. The climate is harsher than in the Arctic, with average temperatures of between −25 and −60°C; in the interior of the plateau, winter temperatures below −80°C have been recorded. This is mainly due to the weakness of the Sun's rays and the considerable heat losses brought about by reflection from the ice sheet. Apart from the sharpest peaks, there are very few areas not blanketed with snow and ice. There are some valleys, known as 'dry valleys', where a higher temperature is recorded, probably caused by the activity of volcanoes. The Antarctic coast has two main features, the Weddell Sea and the Ross Sea. These regions are completely covered in ice.

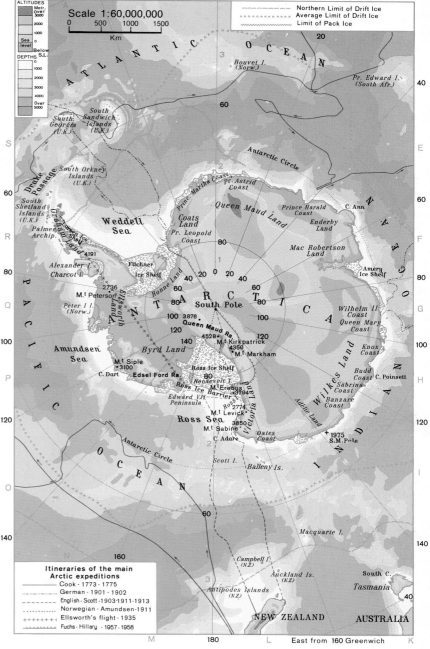

Roald Amundsen
The Norwegian explorer Roald Amundsen (left) reached the South Pole on 14 December 1911. The British Captain Robert Falcon Scott reached the South Pole one month later, but his expedition perished on the return journey.

Scott's hut (below)
The unfortunate explorer's hut was found in a perfect state of preservation in 1955.

Scientific bases
There are more than 50 scientific bases in the Antarctic, set up by countries such as the United States, the USSR, Great Britain, Chile and Argentina. One American base is situated right on the South Pole. Special machinery, techniques and modern equipment make possible the gathering of information on ice thickness, temperature and solar radiation.
Right, an ice-breaker carrying supplies to the American McMurdo Base.
Below right, a plane with special 'skates' landing on the ice runway at the same base.

International treaties
In 1959, following the International Geophysical Year (1957-58) which led to the setting up of numerous scientific bases on the surface of the Antarctic ice, a treaty was signed by the various nations which had participated, laying down that the continent should be kept exclusively for exploration and scientific research purposes, and allocating specific areas to certain countries such as Great Britain and France.

Resources
The 1959 Agreement does not appear to take account of economic realities in the Antarctic. This continent of ice has in fact proved to contain very many desirable resources, and if these are to be mined, fresh legislation will have to be formulated in order to prevent serious dispute between the various powers. The main resources of the Antarctic are the immense iron and oil deposits, though access to these is at present not easy.

Major international organisations

After the Second World War many international organisations were set up with the object of reinforcing co-operation between the countries of the world, and in order to stabilise economic, political and in some cases military links within various areas. An organisation with a universal character is the UNO (United Nations Organisation), set up in 1945 to keep peace in the world and to promote the progress of various countries on the social, economic and cultural fronts. UNO, to which almost all the countries in the world belong, operates through various bodies such as the General Assembly and the Security Council. Various organisations are linked with UNO, and active in different sectors, like the FAO (Food and Agriculture Organisation), UNESCO (United Nations Educational, Scientific and Cultural Organisation), and the WHO (World Health Organisation).

Europe
The European Economic Community has been set up to promote economic co-operation between various countries in western Europe (France, Germany, Italy, the Netherlands, Belgium, Luxembourg, the United Kingdom, the Republic of Ireland and Denmark). Some of the other important bodies in the community are:
the ECSC (European Coal and Steel Community);
EURATOM (European Atomic Energy Community);
BENELUX, set up in 1958 to promote economic unity between Belgium, the Netherlands and Luxembourg;
COMECON (Council for Mutual Economic Aid), which co-ordinates the economic development of the countries of eastern Europe;
COUNCIL OF EUROPE, designed to promote and co-ordinate social and economic development, was set up in 1949 and includes, apart from the EEC countries, many other countries in western Europe;
NORDIC COUNCIL, which links Denmark, Iceland, Sweden, Norway and Finland in development and co-operation on the social and economic fronts;
NATO (North Atlantic Treaty Organisation), also known as the Atlantic Pact, was set up in 1949 for the purposes of western military defence, and including various non-communist countries in eastern Europe;
WARSAW PACT, which links the countries of eastern Europe, is an organisation for co-operation and mutual aid which has a united armed force.

Asia
COLOMBO PLAN (Plan for Development and Co-operation in southern Asia, and the south-east). This was set up in 1951 and links many developing Asiatic countries and some industrialised countries;
ARAB LEAGUE, an organisation which is military and political in character, and links the Arab states of Asia and Africa.

Africa
OAU (Organisation of African Unity) was set up in 1963. It aims at furthering African unity and co-ordinating many aspects of policy, and opposing colonialism.

Latin America
OAS (Organisation of American States) covers many countries in Central and South America, with the object of encouraging peace and progress.

Oceania
ANZUS (the initial letters of the countries) links Australia, New Zealand and the United States in a mutual defence agreement.

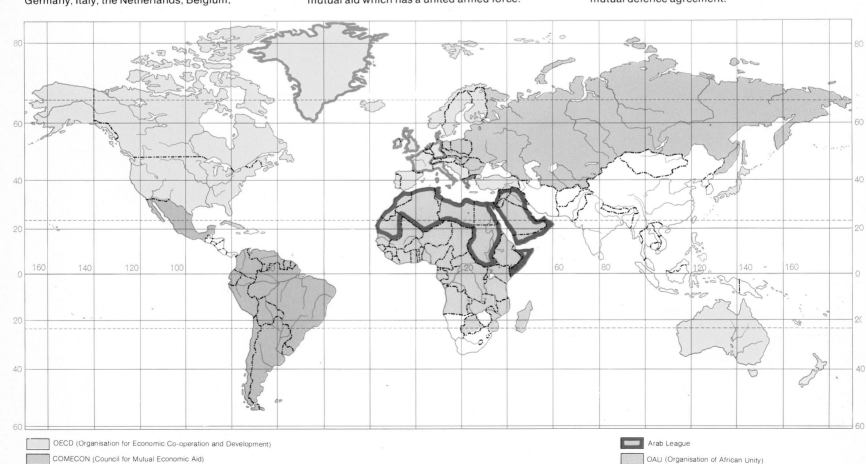

☐ OECD (Organisation for Economic Co-operation and Development)

☐ COMECON (Council for Mutual Economic Aid)

☐ EEC (European Economic Community)

☐ LAFTA (Latin-American Free Trade Association)

☐ Arab League

☐ OAU (Organisation of African Unity)

Countries of Europe

ALBANIA *Area 10,630 sq miles (27,532 sq km); population 2,400,000; capital, Tirana (pop. 200,000); currency, lek (100 qindarka); official language, Albanian.*

Independent since 1912, formerly Turkish. A small People's Republic, Albania lies to the south of Yugoslavia, with a western coastline on the Adriatic Sea. The country is mountainous, with lime soils and karst in the north. Grain and citrus fruits are grown, and sheep and goats are reared.

ANDORRA *Area 191 sq miles (495 sq km); population 25,000; capital, Andorra La Vella (pop. 8,500); currency, franc and peseta.*

A tiny state in the Pyrenees between France and Spain, Andorra consists of wild and rugged tree-covered mountains. Since 1278, the protecting powers have been France and the Spanish Bishopric of Urgel. The main product is tobacco. French and Spanish are spoken, as well as the native Catalan.

AUSTRIA *Area 32,373 sq miles (83,846 sq km); population 7,457,000; capital, Vienna (pop. 1,615,000); currency, schilling (100 groschen); official language, German.*

After the collapse of the Austro-Hungarian Monarchy, the first republic lasted from 1918 to 1938. Then came the *Anschluss* with the German Reich, lasting until 1945, when Austria again became a federal republic.

The south is mountainous, but to the north and north-east the land slopes gently down to the Danube. Cereal crops are cultivated there. The mountain forests produce wood that is used for export or goes to paper factories. Mineral products include iron, magnesium, lead, zinc, copper, and oil. The metal processing and machine industries are prosperous.

BELGIUM *Area 11,774 sq miles (30,495 sq km); population 9,788,000; capital, Brussels (pop. 1,075,000); currency, franc (100 centimes); official languages, French (south), Flemish (north), Dutch, and German.*

An independent monarchy since 1830, formerly linked with the Netherlands, Belgium is thickly populated, with 823 people to the square mile (318 per sq km). The country consists mainly of lowland. Agriculture has been developed to a high degree, and modern farming methods take advantage of the fertile soil and damp climate. Grain, sugar-beet, and potatoes are grown, and vegetables and flowers are cultivated under glass. Cattle and pigs are reared. The main industries are chemicals, textiles, and metals, and the production of glass for mirrors and windows.

BULGARIA *Area 42,858 sq miles (111,002 sq km); population 8,760,000; capital, Sofia (pop. 928,000); currency, lev (100 stotinki); official language, Bulgarian.*

Bulgaria won independence from Turkey in 1878, and in 1946 decided by plebiscite to become a Socialist People's Republic. The country has a varying landscape, with mountain ranges (Balkans and Rhodope Alps) and lowland stretching away in the north to the River Danube. Cereals, fruit, vines, tobacco, sunflowers, and strawberries are cultivated. There are deposits of coal, petroleum, lead, and zinc.

CZECHOSLOVAKIA *Area 49,377 sq miles (127,886 sq km); population 14,974,000; capital, Prague (pop. 1,082,000); currency, koruna (100 haléru); official languages, Czech and Slovak.*

The state of Czechoslovakia was constituted in 1918 out of the union of Bohemia and Moravia (the inhabitants of both of which were known as 'Czechs') and Slovakia. After World War II, the country became a Socialist Federal Republic. Bohemia, in the northwest, is bordered by forest and mountains. The plains are well cultivated. Slovakia is mountainous, and has extensive meadowland and thick forestland. The country was highly industrialized even before the war, especially in Bohemia and Moravia.

DENMARK *Area 16,620 sq miles (43,045 sq km); population 5,080,000; capital, Copenhagen (pop. 1,378,000); currency, krone (100 öre); official language, Danish.*

Denmark has a monarchy dating back to before AD 1000. The country consists of the peninsula of Jutland, which extends northwards from West Germany, and 483 large and small islands. Danish agriculture is one of the most highly developed in the world. There is extensive pig and cattle rearing, and milk, butter, and cheese are exported.

FINLAND *Area 130,165 sq miles (337,126 sq km); population 4,703,000; capital, Helsinki (pop. 885,000); currency, markka (100 penniä); official languages, Finnish and Swedish.*

Finland is a land of lakes and forests. There are some 55,000 lakes, which cover a tenth of the country, and forestland covers as much as two-thirds. The wood processing industry is of prime importance, and Finnish furniture and ready-made houses are highly prized everywhere. Cattle rearing and dairy produce also provide export surpluses, especially butter.

FRANCE *Area 211,200 sq miles (547,000 sq km); population 53,200,000; capital, Paris (pop. 2,590,000); currency, franc (100 centimes); official language, French.*

France, which lies between the Atlantic and the Mediterranean, is separated from Switzerland by the Jura Mountains, from Italy by the Alps, and from Spain by the Pyrenees. There are extensive plains along the Loire and the Garonne, and in the Paris basin. The climate is extremely favourable and agriculture is profitable. Cereals (especially wheat), vegetables, fruit, wine, and sugar-beet are the main crops. Cattle rearing is not quite as comprehensive, but the many varieties of delicious French cheeses are famous. The manufacture of machinery and cars, the aircraft industry, textile mills, and chemical works are all evidence of the country's increasing industrialization.

France is a favourite tourist country by reason of its beautiful scenery and sea coasts, its excellent cuisine, its charming towns, and the wealth of its historical architecture.

GERMANY, EAST (German Democratic Republic) *Area 41,660 sq miles (107,900 sq km); population 17,043,000; capital, East Berlin (pop. 1,200,000); currency, mark (100 pfennigs); official language, German.*

A People's Republic since 1949, East Germany was the Soviet-occupied zone of Germany after World War II. A new 'socialist constitution' was approved in 1968.

The country may be divided up into a flat region in the north and a region of fairly low mountains in the south. Agricultural products include cereals (wheat, rye, barley), potatoes, vegetables, root crops, hops, and flax. Cattle rearing is an important industry. Mineral deposits include coal, lead, zinc, radioactive minerals, potash, and mineral salts. There was considerable industrial development after World War II, and this led to the export of a large number of finished products.

GERMANY, WEST (German Federal Republic) *Area 95,980 sq miles (248,590 sq km); population 61,809,000; capital, Bonn (pop. 279,000); currency, Deutsche mark (100 pfennigs); official language, German.*

The Federal Republic of West Germany was proclaimed in 1949, comprising American, British, and French zones after World War II. A mainly fertile plain covers the northern part of the country. To the south, highlands give way to the foothills of the Alps. Crops grown include cereals (rye, wheat, barley), root crops, vegetables, hops, and potatoes. The dairy industry and cattle and pig rearing are particularly flourishing. Coal mining is important in the Ruhr, and lead, zinc, and potash are also extracted.

West Germany is among the most highly industrialized countries of the world, the most prominent sectors being metallurgy, mechanical engineering, automotive engineering, the chemical industry (especially the manufacture of medicinal products), precision engineering, and the manufacture of optical instruments. Economic development has been greatly assisted by easily navigable rivers, the greatest of which is the Rhine. The more important rivers are linked by canals.

GIBRALTAR *Area 2·25 sq miles (5·83 sq km); population 27,000; capital, Gibraltar (pop. 20,000); currency, pound (100 pence); official language, English.*

At the southern end of the Iberian Peninsula, the rocky promontory of Gibraltar occupies a strategic position at the entrance to the Mediterranean. It has been a British colony since 1713, and in a referendum held in 1967 the people voted almost unanimously to retain the link with Britain rather than return to Spain.

GREECE *Area 50,944 sq miles (131,944 sq km); population 9,200,000; capital, Athens (pop. 2,540,000); currency, drachma (100 lepta); official language, Greek.*

This politically troubled land became a 'presidential parliamentary republic' in 1973, when the 'crowned democracy' was declared at an end. Greece is a country of peninsulas and islands, reaching out from the Balkans into the eastern Mediterranean. Most of the country is mountainous. The mild climate is favourable for the cultivation of the vine, fruit, olives, and tobacco. Marble and emery are the most important mineral products. Tourism is an important economic activity, for the products of the art of Ancient Greece attract visitors from all over the world.

HUNGARY *Area 35,919 sq miles (93,030 sq km); population 10,671,000; capital, Budapest (pop. 1,959,000); currency, forint (100 fillér); official language, Hungarian (Magyar).*

Until 1918, when it was proclaimed a republic, Hungary formed a joint monarchy with Austria. Since 1949, it has been a People's Republic. Apart from the northern part of the country bordering on Czechoslovakia, Hungary is a tableland. Along the Danube (Duna) and the Tisza, the land is very fertile, but in the east it is dry and steppe-like. The main source of revenue is agriculture, and in the north vines are grown. Petroleum, brown coal, and rich bauxite deposits are exploited. There is considerable chemical and engineering industry around Budapest.

ICELAND *Area 39,709 sq miles (102,846 sq km); population 220,000; capital, Reykjavik (pop. 84,000); currency, króna (100 aurar); official language, Icelandic.*

Iceland formerly belonged to Denmark, but became an independent kingdom in 1918 and then, in 1944, a republic. Most of the ground consists of solid lava, and there are still a few volcanic vents. Little land is left that can be used for agriculture. The most important source of revenue is fishing. The houses are heated by the numerous hot springs.

IRELAND, REPUBLIC OF *Area 27,135 sq miles (70,279 sq km); population 2,978,000; capital, Dublin (pop. 566,000); currency, pound (100 pence); official languages, English and Gaelic.*

Ireland lies west of Great Britain, across the Irish Sea, and consists of the Republic of Ireland, which has been independent since 1948, and the north-eastern part, Northern Ireland, which is part of the United Kingdom. There is an extensive flat stretch of land with lakes, bordered on north and south by highland country. Ireland is called the 'Emerald Isle' because of its lush pastures—the essential raw material for the prosperous cattle rearing industry. The main agricultural products are cereals and potatoes. The manufacture of foodstuffs is an important industry.

ITALY *Area 116,303 sq miles (301,223 sq km); population 54,841,000; capital, Rome (pop. 2,843,000); currency, lira; official language, Italian.*

Italy as we know it today was not unified until 1861. It remained a monarchy until after World War II, when, in 1946, the people voted to make it a republic.

The Italian peninsula is bounded in the north by the Alps, and is traversed by the Apennines, running from north-west to south-east, for the whole of its length. In the north, south of the Alps, the fertile plain of the Po stretches to the Adriatic Sea.

The most important agricultural products are wheat, rice, maize, vegetables, olives, citrus fruits, and the vine. Italy produces and exports more wine than any other country.

There are abundant supplies of marble. Important industries include metal-working, mechanical engineering (especially motorcars), the processing of foodstuffs, and oil refining. Tourism is a major source of revenue, for no other country in the world possesses so many ancient art treasures.

LIECHTENSTEIN *Area 62 sq miles (161 sq km); population 24,000; capital, Vaduz (pop. 4,000); currency, franc (Swiss); official language, German.*

Liechtenstein has been a hereditary principality since the 1340s, and became an independent state in 1719. It is a tiny country, consisting of nothing but mountains, between Austria and Switzerland. It is almost completely covered with forests.

LUXEMBOURG *Area 999 sq miles (2,587 sq km); population 357,000; capital, Luxembourg (pop. 78,000); currency, franc (100 centimes); official languages, French, Luxembourgeois, and German.*

The Grand Duchy of Luxembourg has been independent since 1890. It is a hilly country, and potatoes, cereals, and fruit are cultivated. The main source of revenue comes from the mining of iron ore.

MALTA *Area 122 sq miles (316 sq km); population 304,000; capital, Valletta (pop. 16,000); currency, pound (100 cents); official languages, Maltese and English.*

An island in the middle of the Mediterranean to the south of Sicily, Malta (which also includes the smaller islands of Gozo and Comino) became an independent country in 1964, after 150 years of British rule. The island has a mountainous landscape. Cereals, vines, and vegetables are cultivated.

MONACO *Area 0.7 sq miles (1.8 sq km); population 24,000; capital, Monaco (pop. 2,000); currency, franc (French); official languages, French and Monégasque.*

This little principality lies on the French Mediterranean coast to the east of Nice. Its favourable climate and the well-known Monte Carlo casino attract many tourists.

NETHERLANDS *Area 15,771 sq miles (40,844 sq km); population 13,800,000; capital, Amsterdam (pop. 807,000); currency, guilder (100 cents); official language, Dutch.*

After a period of domination by France, the Netherlands became an independent constitutional monarchy in 1815. At that time it also included what are now Belgium (broke away in 1830) and Luxembourg (1890).

The land is a plain, partly below sea level and protected by high dykes. The port of Rotterdam (pop. 654,000) has the largest turnover of merchandise in the world.

The marine climate brings heavy rainfall, and the fertile soil bears rich crops of vegetables, flowers, and potatoes. Cereals are grown principally as fodder for the abundant cattle, which produce milk and cheese. The foodstuffs processing industry is highly developed. There are large margarine factories, electrical engineering works, and petroleum refineries.

NORWAY *Area 125,181 sq miles (324,217 sq km); population 4,035,000; capital, Oslo (pop. 477,000); currency, krone (100 öre); official languages, Bokmål (or Riksmål) and Nynorsk (or Landsmål).*

Norway was at various times united with Denmark or Sweden, and has a monarchy that goes back a thousand years. Most of the country is mountainous, with deep fjords along the coast. The Gulf Stream provides a mild climate for the latitude, so that the Atlantic ports remain free of ice throughout the winter. The most important economic activity is fishing. Huge pine forests provide wood for the paper industry. In the tundra of the far north, there are 22,000 nomadic Lapps, who keep reindeer. Hydraulic power is drawn from the numerous waterfalls, and these provide even the smallest villages with electricity. Iron ore is mined, and oil began to be extracted from the North Sea fields in the 1970s.

POLAND *Area 120,360 sq miles (311,730 sq km); population 34,528,000; capital, Warsaw (pop. 1,308,000); currency, zloty (100 groszy); official language, Polish.*

A People's Republic, Poland was once a monarchy, but its powerful neighbours several times forced it into accepting partial or total partitioning of its territory. After World War II, the victorious powers fixed Poland's new borders.

Most of Poland lies in the plain that stretches from Russia to northern Germany. Only towards the south does the land become at all mountainous. The most important economic activity is still agriculture, and the potato harvest is the second largest in the world. Cattle rearing provides meat exports as well as covering Poland's own needs. Silesia has rich mineral deposits, including

considerable resources of coal, iron, lead, and zinc.

PORTUGAL *Area 34,240 sq miles (88,680 sq km); population 8,740,000; capital, Lisbon (pop. 783,000); currency, escudo (100 centavos); official language, Portuguese.*

Portugal was a monarchy until 1910, and has been an independent country since the 12th century. A military coup in 1974 saw the return of a multi-party system after a period of authoritarian rule.

The country occupies most of the western part of the Iberian Peninsula, and is traversed by mountain ranges and by rivers such as the Douro and Tagus (Tejo) that rise in Spain and flow into the Atlantic. Nearly half the people work on the land and in the forests. The mild climate is favourable to the cultivation of vegetables, cereal crops, olives, and, above all, the vine. Port, a fortified wine, is exported to countries all over the world. Fishing is an important industry, most of the catch (especially sardines and tuna) being canned. The harbour towns of Lisbon and Oporto have large industrial areas. Portugal has the most extensive cork forests in the world. The lovely coastline and picturesque forests attract large numbers of tourists.

ROMANIA *Area 91,700 sq miles (237,500 sq km); population 21,559,000; capital, Bucharest (pop. 1,488,000); currency, leu (100 bani); official language, Romanian.*

After being under Turkish control for a number of years, Romania became fully independent in 1878. It was a monarchy until 1947, and a year later a communist government was set up. The country is traversed by two crescent-shaped and wooded ranges of the Carpathians. Between them lies the Transylvanian plateau. The plains of Walachia and Moldavia extend towards the south and east, broken by the tributaries of the Danube and a number of lakes. In the south-east, the country reaches the Black Sea. Most workers are employed on the collective farms, but the country's main wealth stems predominantly from industry and mining. Romania is one of Europe's leading oil-producing countries.

SAN MARINO *Area 24 sq miles (62 sq km); population 19,000; capital, San Marino (pop. 2,000); currency, lira (Italian); official language, Italian.*

The independence of San Marino, the world's smallest republic, goes back to the 1200s, and it was founded about AD 350. Its status was recognized by Italy in 1862. Entirely surrounded by Italy, the country lies on the eastern slopes of the Apennines. The main sources of revenue are agriculture, stockbreeding, and tourism.

SPAIN *Area 194,885 sq miles (504,750 sq km); population 35,260,000; capital, Madrid (pop. 3,150,000); currency, peseta (100 céntimos); official language, Castilian Spanish (Basque, Catalan, and Galician are spoken in their respective regions).*

A monarchy for many centuries, Spain became a republic in 1931. After the parties of the left had been successful in the 1936 elections, civil war broke out. It lasted three years, and the victorious General Franco became head of state. In 1947, he declared that Spain would revert to a monarchy, which it did when he died 28 years later.

Spain has two large plains—the Ebro basin in Aragon and the dry basin of the Guadalquivir in lower Andalusia. The rest of the country is mountainous, with, in the centre, the largely rainless Meseta plateau, which covers three-quarters of the country. Cereal crops, vines, and olives are grown there. A third of the work force is engaged in agriculture, either as labourers on private estates or as smallholders. One big problem is the migration of young people to the towns and tourist centres.

SWEDEN *Area 173,400 sq miles (449,110 sq km); population 8,236,000; capital, Stockholm (pop. 1,307,000); currency, krona (100 öre); official language, Swedish.*

The Swedish monarchy has existed for nearly a thousand years. For more than the last 150 of these, Sweden has been involved in no wars. The social welfare and schools systems are exemplary.

The eastern half of the Scandinavian mountain chain lies in Sweden. The land falls away gradually to the south-east until it reaches the Baltic. Numerous waterfalls are exploited for electric power. One-twelfth of the country is covered by lakes. In the plains, vast fields of wheat, sugar-beet, and potatoes are to be seen, and the forests of central Sweden provide immense quantities of timber. What is not exported is processed for furniture, cellulose, and paper. Sweden is a highly industrialized country, manufacturing, in particular, high-quality steel. Other important industries are shipbuilding, car and ball-bearing manufacture, and chemicals. The northern parts are peopled by several thousand Lapps, who live largely by rearing reindeer.

SWITZERLAND *Area 15,940 sq miles (41,284 sq km); population 6,385,000; capital, Bern (pop. 162,000); currency, franc (100 centimes); official languages, German, French, and Italian.*

The Federal Government consists of 22 basically independent *cantons,* whose parishes also enjoy the right to a considerable amount of self-administration. The country has been neutral for some 150 years. Sandwiched between Austria and France in one direction, and between Italy and West Germany in another, Switzerland lies squarely in the Alps, and half of the country is higher than 3,300 feet (1,000 metres). The northern part, the so-called *Mittelland* (the Swiss plateau), has a surface broken by many lakes and rivers. The main crop there is wheat, but on the mountain slopes cattle are reared and there is much dairy farming. Swiss industry is highly specialized, being concentrated on foodstuffs, pharmaceutical products, and precision engineering (especially watches and clocks). Tourism is very important, particularly in the many areas suitable for skiing.

UNITED KINGDOM *Area 94,216 sq miles (244,018 sq km); population 55,522,000; capital, London (pop. 6,918,000); currency, pound (100 pence); official language, English.*

The United Kingdom of Great Britain and Northern Ireland is governed by a system of parliamentary democracy. The country is generally hilly, and Scotland and Wales are mountainous. The rivers are not very long, but they are for the most part navigable. The climate tends to be unsettled. Britain imports much food, especially from its former colonies, which today belong to the Commonwealth, of which Britain is the head. Sheep rearing is an important industry, producing meat and wool. Fishing is also important, and coal and other minerals produce considerable revenue. It was in Britain that the Industrial Revolution began in the 18th century, and this led to economic prosperity—textiles, engineering, motor-car and aeroplane manufacturing, and shipbuilding. Britain has also played a leading role in the development of rail traffic, and its merchant navy is one of the finest in the world. The country's insular situation, its many excellent river ports, and its frontage on the Atlantic Ocean, have made of the British a nation of mariners. In the 1970s, Britain, with its dwindling prosperity and severe balance-of-trade deficits, saw a possible solution in the development of its considerable North Sea oil resources.

USSR (Russia) *Area 8,650,000 sq miles (22,403,000 sq km); in Europe, 2,150,000 sq miles (5,568,000 sq km); in Asia, 6,500,000 sq miles (16,835,000 sq km); population 238,371,000 (in Europe 179,407,000; in Asia 58,964,000); capital, Moscow (pop. 7,172,000); currency, rouble (100 copecks); official language, Russian.*

The USSR (Union of Soviet Socialist Republics) is a multi-national state consisting of 15 Union Republics, 20 Autonomous Republics, 8 Autonomous Regions, and 10 National Areas. The 'Russians' themselves constitute the majority of the population. Originally the Russians lived only in the heartland of the Soviet Union, but now they are to be found all over, especially in Siberia. There are major distinctions between Great Russians, Little Russians (Ukrainians), and White Russians, but, apart from these, there are more than a hundred races: Uzbeks, Tartars, Armenians, Georgians, Turkomans, Kazakhs, and others, all with their own languages.

In area, the Soviet Union is the largest country in the world, occupying more than half the continent of Europe and about a third of Asia. The centre and north of the European part is tableland. In the south, the frontier is formed by the Caucasus Mountains. The Volga is the longest river in Europe, and the most important in Russia. Beyond the Ural Mountains, the Asian part of the USSR consists of the western Siberian lowlands, the mountainous area of central and eastern Siberia, the flat and partially desert area of central Asia reaching as far as the Pamirs, and the Far East, bounded by the Sea of Okhotsk and the Sea of Japan.

As may be expected from the extent of the country, there is a wide range of climate. In the tundra of the extreme north, the ground never really thaws out, whereas vines and tea plants grow in the south. Inland, the summers are hot and the winters extremely cold.

Once an agricultural country, the Soviet Union is now an industrial world power. Even the extensive collectivized agriculture is largely automated. The country is rich in mineral resources, the conditions for the exploitation of which in the eastern areas are being constantly improved. Scientifically and technically, the USSR is one of the leading nations of the world.

VATICAN CITY STATE *Area 0·17 sq mile (0·44 sq km); population 1,000; capital, Vatican City; currency, lira (Italian); official languages, Latin and Italian.*

The present-day frontiers of the Vatican, which lies wholly within Rome, were recognized by Italy in 1871, and the full and independent sovereignty of the Holy See was ratified in 1929. The museums of the Vatican are visited by hundreds of thousands of tourists every year.

YUGOSLAVIA *Area 98,750 sq miles (255,760 sq km); population, 21,500,000; capital, Belgrade (pop. 1,204,000); currency, dinar (100 paras); official languages, Serbo-Croatian, Slovene, and Macedonian.*

The present-day Socialist Federal Republic consists of six republics: Serbia, Slovenia, Croatia, Bosnia-Herzegovina, Montenegro, and Macedonia. Up to 1918, most of the country belonged to the Austro-Hungarian monarchy.

Bare karst mountains fringe the Adriatic Sea. Inland, most of the agriculturally exploitable plains lie along the Danube and its tributaries. The main crops are wheat, maize, tobacco, and vines, and stone fruits (plums, cherries) that are used in making highly popular alcoholic beverages. There are rich deposits of bauxite, lead, and zinc. The beautiful Adriatic coast has become an important centre of tourism.

Countries of Asia

AFGHANISTAN *Area 250,000 sq miles (647,000 sq km); population 21,900,000; capital, Kabul (pop. 500,000); currency, afghani (100 puls); official languages, Dari Persian and Pushtu.*

The great mountain range of the Hindu Kush extends north-east to south-west across the country, some of its peaks rising to about 25,000 ft (7,600 m). The longest of the many rivers is the Helmand. Only some 4 per cent of the land is cultivated, and many people live as nomadic herdsmen, wandering over the mountain pastures with their herds of goats and karakul sheep. In the villages, cereals, sugar-beet, fruit, and cotton are grown. Exports include lambskins, carpets, and fruit. Manufacturing industries are being developed.

BAHRAIN *Area 420 sq miles (1,080 sq km); population 320,000; capital, Manama (pop. 90,000); currency, dinar (1,000 fils); official language, Arabic.*

The state consists of several islands in the Persian Gulf, the largest of which is Bahrain Island. Once famous for its pearl fisheries, it has become rich by oil production. Its social services are highly developed.

BANGLADESH *Area 55,126 sq miles (142,776 sq km); population 86,498,000; capital, Dacca (pop. 1,700,000); currency, taka (100 paise); official languages, Bengali and Bihari.*

Until 1971, the country was East Pakistan, but in that year it broke away from Pakistan after a bloody civil war. Its territory consists of part of Assam and the old province of East Bengal. Much of it is an alluvial plain formed by the Ganges and the Jamuna. The delta of the Ganges, on the Bay of Bengal, is the world's largest. The chief products are jute, rice, tea, and tobacco.

BHUTAN *Area 18,000 sq miles (46,000 sq km); population 1,150,000; capital, Thimphu (pop. 8,000); currency, rupeé (100 paise) and ngultrum; official language, Dzongka.*

Small kingdom in the Himalayas, lying between Tibet (China) and India. Most of its people live in the fertile valleys in the centre of the country. The south has forested lowlands, and the north is fringed by high mountain peaks. The way of life is very similar to that of Tibet. Most of the people live by farming; their chief crops are rice, wheat, and barley.

BRUNEI *Area 2,226 sq miles (5,765 sq km); population 177,000; capital, Bandar Seri Begawan (pop. 38,000); currency, dollar (100 sen); languages, Malay, Chinese, and English.*

Brunei, on the northern coast of Borneo, is a self-governing sultanate. It is under British protection.

BURMA *Area 262,000 sq miles (679,000 sq km); population 30,100,000; capital, Rangoon (pop. 3,187,000); currency, kyat (100 pyas); official language, Burmese.*

The country became independent in 1948 after several generations of British rule. The Arakan Mountains extend along the western side of the country, and the eastern half is a high plateau, the Shan Massif. Between the mountains and the plateau is a lowland drained by the Irrawaddy and Sittang rivers. Another great river, the Salween, flows near the eastern border. A narrow strip of land, the Tenasserim Coast, stretches southwards to the Malay Peninsula. Burma is rich in mineral resources—oil, precious stones, and metals. The chief crops are rice, wheat, millet, sugarcane, ground-nuts, and tobacco. The forests yield teak and other woods. Most of the people are Burmans.

CHINA *Area 3,700,000 sq miles (9,600,000 sq km); population 894,531,000; capital, Peking (pop. 7,570,000); currency, yuan (10 chiao; 100 fen); official language, Chinese (Mandarin).*

The People's Republic of China, occupying more than one-fifth of Asia, is the home of about one-fifth of all the people in the world. Its history goes back nearly 4,000 years, and it has one of the oldest and most highly-developed civilizations. Vast areas of the country are almost uninhabited, but there are also many huge cities. In the east, there is a 4,250-mile (6,800-km) coastline on the Pacific Ocean. The Formosa Strait separates China from another Chinese country, Taiwan. On the south, west, and north, lofty mountain ranges form natural frontiers. The high plateau of Tibet in the south-west lies between the Kunlun Mountains (to the north) and the Himalayas, the world's highest mountain range (to the south). Beyond the Kunlun Mountains is the Takla Makan Desert. In the north, in Inner Mongolia, is part of another great desert, the Gobi.

The eastern part of China, the part where most of the people live, consists of two great river basins separated by the Chin Ling range. To the north of this range is the plain crossed by the Hwang Ho—the Yellow River, so called because of the yellow mud that colours its waters. To the south is the plain of the Yangtze-Kiang. These lowland regions are the historic China, the part of the country that the Great Wall was built to protect.

In the north and in the mountains the winters are bitterly cold. In the south, the climate is tropical or sub-tropical. The south-eastern coast suffers from typhoons and other destructive storms. In the interior, the rainfall is irregular and droughts and floods have caused famine from time immemorial. Today, dams and irrigation give some measure of protection. Rice and wheat are the chief crops. In the Yangtze valley as many as three rice crops are harvested each year. The government encourages the development of industry, but the economy is still mainly agricultural.

CYPRUS *Area 3,572 sq miles (9,251 sq km); population 640,000; capital, Nicosia (pop. 108,000); currency, pound (1,000 mils); official languages, Greek and Turkish.*

The island republic of Cyprus, in the Mediterranean Sea, was under British rule until 1960. Since independence it has suffered from conflict between the Greek majority (four-fifths of the population) and the Turkish minority. The island, the third largest in the Mediterranean, has two mountain ranges: the Kyrenia Range in the north, and the Troodos Mountains in the centre and west. Between these ranges lies a fertile plain, the Mesaoria. The country is rich in minerals, including copper and asbestos. Agricultural products, such as cereals, wine, fruit, and tobacco, are the chief source of income.

HONG KONG *Area 398 sq miles (1,031 sq km); population 4,478,000; capital, Victoria (pop. 670,000); currency, dollar (100 cents); languages, English and Chinese.*

The British crown colony of Hong Kong, on the southern coast of China, consists of Hong Kong Island, more than 200 other small islands, and Kowloon and the New Territories on the mainland. It is an important financial, industrial, and trading centre.

INDIA *Area 1,262,000 sq miles (3,268,400 sq km); population 667,183,000; capital, New Delhi (pop. 4,070,000); currency, rupeé (100 paise); official language, Hindi.*

Once 'the brightest jewel in the British crown', India has been independent since 1947. It has more people than any other country except China. India's civilization is one of the world's oldest, dating back to at least 2500 BC. The country occupies the greater part of the Indian Peninsula, its neighbours in the peninsula being Pakistan and Bangladesh. Its coastline on the Indian Ocean measures some 4,250 miles (6,800 km). The terrain is very varied. Foothills of the Himalayas extend along 1,500 miles (2,400 km) of the northern border. To their south, the alluvial lowlands of the Northern Plains stretch right across the widest part of the peninsula. They have India's richest farming land, and are heavily populated. Still farther south is the Deccan Plateau, occupying the greater part of the peninsula. On both coastal edges it rises to mountain ranges called the *Ghats*. Almost all parts of the country are crossed by great rivers, but the most important are in the north: the Indus, the Ganges, and the Brahmaputra. In most areas, the south-west monsoon brings heavy rains each year from June to September. Much of the country is very hot, the coolest areas being in the hills and on the west coast. Rice and wheat are the most important crops. Other crops are millet, ground-nuts, bananas, cotton, rapeseed, linseed, and jute. There are great numbers of cattle, sheep, and goats; cattle are sacred to the Hindus and are not used for food. The most important manufactures are textiles, but the development of other industries is a major part of government planning. One of the country's most serious problems is over-population.

INDONESIA *Area 782,700 sq miles (2,027,100 sq km); population 155,000,000; capital, Djakarta (pop. 6,000 000); currency, rupiah (100 sen); official language, Bahasa Indonesia.*

The country consists of about 3,000 islands grouped between the Indian and Pacific oceans. The largest are Sumatra, Celebes, and Java. Indonesia shares two other large islands: Borneo with Malaysia, and New Guinea with Papua New Guinea. Most of the larger islands are mountainous and volcanic. There are more than 200 volcanoes, of which about 60 are active and 125 more eject sulphur fumes. The most densely populated island is Java: more than half of all Indonesians live on it and it is the seat of the government. It has rich agricultural land in the north, and it is well known for its wax-printed fabric, called *batik*. Many of the other, lightly-populated islands are thickly forested, and some are swampy. The climate is generally humid and sultry, the hottest regions being on the islands that lie on the equator —Sumatra and Kalimantan (the Indonesian part of Borneo), for example. All the islands are affected by the monsoons. Indonesia has rich mineral deposits, chiefly petroleum, tin, and bauxite. Rubber, tea, coffee, tobacco, and sugar are grown on plantations. The chief subsistence crops are rice and other cereals, bananas, spices, and beans.

IRAN *Area 680,000 sq miles (1,626,500 sq km); population 34,000,000; capital Tehran (pop. 4,496,000); currency, rial (100 dinars); official language, Farsi (Persian).*

The Islamic republic of Iran lies between the Caspian Sea in the north, and the Persian Gulf and Arabian Sea in the south. It is often called *Persia*. It is mostly a vast, mountain-fringed plateau, averaging some 4,000 ft (1,200 m) above sea-level. However, part of the Great Sand Desert, the Dasht-i-Lut, in the east-centre is some 800 ft (250 m) below sea-level. This desert is one of the hottest in the world. To its north is the Great Salt Desert, the Dasht-i-Kavir. The northern coastal strip is the only major agricultural area, and the chief crops are cereals, tea, fruit, and cotton. Several million people live nomadic lives as herdsmen. The rich mineral deposits include petroleum.

IRAQ *Area 172,000 sq miles (445,500 sq km); population 13,505,000; capital Baghdad (Pop. 3,206,000); currency, dinar (1,000 fils); official language, Arabic.*

The country has been independent since 1958; previously it had been under Turkish and, from 1920, British rule. The lowlands in the centre of Iraq are the basins of the Tigris and Euphrates rivers. These great rivers are the frontiers of the historic region of *Mesopotamia*, 'the country between the rivers'. On the north, the lowlands are bordered by wooded hills, which are part of *Kurdistan*. The people of this region, the Kurds, look upon themselves as a separate nation. In the west of Iraq are the barren wastes of the Syrian Desert. The country's chief source of revenue is petroleum, and it has other minerals, too. Cereals, cotton, vegetables, and tobacco are the principal agricultural products.

ISRAEL *Area 7,992 sq miles (20,700 sq km); population 3,670,000; capital Jerusalem (pop. 400,000); currency, shekel (100 agora); official languages, Hebrew and Arabic.*

Since its foundation in 1948, Israel has fought a continuing war against some of its hostile Arab neighbours. About half of the country is occupied by the Negev Desert, but the north is mountainous and there is also a low-lying coastal strip. Much desert land has been made arable by being cleared and irrigated. This pioneer work was carried out by *kibbutzim*, community settlements. Intensive agriculture is of major importance to the economy. The chief products are cereals, citrus fruits, grapes (for eating and for wine), and vegetables. There are textile, engineering, and chemical industries in addition to food processing. Mineral resources include potash, phosphates, oil, and natural gas.

JAPAN *Area 142,810 sq miles (369,880 sq km); population 118,362,000; capital Tokyo (pop. 11,600,000); currency, yen; official language, Japanese.*

Nippon Koku, 'the Land of the Rising Sun', has an emperor who belongs to one of the world's oldest ruling dynasties. The country consists of an archipelago in the Pacific Ocean, separated from the Asian mainland by the Sea of Japan. There are four main islands: Honshu, Hokkaido, Kyushu, and Shikoku. Among the more than 3,000 smaller islands there are two major groups: the Ryukyus and the Bonins. Most of the islands are mountainous, the highest peaks being on Honshu. Among them is Fujiyama, the highest mountain in Japan, which rises to 12,388 ft (3,776 m). This snow-mantled peak is a volcano, but not active. There are nearly 200 other volcanoes, some of which erupt from time to time. Earthquakes are frequent, but generally they cause only minor damage. The islands have many rivers, some of which are very fast-flowing, and are consequently suitable for the production of hydro-electricity. Most of Japan's farms are small. The chief crops are rice and other cereals, fruit, and vegetables. But because only a small part of the land can be cultivated, Japan has to import much of its food. It also has to import most of the raw materials that feed its industries. In spite of this, the country has raised itself to the front rank of industrial powers, and has a leading place among producers of optical goods, cameras, radio and television equipment, and motor vehicles, including motor-cycles. It is also a major shipbuilding country, and it has built up one of the world's largest fishing fleets. Japan is very densely populated but—in contrast to most other Asian countries—its population has risen slowly in recent years.

JORDAN *Area 37,700 sq miles (97,600 sq km); population 2,497,000; capital, Amman (pop. 584,000); currency, dinar (1,000 fils); official language, Arabic.*

The Hashemite Kingdom of the Jordan is a mountainous country lying mainly to the east of the Jordan River. At the southern end of the river is the Dead Sea, the Earth's lowest surface point. The north-east of the country is part of the barren Syrian Desert. Only one-tenth of the land is agriculturally productive. The chief crops are cereals, olives, citrus fruits, and tomatoes. Phosphates and some other minerals are exported, and there are manufacturing industries and oil refining.

KAMPUCHEA, DEMOCRATIC *Area 70,000 sq miles (181,000 sq km); population 9,377,000; capital, Phnom Penh (pop. 2,000,000 in 1973); currency, riel (100 sen); official language, Khmer.*

Kampuchea in Indochina was formerly the kingdom of Cambodia. Much of the country lies in the fertile alluvial basin of the Mekong River, but there are mountains in the north and south-west. Most people live by farming or fishing. The chief subsistence crop is rice, and other crops include cotton, pepper, tobacco, and rubber. Fish are taken from the Tonle Sap, the 'Great Lake', in the west.

KOREA, NORTH *Area 46,800 sq miles (121,200 sq km); population 16,000,000; capital, Pyongyang (pop. 1,500,000); currency, won (100 jun); official language, Korean.*

The peninsula of Korea on the north-east coast of China is separated from Japan by the Korea Strait. In 1910 it was annexed by Japan, and after World War II was occupied by Russian troops (in the north) and American troops (in the south). In 1948, the two occupation zones became separate states. A conflict between the two states from 1950 to 1953 involved several other countries, too, including the United States, China, Britain, and France. It ended with agreement that the 38° parallel should form the boundary between the two Koreas. North Korea, the Democratic People's Republic of Korea, is mountainous and is very rich in minerals. It also has textile and engineering industries. The small amount of arable land is productive, the chief crops being cereals and cotton.

KOREA, SOUTH *Area 38,400 sq miles (99,460 sq km); population 38,439,000; capital Seoul (pop. 6,879,000); currency, won (100 jun); official language, Korean.*

The Republic of Korea occupies the southern part of the Korean Peninsula. It is generally mountainous, but the valleys and the southern plains are fertile. The chief crops are rice, vegetables, fruit, soya beans, and groundnuts. Manufactures include electrical goods and textiles, and there are some exports of minerals.

KUWAIT *Area 7,500 sq miles (19,000 sq km); population 995,000; capital, Kuwait City (pop. 300,000); currency, dinar (1,000 fils); official language, Arabic.*

The small, desert country of Kuwait has one of the world's highest *per capita* incomes as a result of its production of petroleum. It is believed to have about one-fifth of the world's known oil resources. It also produces natural gas. Much of its labour force consists of foreign workers from Saudi Arabia, Egypt, and other countries. There are highly-developed social services.

LAOS *Area 91,400 sq miles (236,725 sq km); population 3,500,000; capital, Vientiane (pop. 174,000); currency, kip (100 ats); official language, Lao.*

Laos, fully independent since 1954, was formerly part of French Indochina. The country is landlocked, and its northern part is mountainous and heavily forested. In the south the land descends to the Mekong River; this region is relatively fertile. The chief subsistence crops are rice and other cereals, but coffee, cotton, tea, and tobacco are also grown. The most important export is tin. Teak and other woods are exported, too.

LEBANON *Area 4,300 sq miles (11,000 sq km); population 2,780,000; capital, Beirut (pop. 600,000); currency, pound (100 piastres); official language, Arabic.*

Lebanon became an independent country in 1946. Earlier, it had been part of the Ottoman Empire and, after World War I, a French mandated territory. It has a narrow coastal strip on the eastern Mediterranean, behind which rise the Lebanon Mountains. Farther inland is the fertile Bekaa Valley, and then the heights of the Anti-Lebanon Mountains along the frontier with Syria. Only about one-third of the land is suitable for agriculture, the chief crops being citrus fruits, apples, grapes, olives, bananas, and tobacco. The country has many industries, and is an important financial and commercial centre. It is the only Arab state in which the Christian population is influential.

MACAO *Area 6 sq miles (16 sq km); population 320,000; capital, Macao (pop. 320,000); currency, pataca (100 avos); languages, Portuguese and Cantonese.*

Macao is an overseas province of Portugal. It consists of two small islands and a mainland peninsula at the mouth of the Canton River in southern China. It is a popular tourist centre.

MALAYSIA *Area 130,000 sq miles (337,000 sq km); population 13,688,000; capital, Kuala Lumpur (pop. 770,000); currency, dollar (100 cents); official language, Malay.*

The Federation of Malaysia became an independent country in 1963. Its territory consists of former British-ruled states in the southern part of the Malay Peninsula and the northern part of the island of Borneo. The peninsula regions are called *West Malaysia*, and those in Borneo *East Malaysia*. West Malaysia is separated by the Johore Strait from Singapore, which was part of the Federation until 1965. The peninsula has a mountain backbone; the western coastal plain is considerably wider than that in the east.

East Malaysia is extremely mountainous, its highest peak, Mount Kinabalu, rising to 13,450 ft (4,100 m). About two-thirds of Malaysia is covered by thick rain forest. Rubber and timber are among the valuable forest products; Malaysia is one of the two leading rubber producers in the world. There are rich deposits of tin, as well as mineral oils, iron, and bauxite. On the lowlands rice, peppers, and pineapples are grown.

MALDIVES *Area 115 sq miles (298 sq km); population 129,000; capital, Malé (pop. 14,000); currency, rupeé (100 laris); official language, Maldivian.*

The Maldives, a former British protectorate, consist of a chain of 12 atolls about 400 miles (640 km) south-west of Sri Lanka in the Indian Ocean. Altogether, there are about 2,000 coral islands of which some 200 are inhabited. No point is more than 8 ft (2·4 m) above sea-level.

MONGOLIA *Area 600,000 sq miles (1,550,000 sq km); population 1,467,000; capital Ulan Bator (pop. 250,000); currency, tugrik (100 möngö); official language, Khalkha Mongolian.*

From the 1600s to 1912, Mongolia was a Chinese province; its status was then in doubt until 1946 when China recognized its independence. It is now called the *Mongolian People's Republic*. Most of it consists of vast plateaux ringed by chains of mountains in the north and east. In the south-east is part of the Gobi Desert. Many of the people are herdsmen, but in recent years efforts have been made to develop agriculture. The country's mineral resources include coal, oil, and non-ferrous metals.

NEPAL *Area 54,362 sq miles (140,797 sq km); population 14,063,000; capital, Katmandu (pop. 354,000); currency, rupee (100 pice); official language, Nepali.*

The Hindu kingdom of Nepal lies on the southern flank of the Himalayas, and Mount Everest (29,028 ft; 8,848 m) towers above its northern frontier. Most of the country is mountainous, and it has also thick jungles and swamps. The chief crops are rice and other cereals, and jute. In the villages, textiles and other woven goods are produced.

OMAN *Area 82,000 sq miles (212,000 sq km); population 750,000; capital, Muscat (pop. 7,000); currency, rial Omani (1,000 baiza); official language, Arabic.*

The sultanate of Oman, in the south-east of the Arabian Peninsula, has a long coastline on the Arabian Sea. The centre is low-lying but barren. In the north-east there are hills, and in the south-west the hot Dhofar Plateau. The chief exports are oil, dates, fish, and pearls.

PAKISTAN *Area 310,400 sq miles (804,000 sq km); population 82,738,000; capital Islamabad (pop. 235,000); currency, rupee (100 paisas); official language, Urdu.*

Until 1947, the land that is now Pakistan was part of the British-ruled Indian Empire. In 1971, part of Pakistan—separated from the rest of the country by 900 miles (1,500 km) of Indian territory—broke away and formed the independent nation of Bangladesh after a bloody civil war. Great mountain ranges rise along the north and north-west frontiers—the Himalaya, Hindu Kush, and Karakoram systems. On the boundary with Afghanistan is the Khyber Pass. About one-third of the country is a great plain, watered by the Indus. This plain was the site of one of the earliest civilizations. The climate is strongly affected by the monsoons. Much of the country's

agriculture depends on artificial irrigation. Cotton and rice are exported. There are textile, chemical, and other industries.

PHILIPPINES *Area 115,800 sq miles (299,900 sq km); population 49,060,000; capital, Manila (pop. 1,580,000); currency, peso (100 centavos); official language, Pilipino.*

The Philippines has been independent since 1946. Before that, it was ruled by Spain for 300 years, and, after 1898, by the United States. The country consists of more than 7,000 islands, extending for some 1,000 miles (1,600 km) between the Pacific Ocean and the South China Sea. The three largest islands are Luzon, Mindanao, and Palawan. About 700 islands are inhabited. Most of the islands are mountainous, and some have volcanoes. The chief crops are cereals, fruits, sugar, sweet potatoes, and hemp. There are valuable mineral deposits.

QATAR *Area 4,000 sq miles (10,300 sq km); population 200,000; capital, Doha (pop. 90,000); currency, riyal (100 dirhams); official language, Arabic.*

The sheikdom of Qatar occupies a 120-mile (190-km) long peninsula jutting northwards from the coast of Saudi Arabia into the Persian Gulf. Once a land of nomadic herdsmen, fishermen, and pearl divers, it has become a rich and important oil-producing state.

SAUDI ARABIA *Area 920,000 sq miles (2,383,000 sq km); population 10,405,000; capital, Riyadh (pop. 667,000); currency, riyal (20 qursh); official language, Arabic.*

The kingdom of Saudi Arabia occupies the greater part of the Arabian Peninsula. The mountains of the Hejaz and Asir ranges extend along the west coast. Inland are rocky plateaux and deserts, the largest deserts being the An Nafud in the north, and the Rub'al Khali, the Empty Quarter, in the south. There are no permanent rivers. Many nomads roam the sandy wastes. The country has enormous revenues from oil production.

SINGAPORE *Area 224 sq miles (580 sq km); population 2,322,000; capital, Singapore (pop. 1,240,000); currency, dollar (100 cents); official languages, Malay, Chinese, Tamil, and English.*

The island country of Singapore is separated from the southern tip of the Malay Peninsula by the narrow Johore Strait. Until 1965 it was part of Malaysia, and before that was a British crown colony. Most of the island is low-lying. It owes its importance to its fine harbour and its usefulness as a trade centre. In recent years it has greatly developed its industries. Its population is predominantly Chinese. The next largest group is Malay.

SRI LANKA *Area 25,332 sq miles (65,610 sq km); population 14,652,000; capital, Colombo (pop. 565,000); currency, rupee (100 cents); official language, Sinhala.*

Island country in the Indian Ocean, off the southern tip of India. It was formerly called *Ceylon* and was British-ruled until 1948. Most of the island is a fertile plain, but the southern part has mountains that rise to 8,400 ft (2,550 m). Rice, tea, palms, and fruit grow in the tropical monsoon climate, and the forests provide rubber and valuable woods. Most of the people are Sinhalese, but there is a large Tamil minority. Unlike the Buddhist Sinhalese, the Tamils—who emigrated to Sri Lanka from southern India—are Hindus.

SYRIA *Area 71,800 sq miles (185,960 sq km); population 7,500,000; capital, Damascus*

(pop. 1,097,000); currency, pound (100 piastres); official language, Arabic.

Syria became independent in 1946. Before that it had been ruled as a mandated territory by the French, and, until 1919, as part of the Ottoman Empire. The south of the country is in the Syrian Desert, to the north of which is the broad and fertile valley of the River Euphrates. Beyond the valley is a region of rough plains. The chief crops are wheat, barley, cotton, fruit, and tobacco. A number of cattle and sheep are also raised, and in the desert areas there are many nomadic herdsmen. Industries include food processing, and the manufacture of textiles and cement. Oil pipelines cross the desert from Iraq to the Mediterranean ports.

TAIWAN *Area 13,885 sq miles (35,962 sq km); population 16,150,000; capital, Taipei (pop. 1,920,000); currency, dollar (100 cents); official language, Chinese (Mandarin).*

The island of Taiwan, or Formosa, in the Pacific Ocean is separated from the Chinese mainland by the Formosa Strait. In 1895, it was ceded to Japan by treaty, but it was returned to China in 1945 after World War II. In 1949, Chiang Kai-shek withdrew to Taiwan after the civil war in which he and his supporters were defeated by the communists. He established a Chinese Nationalist republic with the military protection of the United States. Two-thirds of the island is mountainous. The inhabitants live mainly on the fertile western coastal plain. The chief crops are rice, sugar, fruit, and vegetables. Fishing is important, and there are many manufacturing industries, such as textiles, chemicals, food processing, and the manufacture of electrical goods.

THAILAND *Area 198,460 sq miles (513,810 sq km); population 47,843,000; capital, Bangkok (pop. 4,870,000); currency, baht (100 satangs); official language, Thai.*

Thailand was formerly known as *Siam*. The northern part of the country is on the Asian mainland, but a southern 'tail' stretches into the Malay Peninsula. In the far north, between the Mekong and Salween rivers, Thailand is mountainous. In the east is a high tableland. The centre heartland is the vast, fertile floodplain of the Chao Phraya (Menam) River. Rain and monsoon forests cover two-thirds of the country, and there are mangrove swamps along the wet southern coast. The most important crop is rice, the yield of which has been greatly increased by irrigation works. Rubber is the chief cash crop. Fishing is a major source of food. The country's natural resources include valuable woods, such as teak, from the forests, and tin, tungsten, and other minerals. There are almost no roads; river and canal transport is widely used.

TURKEY *Area 301,300 sq miles (780,360 sq km); population 39,180,000; capital, Ankara (pop. 1,480,000); currency, lira (100 kurus); official language, Turkish.*

Formerly the centre of the Ottoman Empire, Turkey became a republic in 1923. The greater part of the country is in Asia, but a small part is in Europe, across the Dardanelles, the Sea of Marmara, and the Bosporus. European Turkey is mainly low-lying, but the vast, broken Anatolian Plateau occupies much of the Asian section. To the north of the plateau are the Pontine Mountains, and to the south the Taurus Mountains. On the coasts and in the Taurus valleys the climate is mild. Crops include fruit, cereals, cotton, and tobacco. In the rugged highlands there are large flocks of sheep. Textiles and iron and steel are the two most important manufacturing industries in Turkey.

UNITED ARAB EMIRATES *Area 32,000 sq miles (82,000 sq km); population 300,000; capital, Abu Dhabi (pop. 236,000); currency, dirham (100 fils); official language, Arabic.*

The United Arab Emirates is a federation of seven sheikhdoms or emirates on the Persian Gulf, formerly known as the Trucial States. The seven emirates are Abu Dhabi, Dubai, Sharjah, Ajman, Umm al Qaiwain, Ras al Khaimah, and Fujairah. The land is mostly low, flat desert, with some coastal hills. There are vast oil deposits in Abu Dhabi, and oil has also been found in Dubai and elsewhere. Many people live by herding or fishing, and dates are grown.

VIETNAM *Area 128,400 sq miles (332,560 sq km); population 50,000,000; chief cities, (north) Hanoi, the capital (pop. 1,444,000), (south) Ho Chi Minh City (Saigon, pop. 3,461,000); currency, dong (100 xu); official language, Vietnamese.*

Formerly part of French Indochina, Vietnam was divided from 1954 to 1975 into a communist state in the north and a non-communist state in the south. Then, a protracted and bloody war ended in a communist victory. The country is about 1,000 miles (1,600 km) long, but is less than 50 miles (80 km) across at its narrowest point. The centre of Vietnam is a fertile coastal plain. In the north is the delta of the Red River, and in the south the delta of the Mekong River. There are many forests and marshes. The chief crop is rice, and other crops are coffee, tea, sugar, tobacco, and sweet potatoes. Rubber, quinine, and cinnamon are exported.

YEMEN (Aden) *Area 128,600 sq miles (333,000 sq km); population 1,797,000; capital, Aden (pop. 250,000); currency, dinar (1,000 fils); official language, Arabic.*

The People's Democratic Republic of Yemen was formerly under British rule, and became independent in 1967. It is on the south-west coast of the Arabian Peninsula. Its sandy coastal plain is separated from the interior desert by highlands. Many of the people are nomadic herdsmen, and fishing is important. Cotton, coffee, and skins are exported.

YEMEN (San'a) *Area 75,000 sq miles (194,000 sq km); population 6,700,000; capital, San'a (pop. 448,000); currency, riyal (40 bogaches); official language, Arabic.*

The Yemen Arab Republic has a broad, sandy coastal strip along the Red Sea; this gives way to highlands, which occupy most of the interior of the country. Coastal areas have little rain, and are unproductive agriculturally. But the highlands have higher rainfall and have many fertile river valleys. Most of the people are herdsmen or subsistence farmers. Coffee, skins, and gum arabic are exported. The only important mineral product is salt.

Countries of Africa

ALGERIA *Area 918,000 sq miles (2,378,000 (sq km); population 19,685,000; capital, Algiers (pop. 1,503,000); currency, dinar (100 centimes); official language, Arabic.*

Algeria has been independent since 1962. Nine-tenths of the country is in the Sahara, and is inhabited only around oases or by nomads. But the coastal strip between the Mediterranean Sea and the northern flank of the Atlas Mountains is fertile and thickly populated. Most of the towns are in this region, which has rich crops of cereals, vegetables, and early fruits. Wine is important, too. Algeria has valuable deposits of petroleum, natural gas, and phosphates.

ANGOLA *Area 481,350 sq miles (1,246,700 sq km); population 5,700,000; capital, Luanda (pop. 475,000); currency kwanza (100 lweis); official language, Portuguese.*

Until 1975, Angola was a Portuguese colony. Apart from a long coastal plain, the country consists mainly of the vast Bié Plateau. Important crops include coffee, sugar-cane, cotton, and oil palms, and there are deposits of oil, iron, and other minerals.

BENIN *Area 44,696 sq miles (115,762 sq km); population 3,559,000; capital, Porto Novo (pop. 85,000); currency, franc; official language, French.*

Independent since 1960, Benin was previously a French colony and was called Dahomey. The centre of Benin is a high plateau, and there are lowlands in the north and south. The majority of the people live in the coastal region. Palm oil, coffee, tobacco, and cotton are exported.

BOTSWANA *Area 220,000 sq miles (570,000 sq km); population 766,000; capital, Gaborone (pop. 37,000); currency, pula (100 thebe); official language, English.*

The republic of Botswana, which became independent in 1966, was formerly the British protectorate of Bechuanaland. The country is a plateau, the southern part of which is occupied by the Kalahari Desert, where Bushmen and small groups of Bantu live. The huge, swampy Okovango Basin in the north is formed by the Okovango River. Minerals and livestock are important.

BURUNDI *Area 10,747 sq miles (27,835 sq km); population 3,700,000; capital, Bujumbura (pop. 70,000); currency, franc; official languages, French and Kirundi.*

Burundi lies on the north-eastern bank of Lake Tanganyika. It was once a German colony, and later a Belgian mandated territory. Most of the country lies on a plateau, but there are mountains in the west; these mark the edge of the African Rift Valley, in which Lake Tanganyika lies. The savanna highlands have good pastures. Rice and other cereals are grown, as well as coffee and cotton.

CAMEROON *Area 183,570 sq miles (475,444 sq km); population 7,633,000; capital, Yaoundé (pop. 180,000); currency, franc; official languages, French and English.*

The Federal Republic of Cameroon was formed in 1961 from French and British trust territories that had previously been part of the German colony of Kamerun. The coastal plain on the Gulf of Guinea is marshy, and slopes upwards to the mountainous plateau that occupies most of the country. In the centre, the Adamawa Highlands rise to some 6,000 ft (1,800 m). Half the country is thickly forested. Palm oil, rubber, and timber are important. The chief crops are cocoa and coffee.

CANARY ISLANDS *Area 2,807 sq miles (7,270 sq km); population 1,165,000; capital, Las Palmas (on Gran Canaria; pop. 287,000); currency, peseta; official language, Spanish.*

Group of thirteen islands some 60 miles (97 km) off the north-west coast of Africa, making up two provinces of Spain.

CAPE VERDE *Area 1,516 sq miles (3,926 sq km); population 272,000; capital, Praia (pop. 45,000; currency, escudo (100 centavos); official language, Portuguese.*

This archipelago off the west coast of Africa gained its independence from Portugal in 1975. The islands are mountainous and have a tropical climate, but droughts are common as the rainfall is uncertain. The main export is coffee.

CENTRAL AFRICAN REPUBLIC *Area 234,000 sq miles (606,000 sq km); population 3,200,000; capital, Bangui (pop. 300,000); currency, franc; official languages, French and Sango.*

The republic was a French colony before independence in 1960. It lies in the centre of the continent. It is mainly a hilly plateau, forested in the south. The chief rivers are the Ubangi and the Bomu. Cotton, coffee, and ground-nuts are exported. Minerals include gold and industrial diamonds.

CHAD *Area 495,750 sq miles (1,284,000 sq km); population 4,000,000; capital, N'djaména (Fort Lamy; pop. 126,000); currency, franc; official language, French.*

Chad, a former French colony, became independent in 1960. It is named after Lake Chad, on its western border. The northern part of the country, in the Sahara, includes the high Tibesti Mountains. The south is savanna, some of it plateau country. Cotton and ground-nuts are exported.

COMOROS *Area 838 sq miles (2,170 sq km); population 320,000; capital, Moroni (pop. 14,000); currency, franc; official language, French.*

The Comoros Islands became independent in 1974. They are mainly mountainous, and densely forested. The main crops are coffee and sugar-cane, which are exported, and also vanilla, copra, and oils.

CONGO *Area 129,000 sq miles (334,000 sq km); population 1,900,000; capital, Brazzaville (pop. 156,000); currency, franc; official language, French.*

The People's Republic of the Congo was a French colony before independence in 1960. It lies across the equator in western Africa, and has a short coastal plain on the Atlantic. Most of the country is high; the broad Batéké Plateau is savanna, but the northern region is covered with thick tropical forest. The Congo and Oubangui rivers form the eastern boundary. The chief crop is sugar-cane. There are various mineral resources.

DJIBOUTI *Area 9,000 sq miles (23,300 sq km); population 240,000; capital, Djibouti (pop. 62,000); currency, franc; official language, French.*

Formerly known as the French territory of

Afars and Issas, it was renamed in 1967 and granted its independence in 1976. It is an arid, hilly, desert land, but swampy in coastal districts. Farming is at a subsistence level, heavily dependent on livestock.

EGYPT *Area 386,000 sq miles (999,700 sq km); population 41,355,000; capital, Cairo (pop. 5,300,000); currency, pound (100 piastres); official language, Arabic.*

Egypt—now called the Arab Republic of Egypt—was a monarchy from 1923 to 1952. Earlier, it had been a British protectorate, and, until 1914, part of the Ottoman Empire. Though most of Egypt's territory is in Africa, a small section, the Sinai Peninsula, is in Asia. The Suez Canal passes through Egypt, and by connecting the Mediterranean Sea with the Red Sea provides a short route for shipping between Europe and Asia. Most of the land is desert: the Libyan Desert in the west, and the Arabian Desert in the east, rising to the Red Sea Mountains. Between the deserts is the valley of the Nile, the world's longest river. The Nile has no tributaries during the whole of its 900-mile (1,450-km) course through Egypt. Agriculture is possible only in the valley, and, in particular, in the great delta of the Nile on the Mediterranean. The amount of arable land has been increased by building dams for irrigation. The most important dam, the Aswan High Dam, also provides hydro-electricity. Most of the people live in the valley; those in the desert live in oases or are nomads. Among the country's chief crops are cotton, sugar, citrus fruits, and rice.

EQUATORIAL GUINEA *Area 11,000 sq miles (28,000 sq km); population 300,000; capital, Malabo (Santa Isabel; pop. 9,000); currency, ekpwele; official language, Spanish.*

The small country of Equatorial Guinea consists largely of the former Spanish possessions of Rio Muni and Bioko; it gained independence in 1968. Rio Muni is on the African mainland. Fernando Pó (Macias Nguema) is a mountainous island in the Gulf of Guinea. Cocoa and coffee are exported.

ETHIOPIA *Area 450,000 sq miles (1,165,000 sq km); population 30,967,000; capital, Addis Ababa (pop. 1,133,000); currency, birr (100 cents); official language, Amharic.*

Until 1974, Ethiopia was ruled by an emperor who belonged to one of the oldest royal dynasties in the world; but in that year it became a republic. It is often called *Abyssinia*. Most of the country consists of high and broken plateaux, divided into two regions by the African Rift Valley. To the west of the valley are the Ethiopian Highlands, which are wild and rugged and are cut by many river valleys. To the east is the Somali Plateau, which is generally more level. The country has little industry, though it has some mineral resources including gold, platinum, and pot-ash. Cereals, coffee, cotton, sugar-cane, fruit, and tobacco are grown; coffee is exported.

GABON *Area 103,100 sq miles (267,000 sq km); population 1,000,000; capital, Libreville (pop. 150,000); currency, franc; official language, French.*

Gabon has been independent since 1960. Before that, it was a French colony. Its coastal plain on the Atlantic is broad around the mouth of the River Ogooué. But most of the country is a mountainous plateau, which has extensive rain forests in which mahogany and other valuable timbers are cut. The most important crops are cocoa and coffee, and recently rice cultivation has begun. Gabon's mineral resources include deposits of oil, iron, and manganese.

GAMBIA *Area 4,000 sq miles (10,500 sq km); population 494,000; capital, Banjul (Bathurst; pop. 40,000); currency, dalasi (100 bututs); official language, English.*

The small country of Gambia was British-ruled before it became independent in 1966. It consists of a narrow strip of territory along the Gambia River. Some of the land is swampy or under water for part of the year. There are few mineral resources. The chief exports are ground-nuts and fruit.

GHANA *Area 92,100 sq miles (238,538 sq km); population 11,380,000; capital, Accra (pop. 900,000); currency, cedi (100 pesewas); official language, English.*

The former British colony of the Gold Coast, Ghana has been independent since 1957. Most of eastern Ghana is in the basin of the Volta River and, like the coastal areas, is low-lying. But there are hills in the east, and a high escarpment extends across the country. The building of the Akosombo Dam on the Volta has produced the largest artificial lake in the world, covering more than 3,000 sq miles (7,800 sq km). This project has aided irrigation and has provided much-needed electrical power. Gold, diamonds, manganese, and bauxite are mined, and there is an aluminium-smelting industry. The chief export crops are cocoa, coffee, and copra.

GUINEA *Area 96,900 sq miles (250,970 sq km); population 6,003,000; capital, Conakry (pop. 526,000); currency, syli; official language, French.*

Guinea, which became independent in 1958, was formerly a French colony. The land rises from the broad, marshy coastal plain on the Atlantic to the Fouta Djallon, a rugged plateau. In the south-east, the thickly forested Nimba Mountains rise to some 5,800 ft (1,800 m). The chief rivers are the Niger and the Gambia, both of which have their sources in Guinea. There are rich deposits of bauxite and iron. The chief export crops are bananas, pineapples, kola-nuts, and coffee.

GUINEA-BISSAU *Area 14,000 sq miles (36,000 sq km); population 580,000; capital, Bissau (pop. 109,000); currency, peso (100 centavos); official language, Portuguese.*

Until 1974 a Portuguese possession (called Portuguese Guinea), Guinea-Bissau consists of a mainland territory and a number of islands on the Atlantic coast of Africa. It is mostly low-lying, but the high plateau of the Fouta Djallon projects into the south-east. Crops are rice, ground-nuts, and palm oil.

IVORY COAST *Area 125,000 sq miles (323,700 sq km); population 7,380,000; capital, Abidjan (pop. 600,000); currency, franc; official language, French.*

Ivory Coast became independent in 1960; previously it was a French colony. The northern two-thirds of the country is a savanna-covered plateau. The coastal plain is broad and wooded. The most valuable export crops are cocoa and coffee; and bananas and pineapples are also exported. Timber is an important source of revenue.

KENYA *Area 224,960 sq miles (582,644 sq km); population 15,942,000; capital, Nairobi (pop. 510,000); currency, shilling (100 cents); official languages, English and Swahili.*

Kenya became independent in 1963; it had been a British colony since 1895. Much of the northern part of the country is a plateau, a region of wide grasslands. In the south-west, the Kenya Highlands include Kenya's two highest mountains, Mount Kenya (17,057 ft; 5,199 m) and Mount Elgon (14,177 ft; 4,321 m). The Nyanza Plateau, which stretches from the highlands to Lake Victoria, is one of the most favoured agricultural regions. The African Rift Valley cuts through Kenya; Lake Turkana, in the north, lies within it. The lower parts of the country consist of dry and thorn savannas. The chief crops are sisal, cereals, pineapples, tea, pyrethrum, and coffee. Kenya is famous for its wild-life reserves.

LESOTHO *Area 11,716 sq miles (30,344 sq km); population 1,214,000; capital, Maseru (pop. 30,000); currency, loti (100 lisente); official languages, English, Sesotho.*

Lesotho, the former British colony of Basutoland, is an enclave surrounded by the territory of South Africa. It became independent in 1966. Nearly all of the country is high; the Drakensberg Mountains rise in the east. The Orange River has its source in Lesotho. The raising of livestock is important.

LIBERIA *Area 43,000 sq miles (111,370 sq km); population 1,600,000; capital, Monrovia (pop. 110,000); currency, dollar (100 cents); official language, English.*

The Liberian republic was founded in 1847, and is the oldest independent country in western Africa. It developed from a number of settlements for Negroes released from slavery in the United States. The Guinea Highlands and Nimba Mountains in the north descend to savanna plateaux, and then to a marshy coastal plain. Iron and diamonds are mined. Crops include coffee and cocoa.

LIBYA *Area 679,360 sq miles (1,759,534 sq km); population 2,250,000; capital, Tripoli (pop. 550,000); currency, dinar (1,000 dirhams); official language, Arabic.*

Libya became an independent country in 1951. Earlier, it had been an Italian colony (from 1912) and, before that, part of the Ottoman Empire. It is one of the largest countries in Africa, but nine-tenths of it is barren land, part of the Sahara. Most of the people live in the fertile lowlands along the Mediterranean coast. This region has groves of oranges and olives, and also grows cereals, tobacco, and vegetables. The country is rich because of huge deposits of petroleum.

MADAGASCAR *Area 230,000 sq miles (595,700 sq km); population 9,310,000; capital, Antananarivo (pop. 400,000); currency, Malagasy franc; official languages, Malagasy and French.*

The Democratic Republic of Madagascar occupies the island of Madagascar in the Indian Ocean, and a few small islands. It is some 250 miles (400 km) from the coast of the African mainland. France ruled it from 1885 to 1960. The centre of Madagascar is a high plateau, bounded by mountains in the north and south, and by a wide coastal plain on the west. Only one-tenth of the land is suitable for agriculture. Exports include sugar, coffee, pepper, vanilla, and cloves. Graphite, mica, and phosphates are mined.

MALAWI *Area 45,500 sq miles (117,850 sq km); population, 5,669,000; capital, Lilongwe (pop. 103,000); currency, kwacha (100 tambala); official language, English.*

The former British protectorate of Nyasa-land, Malawi became an independent country in 1964. It lies along the western side of Lake Malawi (Lake Nyasa), which is in the African Rift Valley. Most of the people live by farming; and tea, tobacco, and tung-oil are exported. Cattle-rearing and fishing are important.

MALI *Area 465,000 sq miles (1,204,000 sq km); population 5,700,000; capital, Bamako (pop. 400,000); currency, franc; official language, French.*

Mali was formerly the French colony of Sudan. In 1959 it joined with Senegal to form the Federation of Mali; but the federation was dissolved after a year, and Mali and Senegal became separate countries. The loss of Senegal left Mali without an outlet to the sea. The northern part of the country is in the Sahara and is inhabited only by nomads. The south is watered by the Niger and Senegal rivers. Cotton and ground-nuts are exported.

MAURITANIA *Area 419,000 sq miles (1,085,000 sq km); population 1,500,000; capital, Nouakchott (pop. 135,000); currency, ouguiya (5 khoums); official languages, Arabic and French.*

Mauritania became an independent country in 1960; it had been ruled by France since 1920. It is officially called the *Islamic Republic of Mauritania*. Much of the country is in the western Sahara and consists of barren plateaux. Only in the south-west, the flood plain of the Senegal River, is the land fertile. Cereals and ground-nuts are produced. The most important source of income is iron ore.

MAURITIUS *Area 800 sq miles (2,000 sq km); population 867,000; capital, Port Louis (pop. 135,000); currency, rupee (100 cents); official language, English. French and Creole are also spoken.*

The tiny country of Mauritius was a British crown colony until 1968. It consists of a group of islands in the Indian Ocean, the largest of which are Mauritius and Rodrigues. Mauritius Island is mountainous and is of volcanic origin. The main crop is sugar-cane.

MOROCCO *Area 171,000 sq miles (442,888 sq km); population 17,826,000; capital, Rabat (pop. 565,000); currency, dirham (100 centimes); official language, Arabic.*

Morocco, independent since 1956, is dominated by the Atlas Mountains, which rise to 13,661 ft (4,164 m) above sea-level in Mount Toubkal. To the east of the mountains are the wastes of the Sahara. Morocco's coastal plain on the Mediterranean, in the north, is hilly, but the western, Atlantic coast has sandy beaches. The country has rich mineral deposits, and supplies a third of the world demand for phosphates. Crops include cereals, oranges, olives, apricots, grapes (for wine as well as for eating), and nuts.

MOZAMBIQUE *Area 303,000 sq miles (785,000 sq km); population 9,000,000; capital, Maputo (Lourenço Marques; pop. 440,000); currency, escudo (100 centavos); official language, Portuguese.*

The People's Republic of Mozambique, independent since 1975, was formerly ruled by Portugal. It has a coastline of some 1,500 miles (2,400 km) on the Indian Ocean, and the great Lake Malawi is in the north. The country has a wide coastal plain, but most of it consists of highlands through which flow several rivers, including the Zambezi and Limpopo. Cane-sugar, coconuts, cotton, and tea are produced. Coal and iron are mined.

NIGER *Area 459,000 sq miles (1,189,000 sq km); population 4,600,000; capital, Niamey (pop. 100,000); currency, franc; official language, French.*

Niger was ruled by France before independence in 1960. It has no coastline, and most of it is an arid plateau. The northern part is in the Sahara. A few small rivers seep away into the desert; they provide water for scattered patches of green. The south of the country is savanna, and in the south-west there is fertile land around the Niger River. Cereals, coffee, and cotton are grown, and there are deposits of tin, iron, and uranium.

NIGERIA *Area 356,669 sq miles (923,768 sq km); population 79,700,000; capital, Lagos (pop. 1,000,000); currency, naira (100 kobo); official language, English.*

Nigeria, the most heavily-populated country in Africa, was a British colony and protectorate until 1960. The chief feature of the country is the great Niger River, which, with its tributaries, waters most of Nigeria. There are mangrove swamps and lagoons along the coast, particularly in the Niger delta. Some 50 miles (80 km) inland the rain forest begins; beyond this are the plateaux, and, still farther north, a semi-desert tract. Lake Chad is on the north-east frontier. Two-thirds of Nigeria's agricultural produce is exported. The country is the leading producer of ground-nuts in the world, and is among the leaders for cocoa. The rearing of stock is important. Petroleum, tin and coal are extracted. There are food-processing and oil-refining industries, and textiles, steel, and chemicals are manufactured.

RWANDA *Area 10,169 sq miles (26,338 sq km); population 4,120,000; capital, Kigali (pop. 7,000); currency, franc; official languages, French and Kinyarwanda.*

Rwanda was, until 1962, part of the UN trust territory of Ruanda-Urundi, administered by Belgium. It is bounded on the west by Lake Kivu. Most of it occupies a hilly plateau. Mountains in the west, by the lake, divide the River Zaïre (Congo) basin from that of the Nile. Coffee, tea, and tobacco are exported.

SAO TOME and PRINCIPE *Area 372 sq miles (963 sq km); population 75,000; capital São Tomé (pop. 17,000); currency, dobra (100 centimos); official language, Portuguese.*

These islands in the Gulf of Guinea became independent from Portugal in 1975. They are volcanic islands and are mountainous, over half the area being forested. The main exports are cacao, coffee, and rubber.

SENEGAL *Area 77,800 sq miles (201,500 sq km); population 4,000,000; capital, Dakar (pop. 581,000); currency, franc; official language, French.*

Senegal, a former French colony, became part of the Federation of Mali in 1959; but one year later the Federation was dissolved, and Senegal and Mali became separate countries. Cape Vert in Senegal is the westernmost point in Africa. The country has a long, sandy coast on the Atlantic Ocean, and is mostly low-lying. But in the south-east it has hills of the Fouta Djallon. Its rivers include the Senegal and the Gambia. Much of the valley of the Gambia River forms a separate country, called the Gambia, which is an enclave within Senegalese territory. The chief crops are rice and ground-nuts. Phosphates are mined.

SEYCHELLES *Area 108 sq miles (280 sq km; population 62,000; capital, Victoria (pop. 14,000); currency, rupee (100 cents); official language, English.*

A British colony until 1976, the Seychelles consists of two groups of islands: one flat, the other mountainous. Coconut palms flourish on the fertile volcanic soils. The main exports are copra, vanilla, cinnamon, and guano.

SIERRA LEONE *Area 27,925 sq miles (72,325 sq km); population 3,000,000; capital, Freetown (pop. 274,000); currency, leone (100 cents); official language, English.*

Sierra Leone, which became independent in 1961, was formerly a British colony; the colony was founded around a settlement at Freetown for escaped slaves. Most of the country is high and mountainous, and consists of a broken plateau that rises to the Fouta Djallon. Freetown is built on a hilly peninsula, but the rest of the coastal region is low-lying and marshy. Nearly three-quarters of the people live by agriculture: palm kernels, coffee, and cocoa are exported. Sierra Leone has useful mineral deposits. They include diamonds, iron, and bauxite.

SOMALIA *Area 246,200 sq miles (637,700 sq km); population 3,354,000; capital, Mogadishu (pop. 220,000); currency, shilling (100 cents); official language, Somali.*

Somalia became an independent country in 1960; it was formed from two British and Italian possessions. It lies on the 'horn' of Africa, and has coastlines on the north, and the east, where the coastal plain is broad. The interior of the country is a plateau, sloping upwards towards the Ethiopian Highlands in the west. Bananas are exported, and other crops are cereals, ground-nuts, and cotton.

SOUTH AFRICA *Area 472,360 sq miles (1,223,410 sq km); population 25,471,000; capitals, Cape Town (legislative capital, pop. 1,100,000) and Pretoria (administrative capital, pop. 562,000); currency, rand (100 cents); official languages, English and Afrikaans.*

South Africa is the richest and the most southerly country in Africa. It is governed by its white population, which, although large, is only about one-fifth of the country's total population. Most of the country consists of plateau land. The eastern plateau, the High Veld, is the most prosperous part of the country, with rich farmlands and highly-developed industry. It also has important mineral resources. To the south-east of the High Veld is the great mountain range of the Drakensbergs, and beyond that is a coastal plain. Two other large plateaux are called karroos—the Great Karroo in the south, and the Upper Karroo in the west. In the far north-east of the country is the *Transvaal*—the region 'beyond the Vaal River'. There are two other large rivers, the Limpopo and the Orange. South Africa's farms are among the most productive in the world. Their crops include cereals, vegetables, fruit, tobacco, and sugar-cane. Livestock, particularly sheep, are important. Vineyards produce fine wines. Textiles, steel, chemicals, and machinery are manufactured. About half of the gold mined in the world comes from South Africa. Diamonds, silver, iron, manganese, and chromium are also extracted.

SOUTH-WEST AFRICA (NAMIBIA) *Area 318,261 sq miles (824,292 sq km); population 746,000; capital, Windhoek (pop. 60,000); currency, rand (100 cents); official languages, English and Afrikaans.*

Now usually called *Namibia*, South-West Africa is a self-governing state under the protection of South Africa, but the U.N. does not recognise its government. The coastal area, called the *Namib*, is desert. Inland is a vast plateau. Much of the country is too dry for crop cultivation, but there are large herds of livestock. Fishing is important and there are mineral deposits.

SUDAN *Area 967,500 sq miles (2,505,800 sq km); population 18,000,000; capital, Khartoum (pop. 135,000); currency, pound (100 piastres); official language, Arabic.*

The Sudan, the largest country in Africa, was ruled by Egypt from 1820 to 1880, and was under joint British and Egyptian rule from 1898 to 1956. The Nile and its tributaries reach out into almost all parts of the country. The Blue Nile and the White Nile meet at Khartoum, and flow northwards to Egypt. Northern Sudan is desert. South of the desert are hills, and beyond them broad plains of scrubby grassland and savanna. The southern parts of the country, near the Equator, have rich vegetation, with alluvial grasslands, tropical forests, and swamp forests. Cotton and other crops are grown in the Nile valley and irrigation works have aided agriculture along the Atbara River. Cereals, fruits, ground-nuts, and sugar-cane are produced. In the drier regions, cattle, sheep, goats, and camels are raised on a nomadic or semi-nomadic basis. Fishing is important, both in the Nile and its tributaries and also on the Red Sea coast.

SWAZILAND *Area 6,704 sq miles (17,363 sq km); population 505,000; capital, Mbabane (pop. 21,000); currency, lilangeni (100 cents); official languages, English and Siswati.*

Swaziland became an independent country in 1968. At that time it was a British protectorate. The Lebombo Mountains rise along the eastern side of the country. The rest of the terrain, except where cultivated, is veld, higher in the west than elsewhere. Crops include sugar-cane, citrus fruits, cotton, and rice. Iron, asbestos, and gold are mined.

TANZANIA *Area 362,820 sq miles (939,700 sq km); population 15,000,000; capital, Dar es Salaam (pop. 870,000); currency, shilling (100 cents); official languages, Swahili and English.*

The United Republic of Tanzania was formed in 1964, its territory being the former British trust territory of Tanganyika in eastern Africa, and some offshore islands of which the largest are Zanzibar and Pemba. On the northern and western frontiers of continental Tanzania there are three great lakes; Victoria, Tanganyika, and Malawi (Nyasa). Most of the country is a hilly plateau, forested in places and covered with scrubby grassland in others. In the north-east of the plateau is Mount Kilimanjaro (19,340 ft; 5,895 m), Africa's highest mountain. The coastal plain is narrow at most points. About a quarter of the land area has been declared nature conservation territory. The mainland has poor soils. The chief exports from Tanzania are coffee, cloves, sisal, cotton, diamonds, and cashew nuts.

TOGO *Area 21,853 sq miles (56,599 sq km); population 2,170,000; capital, Lomé (pop. 148,000); currency, franc; official language, French.*

The small country of Togo became independent in 1960; earlier it had been a French trusteeship territory, and, until 1919, a German protectorate. Much of the country is mountainous and thickly forested, but there is savanna in the north-west. The coastal districts are swampy, with large land-locked lagoons. The people grow some cereals, cassava, and yams. Cocoa, citrus fruits, palm kernels, and coffee are the main crops produced for export.

TUNISIA *Area 63,170 sq miles (163,600 sq km); population 6,065,000; capital, Tunis (pop. 944,000); currency, dinar (1,000 millimes; official language, Arabic.*

A French protectorate from 1883, Tunisia became completely independent in 1956. It is one of the smallest countries of northern Africa, and has the continent's most northerly point, Cape Blanc. The northern part of Tunisia is in the Atlas Mountains, which here rise to a maximum of some 5,000 ft (1,500 m) above sea-level. In the north-east there is a coastal plain. The southern region is in the Sahara. In the west is the vast salt pan called the *Chott Djerid*, which in the rainy season turns into a salty marsh. Vines, olives, vegetables, and citrus fruits grow in the Mediterranean region. In the desert, people live in the oases, where water is available, and nomads keep animals.

UGANDA *Area 93,981 sq miles (243,410 sq km); population, 13,656,000; capital, Kampala (pop. 331,000); currency, shilling (100 cents); official language, English.*

The former British protectorate of Uganda became an independent country in 1962. It is an inland country. In the south-east, it includes part of Lake Victoria, Africa's largest lake. Most of the country is a high plateau, bordered on the east and the west by mountains. In the east, Mount Elgon rises to 14,178 ft (4,321 m); and in the west, the Ruwenzori Mountains rise to 16,794 ft (5,119 m). The chief river is the White Nile. The leading exports are coffee, cotton, tea, copper, and hides and skins.

UPPER VOLTA *Area 105,869 sq miles (274,199 sq km); population 5,611,000; capital, Ouagadougou (pop. 125,000); currency, franc; official language, French.*

The former French colony of Upper Volta became an independent country in 1960. It lies on a sloping plateau, and has the headstreams of the Volta River—the Black, White, and Red Voltas. Despite its rivers, the country has an acute shortage of water, and its soil is poor. The typical vegetation is savanna. Most people are subsistence farmers. The main exports are live cattle, cotton, hides and skins, groundnuts, and sesame.

WESTERN SAHARA *Area 102,710 sq miles (266,000 sq km); population 180,000; capital until 1976, El Aiún.*

Western Sahara was ruled as Spanish Sahara until 1976 when Spain withdrew and the territory was partitioned. Morocco took the northern, phosphates-rich two-thirds, while Mauritania took the southern third. But Saharan rebels proclaimed their country an independent republic. Their guerrilla warfare caused Mauritania to remove its troops in 1979. Morocco then took the whole country, but it could not suppress the rebel forces which were aided by Algeria.

ZAIRE *Area 905,565 sq miles (2,345,402 sq km); population 28,404,000; capital, Kinshasa (pop. 2,500,000); currency, zaïre (100 makuta); official language, French.*

The country was formerly called the *Republic of the Congo*. It was a Belgian colony that gained independence in 1960. Most of the country is a plateau, highest in the south-east, in Katanga. The eastern border, in the African Rift Valley, runs through several great lakes. This part is very mountainous, the Ruwenzori Mountains to 16,794 ft (5,119 m). The Zaïre (Congo) River pursues a course of some 2,800 miles (4,500 km) through the country. Zaïre is rich in minerals, particularly in copper. Diamonds, cobalt, and iron are among the other minerals extracted. Agricultural exports include coffee, tea, sugar, cotton, rubber, and fruit. There are many manufacturing industries.

ZAMBIA *Area 288,130 sq miles (746,253 sq km); population 5,945,000; capital, Lusaka (pop. 401,000); currency, kwacha (100 ngwee); official language, English.*

Zambia, which became independent in 1964, was formerly the British protectorate of Northern Rhodesia. The country is watered by one of Africa's great rivers, the Zambezi. Most of Zambia is a plateau, averaging some 4,000 ft (1,200 m) above sea-level. But some of the country is higher. The Muchinga Mountains in the eastern part rise to more than 7,000 ft (2,130 m). There are many lakes, either in Zambia or on its borders. They include Lake Kariba, in the south, an artificial lake formed by the building of the Kariba Dam. This project supplies hydro-electricity to Zimbabwe as well as to Zambia. The country is rich in mineral resources, especially copper. The chief export crops are cereals, ground-nuts, tea, coffee, and cane sugar, but output is affected by high wages paid in mining.

ZIMBABWE *Area 150,820 sq miles (390,622 sq km); population 7,473,000; capital, Salisbury (pop. 503,000); currency, dollar (100 cents); official language English.*

Zimbabwe was formerly the British colony of Southern Rhodesia, but in 1965 the colonial government declared the country independent. Britain declared this act to be illegal. In the 1970s, African nationalists waged a guerrilla war against the white government. The war ended in 1980 when legal independence was granted. Zimbabwe is a land-locked, mostly plateau region, lying between the basins of the Zambezi River in the north and the Limpopo River in the south-east. Lake Kariba on the border with Zambia is behind the Kariba Dam which was built across the Zambezi River. Hydro-electricity generated at the Dam is supplied to Zimbabwe and Zambia. Zimbabwe has rich mineral resources, including iron, copper, asbestos, and gold. Crops include cereals, fruit, sugar-cane, and tobacco, and beef cattle are important.

Countries of North and Central America

BAHAMAS *Area 5,400 sq miles (13,990 sq km); population 193,000; capital, Nassau (pop. 112,000); currency, dollar (100 cents); official language, English.*

The Bahamas were a British colony from 1649 to 1964, when they became self-governing. They acquired their independence in 1973. The whole group of islands is strung out between Florida and Haiti, and consists of some 700 islands, about 25 of which are inhabited, and over 2,000 reefs and keys. Thanks to the excellent climate, the Bahamas are a great attraction for foreign tourist traffic. The native population consists almost entirely of coloured peoples.

BARBADOS *Area 166 sq miles (430 sq km); population 241,000; capital, Bridgetown (pop. 19,000); currency, dollar (100 cents); official language, English.*

Barbados became a British colony in 1652, attained self-government in 1961, and won its independence in 1966. It is the most easterly island of the Lesser Antilles, and has a tropical and humid climate. The fertile soil is given over almost exclusively to the production of sugar-cane. Tourism is the second most important industry.

BELIZE *Area 8,900 sq miles (23,000 sq km); population 139,000; capital, Belmopan (pop. 5,000); currency, dollar (100 cents); official language, English.*

A British colony as British Honduras since 1884, Belize became a self-governing dependency in 1964. It lies on the Caribbean coast of Central America, to the east of Guatemala. The population is made up largely of Negroes and people of mixed blood, along with about 3,000 Whites and several thousand American Indians. Wood, sugar, and citrus fruits are the most important exports.

BERMUDA *Area 21 sq miles (53 sq km); population 60,000; capital, Hamilton (pop. 2,000); currency, dollar (100 cents); official language, English.*

Bermuda, a group of some 350 small islands in the Atlantic, 580 miles (930 km) from the United States, became a British colony in 1684, and a self-governing dependency in 1968. About 20 of the islands are inhabited, and tourism is the most important source of income.

CANADA *Area 3,851,809 sq miles (9,976,139 sq km); population 23,444,000; capital, Ottawa (pop. 702,000); currency, dollar (100 cents); official languages, English and French.*

After the USSR, Canada is the next largest country in the world. It is, however, relatively thinly populated, and still welcomes immigration. For more than a hundred years, the English and French fought over the possession of this land. The last battle was won by the British in 1759, and in 1763 France resigned all her claims. The French settlers were, however, permitted to remain in the country and retain their own language. In the province of Quebec, the French Canadians still constitute a closed racial group. Canada has been a member of the British Empire and Commonwealth since 1867, but although the British monarch reigns as monarch of Canada, the country is completely independent and self-governing.

In a north-south direction, Canada stretches for some 2,900 miles (4,670 km). As a result, the climate is extremely varied. A narrow coastal strip in the west has a mild maritime climate, whereas in the interior there is a dry and cold continental climate. North of the Arctic Circle, snow lies on the ground almost the whole year through, whereas in Ontario, on Canada's southern border, the vine is cultivated.

About half of Canada is taken up by a land region known as the Canadian Shield. Sparsely populated and made up of hard, ancient rocks, this horseshoe-shaped region stretches down central Canada from the Northwest Territories, round Hudson Bay to the northern coast of Quebec. A swampy, forested lowland separates the Shield from the southern shores of Hudson Bay, and to the east there are the Appalachian regions (Newfoundland, Nova Scotia, etc.) and the St Lawrence-Great Lakes lowlands. The latter is a comparatively small region, but more than half the country's people live there. Its flat and rolling land is extremely fertile. West of the Shield are the interior plains (the prairies, where Canada's vast output of wheat is grown), and the western mountain region, which contains the Canadian Rockies and the Coast Mountains. Canada also has a number of very large islands, which lie almost entirely within the Arctic Circle.

Canada has vast mineral resources in the west, and more recently, oil and natural gas have been found, principally in the centre of the south-west. But although industry is in a leading position in the economy, Canada still remains a land of fishermen, hunters, and farmers. Almost half the land area is covered with forest. Thus, in addition to the trapping and farming of fur-bearing animals, the timber, furniture, and paper industries are very highly developed.

Three-quarters of Canada's people live in the towns. Only small groups of the original inhabitants of the country are still extant: Some 20,000 Eskimoes and 250,000 American Indians (most of whom live on reservations). All others are descendants of immigrants.

COSTA RICA *Area 19,650 sq miles (50,890 sq km); population 2,000,000; capital, San José (pop. 216,000); currency, colón (100 centimos); official language, Spanish.*

Originally a colony of Spain, Costa Rica has been an independent republic since 1821. It lies on the land bridge between North and South America, bordering in the north-east on the Caribbean and in the south-west on the Pacific. Its main products are coffee, sugar, and bananas.

CUBA *Area 44,218 sq miles (114,524 sq km); population 8,553,000; capital, Havana (pop. 1,755,000); currency, peso (100 centavos); official language, Spanish.*

Discovered by Christopher Columbus in 1492, Cuba was a Spanish possession until it became an independent republic in 1898. A revolution in the 1950s saw the communist Fidel Castro come to power in 1959.

A beautiful island, the largest in the Greater Antilles, Cuba lies between Florida and Jamaica. Three-quarters of its inhabitants are Whites, mostly of Spanish descent, while the rest are Negroes or of mixed blood. The 2,100-mile (3,400-km) coastline has many small bays, and numbers of minor islands and coral reefs lie just off it. The eastern part of the island is mountainous, the maximum height being 6,560 feet (2,000 metres). The rest is flat or rolling land. Cuba is the world's third largest producer of sugar-cane.

Tobacco is also an important crop and there are large reserves of nickel.

DOMINICA *Area 290 sq miles (728 sq km); population 80,000; capital, Roseau (pop. 10,200); currency, dollar (100 cents); official language, English.*

A mountainous republic in the Lesser Antilles, Dominica has spectacular scenery and considerable volcanic activity. Cacao, limes, bananas, mangoes, oranges, avocado pears and vanilla are cultivated. The main exports are rum, lime juice and copra. Most of the population are Negroes.

DOMINICAN REPUBLIC *Area 18,800 sq miles (48,700 sq km); population 5,424,000; capital, Santo Domingo (pop. 817,000); currency, peso (100 centavos); official language, Spanish.*

The Dominican Republic has been independent since 1844, after periods of Spanish and French possession. It occupies two-third of the islands of Hispaniola. It has a long history of uprisings and revolutions. The majority of the inhabitants are Negroes, the descendants of slaves. They speak a Creole dialect and practise voodoo. The small ruling class is made up largely of Mulattoes. The land is mountainous, only a third of it being arable. Coffee and sugar are the most important farm products. Bauxite is the most valuable export after coffee.

EL SALVADOR *Area 8,260 sq miles (21,400 sq km); population 4,364,000; capital, San Salvador (pop. 915,000); currency, colón (100 centavos); official language, Spanish.*

The smallest but the most thickly populated of the Central American states, El Salvador has been an independent republic since 1841. From a narrow, hot and humid coastal strip, the land rises to a volcanic mountain region, a 2,000-foot (600-metre) plateau, and another mountain range. Rice, maize, and coffee are the most important agricultural products. About three-quarters of the people are Mestizos (of mixed White/American Indian blood) and a fifth are American Indians.

GREENLAND *Area 840,000 sq miles (2,175,000 sq km); population 50,000; capital, Godthåb (pop. 8,000).*

Greenland, which lies to the north-east of North America, is the largest island in the world. Colonized at various times by Denmark and Norway, it became a province of Denmark in 1953 with equal rights with the rest of the country. About 85 per cent of its surface is covered by a permanent layer of thick ice. After Antarctica, it is the largest frozen expanse of land in the world. A mountainous coastal strip surrounding the ice-cap is free of ice, and has been strongly indented by fjords to form a number of small islands and peninsulas. The highest peak rises 12,139 feet (3,700 metres). Most Greenlanders have both Eskimo and Danish ancestry. They speak Greenlandic, a form of Eskimo language. Many speak Danish. The main occupations are fishing and fish processing. Internal autonomy was granted in 1979.

GRENADA *Area 133 sq miles (344 sq km); population 108,000; capital, St George's (pop. 8,400); currency, dollar (100 cents); official language, English.*

An island of the Lesser Antilles group, Grenada became an independent nation within the Commonwealth in 1974.

GUATEMALA *Area 42,040 sq miles (108,900 sq km); population 6,064,000; capital, Guatemala City (pop. 790,000); currency, quetzal (100 centavos); official language, Spanish.*

The most populous of the Central American states, Guatemala, once a Spanish colony, has been independent since 1821. It has a long history of political troubles. The land is volcanic, and has a tropical climate. Coffee is grown in the fertile mountain districts, and bananas and cotton are also important. About 45 per cent of the people are American Indians.

HAITI *Area 10,700 sq miles (27,700 sq km); population 4,768,000; capital, Port au Prince (pop. 300,000); currency, gourde (100 centimes); official language, French.*

Haiti, today an independent republic, has been a Spanish and French colony in turn, and was, from 1915 to 1934, under the control of the United States. It occupies the western third of the island of Hispaniola. It has a long history of uprisings and revolutions. The majority of the inhabitants are Negroes, the descendants of slaves. They speak a Creole dialect and practise voodoo. The small ruling class is made up largely of Mulattoes. The land is mountainous, only a third of it being arable. Coffee and sugar are the most important farm products. Bauxite is the most valuable export after coffee.

HONDURAS *Area 43,300 sq miles (112,000 sq km); population 2,800,000; capital, Tegucigalpa (pop. 225,000); currency, lempira (100 centavos); official language, Spanish.*

Formerly under Spanish control, Honduras declared its independence in 1838. It lies in northern Central America, on the Caribbean, with a short Pacific coastline in the south. The interior is mountainous, and much of the coastal area is swamp and jungle. Most of the people are of mixed blood, and earn their living on the land. The most important products are bananas and coffee.

JAMAICA *Area 4,400 sq miles (11,400 sq km); population 2,060,000; capital, Kingston (pop. 573,000); currency, dollar (100 cents); official language, English.*

A former British colony, Jamaica became independent in 1962. It is the southernmost island of the Greater Antilles group. The interior is mountainous, and the Blue Mountains in the east rise to a height of 7,402 feet (2,256 metres). There are frequent earthquakes, one of which almost wholly destroyed the capital in 1907. In the fertile coastal plain to the west of Kingston, the principal crop grown is sugar-cane. Jamaica is the world's third largest producer of bauxite (aluminium ore), and its rum is regarded as the finest in the world.

MEXICO *Area 760,000 sq miles (1,968,000 sq km); population 71,616,000; capital, Mexico City (pop. 9,618,000); currency, peso (100 centavos); official language, Spanish.*

Mexico was a Spanish possession until its independence in 1821. Today it is a republic consisting of 31 federal states. The largest Central American country, it lies between the Pacific and the Gulf of Mexico, and borders the United States in the north. The Sierra Madre, an extension of the Rocky Mountains, stretches down from the north in two long chains through the whole of Mexico. Between them lies an elevated plateau, where most of the people live. On the southern edge of this plateau lie a series of volcanoes, some still active. The highest peak is Orizaba, which rises 18,701 feet (5,700 metres). The long arm of Lower California extends in the west, separated from the rest of the country by the Gulf of California. In the east of Mexico is the Yucatán Peninsula, a low limestone plateau. Many famous ruins of the ancient Maya Indian civilization are located there.

Mexico still has some three million pure-blooded American Indians, but most of the people are Mestizos. About three-quarters of the working population is engaged in agriculture, although only an eighth of the land is arable. The country has rich mineral resources. Gold and silver have always been found there, and there are also iron, copper, lead, uranium, and, above all, oil and natural gas. These, of course, form the foundation for the developing manufacturing industries.

NICARAGUA *Area 57,150 sq miles (148,020 sq km); population 2,300,000; capital, Managua (pop. 350,000); currency, córdoba (100 centavos); official language, Spanish.*

Nicaragua was a Spanish colony until 1821, and became an independent republic in 1838. It lies between Honduras and Costa Rica, and is the most thinly populated state in Central America. About 70 per cent of the inhabitants are Mestizos, and the rest are Whites, Negroes, or American Indians. The volcanic mountain region of the interior rises to a height of some 7,000 feet (2,100 metres). The swampy land on the Caribbean is known as the 'Mosquito Coast'. Forests cover four-fifths of the land, and only about a tenth is used for agriculture. The main crops are cotton, coffee, and sugar. Meat is also exported, and there are important deposits of gold and silver.

PANAMA *Area 29,200 sq miles (75,600 sq km); population 1,428,000; capital, Panama City (pop. 418,000); currency, balboa (100 cents); official language, Spanish.*

A small country that forms the narrow land bridge between North and South America, Panama is mountainous, with tropical rain forests, and is divided in two by the Panama Canal. Until 1903, Panama formed part of Colombia, but, with the support of the United States, it declared its independence once the Canal had been built. Much of the population finds employment in connection with the Canal. Important products include bananas and rice.

PUERTO RICO *Area 3,400 sq miles (8,800 sq km); population 3,112,000; capital, San Juan (pop. 851,000).*

An island of the Greater Antilles group, Puerto Rico belonged to Spain for nearly 400 years before being ceded to the United States in 1898. It is not one of the United States, but its inhabitants, who speak Spanish, have the rights of US citizens. The island is thickly populated and poor, which means that many emigrate to the United States. The economy is based on manufacturing and tourism as well as on agriculture.

ST LUCIA *Area 238 sq miles (616 sq km); population 110,780; capital, Castries; currency, dollar; official language, English.*

St Lucia gained its independence from Britain in 1979. It is a volcanic island, and its economy is based on farming and tourism.

ST VINCENT *Area 150 sq miles (388 sq km); population 100,300; capital, Kingstown; currency, dollar; official language, English.*

St Vincent also became independent from Britain in 1979, and its economy has a similar base to St Lucia.

UNITED STATES OF AMERICA *Area 3,615,211 sq miles (9,363,353 sq km); population 214,808,000; capital, Washington DC (pop. 2,861,000); currency, dollar (100 cents); official language, English.*

The United States is a federation of 50 states. The first 13 declared their independence in 1776, after emerging victorious in wars against their colonial masters, Britain and France. The United States is one of the largest and most powerful countries in the world. In the north, it has a long frontier with Canada, the eastern boundary is the Atlantic Ocean, the Pacific Ocean forms the western boundary, and the southern border is with Mexico and on the Gulf of Mexico. Alaska, the 49th state, lies to the west of Canada, and Hawaii, the 50th, lies in the Pacific, some 2,400 miles (3,860 km) west of California.

The mainland may be divided into five natural regions: (1) the Atlantic coastal plain, which gives way in the west to (2) a highland region—the long range of the Appalachians; the land then falls away again to (3) the broad interior plains crossed in a north-south direction by the Mississippi and the Missouri; (4) the western highlands consist of the rocky mountains, with their high plateaux and peaks of over 13,000 feet (4,000 metres), the Sierra Nevada, and other ranges; and (5) the coastal strip along the Pacific, which descends to the Ocean. Despite the size and variety of the country, most parts of the United States have a moderate climate.

The population is about 87 per cent Whites (descendants of immigrants and new immigrants themselves from all the countries of Europe), 11 per cent Negroes (mostly descendants of African slaves), and the others include some half million American Indians, most of whom live on reservations.

The United States is the richest country in the world. A high average standard of living is aimed at, and much is done to provide equality of opportunity, but a small minority still live in varying degrees of poverty.

It is mainly in the north that are found America's giant industrial undertakings. Industrialization has also extended to agriculture, and the working of the frequently huge farms is extensively mechanized and specialized. Nowhere else on Earth is so much maize, oats, tobacco, cotton, soya bean, and citrus fruit produced as in the United States. High productivity is also recorded for wheat, barley, and sugar-beet. The high technical standards of the country are also seen in the harnessing of energy (whether by water, coal, oil, or natural gas), as also in the opening up of access to the rich mineral resources in the ground.

STATES OF THE UNITED STATES
Areas in square kilometres

Alabama	131,333	Montana	377,069
Alaska	1,467,052	Nebraska	198,090
Arizona	293,749	Nevada	284,611
Arkansas	134,537	New Hampshire	23,380
California	404,973	New Jersey	19,479
Colorado	268,753	New Mexico	314,457
Connecticut	12,593	New York	123,882
Delaware	5,133	North Carolina	126,386
Florida	140,092	North Dakota	179,416
Georgia	150,408	Ohio	106,125
Hawaii	16,641	Oklahoma	178,145
Idaho	214,132	Oregon	249,115
Illinois	144,387	Pennsylvania	116,461
Indiana	93,491	Rhode Island	2,717
Iowa	144,887	South Carolina	78,282
Kansas	211,827	South Dakota	196,723
Kentucky	102,693	Tennessee	107,039
Louisiana	116,368	Texas	678,924
Maine	80,082	Utah	212,628
Maryland	25,618	Vermont	24,025
Massachusetts	20,269	Virginia	103,030
Michigan	147,155	Washington	172,416
Minnesota	205,358	West Virginia	62,341
Mississippi	122,496	Wisconsin	141,061
Missouri	178,696	Wyoming	251,755

Countries of South America

ARGENTINA *Area 1,073,000 sq miles (2,779,000 sq km); population 25,384,000; capital, Buenos Aires (pop. 8,353,000); currency, peso (100 centavos); official language, Spanish.*

Argentina has been independent since 1816, and a federal republic since 1853. The country is 2,300 miles (3,700 km) long from north to south, almost half the length of the continent. In the north-west, there is the hot bush and forest lowland of the Gran Chaco, to the south the steppe lowlands of the Pampas, which extend as far as the coast, and in the west the Andes, which contain the highest mountain in South America, the 22,835 feet (6,960 metres) high Aconcagua. The climate varies from almost tropical in the Gran Chaco to cool in the south. In the damp north-eastern marginal areas, there is tropical primeval forest, in which palms, lianas, bamboo, mimosa, and acacia grow.

Ninety per cent of Argentinians are white, mostly of Spanish or Italian descent. A small German minority, however, wields considerable economic influence. Some pure-blooded Amerindians live in the Gran Chaco.

The basis of the economy is agriculture, but huge herds of cattle graze on the Pampas, and beef is an important export. The Pampas merge into a crescent-shaped region, nearly 200 miles (320 km) broad, in which grain is cultivated. Cotton is planted in the Gran Chaco, and the province of Tucumán in the north-west is a sugar-cane growing region. The mountains have considerable mineral resources, but these are largely undeveloped.

BOLIVIA *Area 415,000 sq miles (1,075,000 sq km); population 6,444,000; capital, La Paz (pop. 553,000); currency, peso (100 centavos); official language, Spanish.*

Under the leadership of Simón Bolívar, from whom it took its name, the country declared its independence from Spain and Peru in 1825.

Bolivia is completely landlocked. In the west, ranges of the Andes (the Cordilleras), with peaks rising to 20,000 feet (6,100 metres), border the Altiplano, a treeless plateau some 12,500 feet (3,800 metres) above sea level. Here, in an elevated basin, lies Lake Titicaca. The eastern lowlands have affinities with the grass steppes (llanos) of the Amazon Basin and with the Gran Chaco, and they are sparsely populated. More than half the people live in the Altiplano, particularly on the slopes falling away to the east. Only 15 per cent are Whites, but they constitute the ruling class. More than half are Indians, and the rest are of mixed blood, mostly Mestizos. Two-thirds of the population, especially the South American Indians, are engaged in agriculture, but their primitive methods produce poor results, although the llanos are very fertile. The land has considerable mineral resources, especially of tin, of which Bolivia is the second largest producer.

BRAZIL *Area 3,286,488 sq miles (8,511,964 sq km); population 121,933,000; capital, Brasília (pop. 545,000); currency, cruzeiro (100 centavos); official language, Portuguese.*

Brazil declared its independence from Portugal in 1822, and became a republic in 1889. It is the fifth largest country in the world, taking up almost half the South American continent. The main river is the Amazon, in the north, with some hundred navigable tributaries. The Amazon lowlands have a hot and humid climate and constitute the largest tropical primeval forest region in the world. To the north lie the largely unexplored Guiana Highlands, which are partly covered with primeval forest, partly with savanna vegetation. Rain forests lie along the central coastal regions, while in the south-east there are subtropical forests and savanna. Savanna also dominate extensive regions of the highlands in the interior.

Brazil has a larger population than any other South American country. Until the mid-1600s, there was considerable immigration of Portuguese and Spaniards, and from the end of the 1500s Negro slaves were brought into the country. It was not until the 19th century that free immigration began from all the countries of Europe. Today, barely 60 per cent of the inhabitants are white. About 10 per cent are Negroes and 4 per cent Asian, but a third are Mestizos and Amerindians. Most of the Amerindians live in small bands in the forested Amazon region.

Brazil's wealth comes from agriculture. More than half of the whole work force is engaged in agriculture and forestry. The main crop is coffee. The country also has rich mineral resources, and industrialization is being actively promoted.

CHILE *Area 292,000 sq miles (756,000 sq km); population 10,751,000; capital, Santiago (pop. 4,000,000); currency, peso (100 centésimos); official language, Spanish.*

A former Spanish colony, Chile has been independent since 1818. It is a long, mountainous country, stretching along the Pacific coast for more than half the length of South America. There are three distinct climatic zones: in the north, a dry, desert zone with a rainless coast; in the centre, a subtropical zone; and in the south, a zone with heavy rainfall and low summer temperatures.

Between the Andes—the High Cordilleras in the east and the Coastal Cordilleras in the west—runs a great longitudinal valley. There are earthquake zones, and active volcanoes rising to a height of 22,000 feet (6,700 metres). Tierra del Fuego, the southern tip of the continent, is separated from the mainland by the stormy Strait of Magellan.

Most of the population are Mestizos. Of the original Indian native population, only about 500,000 are left. The small ruling class comes from people of European descent. Almost three-quarters of the inhabitants live in the central area, for this is the only part of the country that is arable. Extensive regions require artificial irrigation. There are rich mineral resources, and of all exported products, 80 per cent are mined (copper, iron, nitrates).

COLOMBIA *Area 439,737 sq miles (1,138,914 sq km); population 27,291,000; capital, Bogotá (pop. 2,512,000); currency, peso (100 centavos); official language, Spanish.*

Colombia won independence from Spain in 1819, and became a republic in 1886. It lies in the north-west of South America, bordering on Panama, which, for some time, formed part of Colombia. The Eastern Cordilleras, a range of the Andes, reach a height of 18,000 feet (5,500 metres). The lowlands of the Amazon valley and the Orinoco occupy large portions of the country, on both the Pacific and Caribbean coasts.

More than two-thirds of the population are Mestizos, a fifth are Whites, and the rest are of Negro or Indian origin. The original Indian population is today represented by only about 7 per cent of the inhabitants.

Although Colombia is developing its industry, it is still largely an agricultural country. Very little of the land is under cultivation. There are large numbers of smallholders. The main product is coffee.

ECUADOR *Area 109,500 sq miles (283,600 sq km); population 7,000,000; capital Quito (pop. 700,000); currency, sucre (100 centavos); official language, Spanish.*

Ecuador has been an independent republic since 1830. It suffers from constant uprisings, revolutions, and putsches, under which the country's economic development has been retarded. As a result, it is amongst the poorest countries of South America. It lies on the west coast of the continent, between Peru and Colombia. The coastal lowlands are from 30 to 90 miles (50-150 km) wide. Through the centre of the country run two parallel mountain chains of the Andes, with heights of 10,000-20,000 feet (3,000-6,000 metres). There are large numbers of active volcanoes in this region. Towards the east, the mountain slopes fall steeply away down to the lowlands of the Amazon valley.

Over a third of the inhabitants are Amerindians, engaged in agriculture. The coastal region is inhabited by Mestizos, Negroes, and Mulattoes. The 10 per cent of Whites, chiefly descendants of the Spaniards, constitute the ruling class. Two-thirds of the population are engaged in agriculture or cattle rearing.

FRENCH GUIANA *Area 34,740 sq miles (89,976 sq km); population 60,000; capital, Cayenne (pop. 20,000); currency, franc (French); official language, French.*

The country, which lies on the northern coast of South America, became an overseas department of France in 1946. Most of the people are Negroes or Creoles, and about 10 per cent are American Indians. Tropical rain forest covers almost nine-tenths of the total area, and is still unexplored. Gold is mined and there are large deposits of bauxite. Crops grown include sugar and maize.

GUYANA *Area 83,000 sq miles (215,000 sq km); population 740,000; capital, Georgetown (pop. 168,000); currency, dollar (100 cents); official language, English.*

Formerly British Guiana, the country became an independent member of the Commonwealth in 1966, the world's first Co-operative Republic. Guyana lies between Venezuela and Surinam on the Atlantic Ocean. The highland region in the west rises to a height of nearly 10,000 feet (3,000 metres). The mountains in the east are much flatter and give way to tropical rain forests. Most of the population live on the coastal strip. About half of them are Asians, many of whose ancestors came from India. The Whites and the American Indians constitute only small groups. There are, however, sizeable Negro and Mulatto communities. Bauxite, alumina, manganese ores, and diamonds are mined and exported. Sugar, rice, shrimps, timber, rum and molasses are also exported.

NETHERLANDS ANTILLES *Area 383 sq miles (993 sq km); population 224,000; capital, Willemstad (pop. 146,000); currency, guilder (Dutch); official language, Dutch.*

These islands, also known as the Dutch West Indies, have independence of administration and enjoy equal rights with the Netherlands themselves. They consist of Aruba, Bonaire, and Curaçao off the Venezuelan coast, and three smaller islands of the Windward group. The inhabitants are principally Negroes and Mulattoes. The economy is based on the refining of oil imported from Venezuela to Aruba and Curaçao.

PARAGUAY *Area 157,000 sq miles (406,600 sq km); population 2,650,000; capital, Asunción (pop. 437,000); currency, guaraní (100 céntimos); official language, Spanish.*

Paraguay won its independence from Spain and became a republic in 1811. The larger, western part of the country lies in the Gran Chaco, whereas the eastern part is bordered by the Paraná and constitutes an undulating tableland with subtropical rain forests. Between the Paraguay and Paraná rivers, there are large marshes. Some 95 per cent of the inhabitants are Mestizos. More than half the people live in or around the capital. And more than half are engaged in agriculture.

PERU *Area 496,000 sq miles (1,285,000 sq km); population 17,526,000; capital, Lima (pop. 3,600,000); currency, sol (100 centavos); official language, Spanish.*

Peru declared its independence from Spain in 1821, and after many internal political troubles eventually became a republic. It has a 1,400-mile (2,250-km) coastal strip on the Pacific Ocean, which is fertile only along the river banks. The country is traversed from north to south by the Cordilleras (Andes), the highest peak being Huascarán, at 22,205 feet (6,768 metres). The eastern chain of the Cordilleras merges into the highland region of the Montana, and this, in turn, gives way to wooded lowlands. The main sources of the Amazon rise in the Peruvian Andes.

Most of the inhabitants are descended from American Indians, but the Whites constitute the ruling class. Quechua and Aymara, American Indian languages, are widely spoken. Half of the working population are engaged in agriculture, forestry, and fishing. On the large arable areas of the coastal district, cotton, sugar-cane, rice, maize, and many other crops are grown on plantations. There are extensive irrigation systems. There is also a flourishing mining industry. Copper, lead, and zinc are particularly important.

SURINAM *Area 63,000 sq miles (163,000 sq km); population 480,000; capital, Paramaribo (pop. 110,000); currency, guilder (100 cents); official language, Dutch.*

Surinam, formerly known as Dutch Guiana, became independent in 1975. It lies on the northern coast of South America. Three-quarters of the land area is covered in forest, still largely unexplored. Half the inhabitants are of mixed blood. Along the coast, sugar-cane, coffee, citrus fruits, and cacao are cultivated, and there are vast desposts of bauxite.

TRINIDAD AND TOBAGO *Area 1,980 sq miles (5,130 sq km); population 1,027,000; capital, Port of Spain (pop. 94,000); currency, dollar (100 cents); official language, English.*

These two islands, the most southerly of the Lesser Antilles, formed a British colony from 1889 until their independence in 1962. They lie off the coast of Venezuela. The population of Tobago, by far the smaller of the two islands, consists almost exclusively of Negroes. On Trinidad, more than a third of the people are Indians, but the majority are Negroes or Mulattoes. Trinidad is a mountainous island and has large stretches of rain forest. Half of the country is cultivated (sugar and cocoa), and there are rich deposits of oil and natural asphalt.

URUGUAY *Area 68,536 sq miles (177,507 sq km); population 2,764,000; capital, Montevideo (pop. 1,173,000); currency, peso (100 centésimos); official language, Spanish.*

Uruguay became an independent republic in 1828, having belonged first to Spain and then to Brazil. It is situated on the Atlantic Ocean and on the Río de la Plata, between Brazil and Argentina. Hilly grassland merges in the south into the Argentinian Pampas. The population consists largely of the descendants of Spanish and Portuguese settlers. The main source of income is the rearing of animals. Meat, meat products, and wool are exported. More than two-thirds of the total area is pastureland, only 10 per cent being arable.

VENEZUELA *Area 352,145 sq miles (912,051 sq km); population 12,500,000; capital, Caracas (pop. 2,184,000); currency, bolívar (100 céntimos); official language, Spanish.*

Venezuela won its independence from Spain in 1821 and became a republic in 1830. It lies in the northernmost part of South America, between Colombia and Guyana. The main river is the Orinoco, which drains four-fifths of the country. Mountain systems break up Venezuela into four distinct regions: the Maracaibo lowlands, the highlands in the north and north-west, the vast Orinoco plains or *llanos*, and the Guiana Highlands. The llanos, in the south-east, cover a third of the country's area.

The population consists mainly of 65 per cent Mestizos, 20 per cent Whites, and 10 per cent Negroes. Only 1 per cent are pure-blooded South American Indians. Half of the inhabitants live in the towns.

For years, agriculture was the only source of revenue, with exports of coffee and cocoa. Now, however, Venezuela has developed into an important supplier of raw materials for industry. It is the fifth largest oil-producing country in the world, and the largest exporter. Its oil resources are found mainly in the Maracaibo basin. Its iron ore deposits are also among the largest in the world, and there are important gold and diamond mines. Along with the development of refineries, the country is also being increasingly industrialized.

Countries of Oceania

AUSTRALIA *Area 2,967,909 sq miles (7,686,848 sq km); population 14,074,000; capital, Canberra (pop. 165,000); currency, dollar (100 cents); official language, English.*

The Australian Commonwealth was founded in 1901, comprising New South Wales, Victoria, Queensland, South Australia, Western Australia, and Tasmania. The Northern Territory was transferred from South Australia 10 years later, at the same time as the Australian Capital Territory was acquired from New South Wales. Australia is a member of the British Commonwealth, and a parliamentary democracy. The head of state is the British monarch, represented by a governor-general, who formally appoints the prime minister and other ministers from the majority party in parliament. Parliament (the House of Representatives and the Senate) is the legislative body.

Australia is the smallest of the continents, but it is sometimes also regarded as the largest island in the world. The area of the mainland (i.e. without Tasmania) is 2,941,526 sq miles (7,618,517 sq km), and it has a coastline of over 11,000 sq miles (28,500 sq km). The eastern and more populated part of the country has a regular coastline, with good harbours and rivers flowing to the sea. The western half has a broken coastline, which is thinly-populated except in the south-west. The Great Barrier Reef, the world's largest coral reef, stretches for about 1,250 miles (2,000 km) parallel to the Queensland coast at a distance of 10-150 miles (15-240 km). It covers an area of some 80,000 sq miles (200,000 sq km). Much of Australia's interior, especially in the west, is desert. But in the east, particularly the south-east, and in the south-west around Perth, the land is fertile.

The country as a whole is generally low and flat, but there are highlands stretching right along the east coast and along most of Victoria on the southern coast, the highest point being Mount Kosciusko, which rises 7,316 feet (2,230 metres) in the Australian Alps, near Canberra. In the centre of the continent, lowlands extend from the Gulf of Carpentaria to the shores of the Great Australian Bight in the south. A vast plateau, with an average height of about 1,000 feet (300 metres), covers most of the western two-thirds of Australia. A largely desert region, it includes Western Australia, the Northern Territory, and much of South Australia, extending even into Queensland and New South Wales.

Australia has a warm, dry climate, the northern third of the country lying in the tropics. Only about a third of the country receives enough rain for good farming. Nevertheless, what good pasture land and arable land there is makes Australia the leading wool producing nation in the world and one of the leading meat and wheat exporting countries. Most of the farms are family concerns covering large areas and run with the help of machinery and seasonal workers. In the Northern Territory, some ranches, or *stations* as they are called, cover several thousand square miles.

But Australia is not just an agricultural and farming country. Mining is becoming increasingly important. The gold deposits have long been known, but rich strata of iron ore have also been discovered, and Australia leads the world in the production of lead. Other important minerals include hard and brown coal, bauxite, copper, and zinc. There are several oilfields in production (in Queensland, Western Australia, and offshore Victoria), which supply about two-thirds of the country's needs. Natural gas deposits are also being exploited. Industry has grown enormously, but there is a shortage of manpower to develop all the possibilities offered by this vast country. Economists believe that Australia could support three times its present population.

Most of the inhabitants of Australia are European immigrants or descendants of immigrants. Only about 100,000 of the original native race, the Aborigines, remain, and most of these live on protected reserves. They used to wander through the country beach-combing and hunting. They used primitive implements and weapons (spears, clubs, boomerangs) made of bone, sea-shells, rock, or wood. The Aborigines have chocolate-brown skin and certain physical characteristics that do not place them easily into any of the major racial stocks. They probably lived originally in south-eastern Asia.

The native animal world of Australia is markedly different from that found in other countries of the world, and this phenomenon can be explained by the development undergone by the Earth's crust. Some 200 million years ago, the great land mass that existed then broke up. As it broke away, each continent naturally carried with it the varieties of animal that lived there. These then developed in isolation from the others. So it is that only in Australia do we find the duckbilled platypus and the spiny anteater (echidna), representing a primitive subspecies of mammals. These lay eggs, hatch them out, and then feed their young on breast milk. A special variety of mammal is also found in Australia, the marsupials. These give birth to living young, which are so small that they slip into the mother's pouch immediately after birth. There they are suckled until they are large enough to live an independent life. The best known of these is the kangaroo, but there are also koalas, wombats, bandicoots, dasyures, Tasmanian wolves, and the cuscus.

FIJI *Area 7,055 sq miles (18,272 sq km); population 588,000; capital, Suva (pop. 54,000); currency, dollar (100 cents); official language, English.*

A group of 322 islands in the South Pacific, some 1,100 miles (1,770 km) north of New Zealand, Fiji came under British control in 1874 and became an independent nation within the Commonwealth in 1970. Only 106 of the islands are inhabited, and the largest two, Viti Levu and Vanua Levu, make up seven-eighths of the total area. About half the people are Indians and some 42 per cent are Fijians. The Indians are largely descended from plantation labourers brought from India between 1880 and 1914. The islands have a favourable oceanic climate, and the main agricultural products are sugar-cane and coconuts. Tourism is becoming an increasingly important source of revenue.

FRENCH POLYNESIA *Area 1,550 sq miles (4,000 sq km); population 130,000; capital, Papeete (pop. 15,000).*

An Overseas Territory of France since 1958, French Polynesia consists of a number of islands scattered over a wide area of the eastern Pacific. These include the Society Islands, the Leeward Isles, and the Marquesas. The capital is located on Tahiti, in the Society group. Most of the people are Polynesians. The most important product is copra.

GUAM *Area 209 sq miles (541 sq km); population 105,000; capital, Agaña (pop. 2,000).*

The largest of the Mariana Islands, in the North Pacific, Guam was acquired by the United States from Spain in 1898. It was granted statutory powers of self-government in 1950, and the people became US citizens. Most Guamanians are Chamorros (of Indonesian and Spanish descent). The island is of vital strategic importance as an air and naval base, and about a third of the inhabitants are military personnel and their families. The interior of Guam is mountainous, and coral reefs lie off the coast.

HAWAII *Area 6,425 sq miles (16,641 sq km); population 832,000; capital, Honolulu (pop. 325,000).*

A group of islands in the central Pacific, about 2,400 miles (3,860 km) west of the US mainland, Hawaii was accepted as the 50th state of the United States in 1959. It had been a US territory since 1900. The group comprises a 1,610-mile (2,591-km) chain of 122 islands formed by volcanoes built up from the ocean floor. Of the eight main islands, located in the south-east, seven are inhabited. They have a mild climate and fertile soil. The largest island is called Hawaii and covers nearly two-thirds of the total area. It has two active volcanoes (Mauna Loa and Kilauea) and the highest peak in the state, Mauna Kea, which rises 13,796 feet (4,205 metres). About 80 per cent of Hawaii's inhabitants live on Oahu, the third largest island on which Honolulu and Pearl Harbor are located.

The original inhabitants of these islands were Polynesians, and 15 per cent of today's population have predominant Hawaiian ancestry. About 40 per cent are of White descent, and 30 per cent have Japanese ancestry. The chief products are cane-sugar and tropical fruits. About 35 per cent of the world's tinned pineapple is produced in Hawaii. The tourist industry is one of the state's largest sources of income.

KIRIBATI REPUBLIC *Area 264 sq miles (684 sq km); population 52,000; capital, Tarawa (pop. 11,000).*

Formerly a British colony known as the Gilbert Islands, the Kiribati Republic became independent in 1979. Until 1975 it was linked with Tuvalu (Ellice Islands) which became independent in 1978. The Kiribati Republic contains the Gilbert, Phoenix and Line Islands, and also Ocean Island. They span about 2,000,000 sq miles of the Pacific Ocean. Most of the atolls rise to no more than 12 ft (3.5 metres) above sea level, and are thickly wooded with coconut palms. A high proportion of the population is Micronesian. Ocean Island, to the west of the Gilbert group, has important phosphate deposits. The only other export from the islands is copra.

NAURU *Area 8 sq miles (21 sq km); population 7,000; capital, Nauru; currency, dollar (Australian); official languages, Nauruan and English.*

A tiny island in the Pacific Ocean, Nauru became an independent republic in 1968, having a special relationship with the Commonwealth. It had been under German control from 1888 to 1914, when it surrendered to Australian forces. It was administered under a mandate until 1947 and then a trusteeship. It lies almost on the equator, north of New Zealand, and is surrounded by a coral reef.

Its importance is due to its valuable deposits of phosphates. About half the people are Nauruans, a quarter are other Pacific islanders, and the rest are Chinese or European.

NEW CALEDONIA *Area 7,375 sq miles (19,103 sq km); population 132,000; capital, Nouméa (pop. 50,000).*

An island in the western Pacific 700 miles (1,127 km) east of Queensland, New Caledonia was annexed by France in 1853, and with its various island dependencies is an Overseas Territory of France. Nearly a half of the inhabitants are Melanesians, and a third are Europeans (mostly French). The island is rich in mineral resources, and is the world's fourth largest nickel producer, after the USSR, Canada, and Australia. Chrome, iron, and other minerals are mined.

NEW ZEALAND *Area 103,736 sq miles (268,675 sq km); population 3,129,000; capital, Wellington (pop. 329,000); currency, dollar (100 cents); official language, English.*

Like Australia, New Zealand is an independent parliamentary democracy on the British model. The head of state is the British monarch, represented by the governor-general. The country became a British colony in 1840 when the Maoris, the original native population, ceded sovereignty to the British Crown, and a dominion in 1907.

North and South Islands, which make up nearly 99 per cent of the territory of New Zealand, lie in the South Pacific, about 1,200 miles (1,930 km) east of Australia. There are a number of smaller islands, and New Zealand has responsibility for a large area in the Antarctic Ocean. North and South Islands are separated by Cook Strait, just 16 miles (26 km) wide. Much of the country is mountainous. The highest point, Mount Cook, rises 12,349 feet (3,764 metres) in the Southern Alps, which extend along the entire length of the South Island. There are several volcanoes, including two active ones, on the North Island, which is also noted for its hot springs and geysers. The countryside has great natural beauty and there are many lakes. The climate is temperate, with a narrow annual range of temperature.

About half of the country is used for agriculture, and 90 per cent of the farmland is used for rearing sheep and cattle. New Zealand is the world's fourth largest sheep-rearing and third largest wool-producing country. The main crops are wheat, barley, and oats. Apart from wool and meat, the chief exports are butter and cheese. New Zealand has few mineral resources, the main ones being coal and gold. The generation of energy is dependent on hydro-electric power.

The development of New Zealand since the 1870s has been marked by the successful integration of the native population with the European immigrants (mostly from Great Britain). The Maoris are a branch of the Polynesian race and make up about 8 per cent of the total population.

PAPUA NEW GUINEA *Area 178,000 sq miles (461,000 sq km); population 2,655,000; capital, Port Moresby (pop. 77,000); currency, kina (100 toea); official language, English.*

Formerly a dependency of Australia, Papua New Guinea became self-governing in 1973 and fully independent in 1975. The country comprises the eastern half of the island of New Guinea (West Irian, part of Indonesia, is the other half) and a number of islands off the northern and eastern coasts. Papua, the southern part of the eastern half of New Guinea, was annexed by Queensland in 1883 and became a British protectorate in 1884. The Germans took possession of the northern part in the same year. The British government handed over control of British New Guinea in 1906 to Australia, who renamed it Papua, and the Australians also gained control of the German territory in 1921. They established joint control of the Territory of Papua and New Guinea in 1949.

Papua New Guinea lies wholly within the tropics, separated from Australia by the Torres Strait. A massive chain of mountain ranges stretches across the mainland, reaching a height of 15,400 feet (4,700 metres) with Mount Wilhelm in the Bismarck Range. The land is varied, with deep, forested valleys, large rivers and hundreds of swiftly flowing streams, and, to the south, one of the most extensive areas of swamp land in the world.

Most of the people are Melanesians, but there are also large groups of Papuans and Negritos. Farming is the principal occupation, and the chief crops are coffee, copra, and cocoa. Rubber and timber are also leading exports, and there is an important copper mine on the island of Bougainville.

SAMOA, AMERICAN *Area 76 sq miles (197 sq km); population 31,000; capital, Pago Pago (pop. 2,000).*

This group of five volcanic islands and two coral atolls in the South Pacific has been a territory of the United States since 1900. The people are Polynesians and are US nationals. The chief products are tuna fish and copra.

SOLOMON ISLANDS *Area 11,500 sq miles (30,000 sq km); population 197,000; capital, Honiara (pop. 11,000).*

Formerly a British protectorate, this island group in the South Pacific became fully independent in 1978. The larger islands are mountainous and forested. The rivers tend to flood. The largest island is Guadalcanal. Most of the people are Melanesians. The chief exports are copra, timber, and fish.

TONGA *Area 270 sq miles (700 sq km); population 92,000; capital, Nuku'alofa (pop. 20,000); currency, pa'anga (100 seniti); official languages, English and Tongan.*

A British-protected state since 1900, Tonga became independent in 1970. The kingdom consists of 169 islands, also known as the Friendly Islands. Most of the islands are coral, but some are volcanic. Farming is the main occupation of the people, who are Polynesians, and copra and bananas are the chief exports. Tourism is being developed.

TUVALU *Area 10 sq miles (26 sq km); population 7,900; capital, Funafuti; currency, dollar (100 cents); official language, English.*

Formerly the Ellice Islands, Tuvalu became independent in 1978. The islands are low, and large expanses are thickly wooded. Most of the people are Polynesians. The most important export is copra.

VANUATU REPUBLIC *Area 5,700 sq miles (14,800 sq km); population 99,000; capital, Vila (pop. 6,000).*

A group of islands in the South Pacific some 500 miles (800 km) west of Fiji, the Vanuatu Republic became independent in 1980. There are many active volcanoes on the islands. Most of the people are Melanesians. The chief product is copra.

WESTERN SAMOA *Area 1,097 sq miles (2,842 sq km); population 151,000; capital, Apia (pop. 25,000); currency, tala (100 sene); official languages, English and Samoan.*

A German protectorate in the early 1900s, Western Samoa was administered by New Zealand from 1920 to 1961, before voting its own independence as from 1962. The country comprises 9 of the 14 islands of the Samoan Archipelago (the others constituting American Samoa). The two large islands, Savaii and Upolu, make up 99·8 per cent of Western Samoa's land area. They are mountainous, with rugged interiors. Most of the people, who are Polynesians, live on the coast. The chief exports are copra, cocoa, and bananas.

Index to the maps of the British Isles

Rosehearty II F3
Rossan Point III BC2
Rosslare III E4
Ross-on-Wye I D5
Rothbury I E1
Rotherham I EF3
Rothes II E3
Rothesay II C5
Rousay II E1
Rugby I E4
Rushden 5 F4
Ruthin I C3
Ryde I EF6
Rye I G6

S

Saffron Walden I G4-5
Saint Abb's Head II FG5
Saint Albans I F5
Saint Andrews II F4
Saint Austell I B6
Saint Bee's Head II BC2
Saint David's Head I A5
Saint George's Channel III EF4-5
Saint Helens I D3
Saint Ives I aB
Saint Ives I A6
Saint Martin's I aA
Saint Mary's I aA
Saint Neots I F4
Salcombe I BC6
Salford I D3
Salisbury I DE5
Saltash I B6
Sanday II F1
Sandown I EF6
Sandringham I G4
Sawel Mountain III DE2
Saxmundham I H4
Scafell Pikes I C2
Scalloway II a
Scalpay II C3
Scarborough I F2
Scarinish II B4
Scilly, Isles of I aA
Scourie II C2
Scunthorpe I F3
Seaham I E2

Selby I F3
Selkirk II EF5
Sevenoaks I G5
Severn I D4
Shaftesbury I DE6
Shannon, River II B4
Shannon, River III C3
Shapinsay II F1
Sheffield I EF3
Sheppey, Isle of I GH5
Shepton Mallet I D5
Sheringham I H4
Shetland Isles II a
Shrewsbury I D4
Sidmouth I CD6
Sittingbourne I G5
Sixmilebridge III C4
Skegness I G3
Skibbereen III B5
Skipton I DE3
Skokholm Island I A5
Skomer Island I A5
Skye II B3
Slaney III E4
Sleaford I F3
Slea Head III A4
Slieve Donard III EF2
Sligo III C2
Slough I F5
Slyne Head III A3
Snaefell I B2
Snowdon I BC3
Solihull I E4
Solway Firth II E6
Solway Firth I C2
Somerset I C5
Southampton I E6
South Downs I F6
Southend-on-Sea I GH5
Southern Uplands II DF5
South Esk II EF4
South Molton I C5
Southport I C3
South Ronaldsay II F2
Southwold I H4
Spalding I F4
Spennymoor I E2
Sperrin Mountains III DE2
Spey II E3
Spurn Head I G3
Stafford I DE4
Staffordshire I DE4
Staines I F5

Stamford I F4
Start Point I C6
Stevenage I FG5
Stewarton II D5
Stirling II DE4
Stockport I DE3
Stockton-on-Tees I E2
Stoke-on-Trent I DE3-4
Stonehaven II FG4
Stornoway II B2
Stowmarket I H4
Stow-on-the-Wold I E5
Stour, River I G4-5
Stour, River I D6
Strabane III D2
Strangford Lough III F2
Stranraer II C6
Stratford-upon-Avon I E4
Strathclyde II C4
Strathy Point II D2
Stromness II E2
Stronsay II F1
Stroud I D5
Suck III C3
Sudbury I G4
Sunderland I EF2
Suffolk I GH4
Sumburgh Head II a
Surrey I F5
Sussex, East I G6
Sussex, West I F6
Sutton-in-Ashfield I EF3
Swadlincote I E4
Swaffham I G4
Swale I E2
Swanage I E6
Swansea I B5
Swindon I E5
Swinford III C3
Swords III E3

T

Tain II D3
Tamar I B6
Tamworth I E4
Tarbert (Outer Hebrides) II B3
Tarbert (Strathclyde) II C5
Taunton I CD5

Tavistock I BC6
Taw I C6
Tay II E4
Tees I E2
Teifi I B4
Teignmouth I C6
Telford I D4
Templemore III D4
Test I E5
Tetbury I DE5
Teviot II F5
Tewkesbury I D5
Thames, River I E5
Thames, River I G5
Thetford I G4
Thomastown III DE4
Thornhill II E5
Thirsk I E2
Thurles III CD4
Thurso II E2
Tilbury I G5
Tipperary III C4
Tipperary, County III CD4
Tiree II AB4
Tiverton I C6
Tobercurry III C2
Tobermory II B4
Tonbridge I G5
Tongue II D2
Torbay I C6
Torridon II C3
Totnes I C6
Towcester I E4
Tralee III B4
Tramore III D4
Trent, River I E4
Trent, River-I F3
Tresco I aA
Trim III E3
Troon II D5
Trowbridge I DE5
Truro I aB
Truro I AB6
Tuam III C3
Tullamore III D3
Tullow III E4
Tunbridge Wells I G5
Turriff II F3
Tyne I DE2
Tyne and Wear I E1-2
Tynemouth I E1
Tywi I C5
Tywyn I B4

U

Uig II B3
Uist, North II AB3
Uist, South II A3
Ullapool II CD3
Ullswater I D2
Ulverston I CD2
Unshin III C2
Unst II a
Upper Lough Erne III D2
Ure I E2

V

Valencia Island III A5
Ventnor I E6
Vyrnwy, Lake I C4

W

Wakefield I E3
Wallingford I E5
Walls II a
Walney, Isle of I C2
Walsall I E4
Warley I E4
Warminster I DE5
Warrenpoint III E2
Warrington I D3
Warwick I E4
Warwickshire I E4
Wash, The I G4
Waterford III DE4
Waterford, County III D4
Watford I F5
Waveney I H4
Wellingborough I F4
Wellington I CD6
Wells I D5
Wells-next-the-Sea I G4
Welshpool I C4
Welwyn Garden City I F5
West Bromwich I E4
Western Isles II AB3
Westmeath III D3
Weston-super-Mare I CD5
Westport III B3
Wexford III E4

Weymouth I D6
Whalsay II a
Wharfe I E3
Whernside I D2
Whitby I F2
Whitehaven I C2
Whithorn II D6
Whitstable I H5
Whittlesey I F4
Wick II EF2
Wicklow, County III E3
Wicklow III EF3
Wicklow Head III F4
Wicklow Mountains III E3-4
Widnes I D3
Wigan I D3
Wight, Isle of I EF6
Wigtown II D6
Wiltshire I DE5
Winchester I E5
Windermere, I CD2
Windermere I D2
Windsor I F5
Winsford I D3
Wisbech I FG4
Witham I G5
Witham, River I F3
Withernsea I G3
Witney I E5
Woking I F5
Wolverhampton I D4
Woodbridge I H4
Woodstock I E5
Worcester I DE4
Workington I C2
Worksop I E3
Worthing I F6
Wrexham I C3
Wye I D4-5
Wymondham I GH4

Y

Yare I H4
Yell II a
Yeovil I D6
York I EF2-3
Yorkshire, North I EF2
Yorkshire, South I E3
Yorkshire, West I E3

General index to the maps

Australia 25 A-B-C4
Australian Bight, Group 25a B-C3
Australian Capital Territory 25a D-E3
Austral Islands see Tubuai Islands
Austria 1 E4
Austvagoy 2 C1
Autun 3 E5
Auxerre 3 D5
Avallon 3 E5
Avellino 6 C2
Aveiro 5 A2
Avesta 2 D3
Avezzano 6 C2
Aviá Terai 24 C-D2
Avignon 5 E2
Avila 5 B2
Avilés 5 B2
Aweil 16 C4
Awjilah 16 C2
Axel Heiberg Island 19 G-H2
Ayacucho 23 B4
Ayadh 10 C4
Ayaguz 9 E3
Ayamonte 5 B3
Aydin 6 F3
Ayion Oros 6 F2
Aylmer, Lake 19 F3
Ayr 3 B3
Ayutthaya 13 B2
Ayvalik 6 F3
Azaòuad 15 C2-3
Azaouak 15 D3
Azbine see Air
Azerbajdzan 10 C1
Azogues 23 B4
Azov 7 F5
Azov, Sea of 7 E-F5
Azuaga 5 B3
Azuero Peninsula 21 D4
Azul 24 D3
Az-Zilfi 10 C3

B

Baba, Cape 6 F3
Babajevo 7 F2
Bab al Mandab 10 C4
Babanusa 16 C3
Babar 13 D-E4
Babuyan, Islands 13 D2
Babylon 10 C2
Bacau 4 F4
Bacolod 13 D2
Badajoz 5 B3
Badalona 5 D2
Badanah 10 C2
Baden-Baden 4 B3
Baffin, Bay 19 I-K2
Baffin, Island 19 I-K2-3
Bafoulabé 15 B-C3
Bafq 10 D2
Bafwasende 17 C1
Bagé 24 D3
Baghdad 10 C2
Baghlan 11 B2
Baghrash Köl 11 D1
Baguio 13 D2
Bahamas, 18 N7
Bahawalpur 11 C3
Bahia 23 E-F4
Bahia Blanca 24 C3
Bahrain 8 D4
Bahr el-Arab 16 C3-4
Bahr el-Ghazal 16 C-D4
Baia-Mare 4 E4
Bai-Bung, Point 13 B3
Baikal, Lake 9 F3
Bairnsdale 25a D3
Baja. 4 D4
Baker 20 B1
Baker, Island 25 E2
Baker, L. 19 G3
Bakersfield 20 A-B2
Baku 10 C-D1-2
Balabac 13 C3
Balabac, Strait of 13 C3
Balasov 7 G4
Balaton, L. 4 D4
Bald Head 25a A-B3
Balearic Islands 5 D-E2-3
Bal Haf 10 C4
Bali 13 C4
Bali, Strait of 13 C4
Balikesir 6 F3
Balikpapan 13 C4
Balkan 6 E-F2
Balkhash, 9 D3
Balkhash, Lake 9 D3
Ballarat 25a D3
Balleny, Islands 27 L2
Balonne 25a D2
Balovale 17 C3

Balsas 21 B3
Balta 7 D4
Baltic Sea 2 D4
Baltijsk 7 A3
Baltimore 20 F2
Baluchistan 10 E3
Bam 10 D3
Bamako 15 C3
Bambari 16 C4
Bamenda 15 E4
Bamiyan 11 B2
Banamba 15 C3
Bandar 11 D4
Bandar-Abbas 10 D3
Bandar-Chah-Bahar 10 D-E3
Bandar-e-Pahlavi 10 C-D2
Bandar-e-Shahpur 10 D2
Bandar Seri Begawan 13 C3
Bandeirante 23 D4
Bandiagara 15 C3
Bandirma 6 F-G2
Bandjarmasin 13 C4
Bandung 13 B4
Bangala 17 B1
Bangalore 11 C4
Bangassou 16 C4
Banggai, Islands 13 D4
Bangka, 13 B4
Bangkok 13 B2
Bangla Desh 8 F4
Bangor (U.K.) 3 C3
Bangor (U.S.) 20 G1
Bangui 16 B4
Bangweulu, L. 17 D3
Ban Hat Yai 13 A-B3
Bani 15 C3
Bani Walid 16 B1
Banja Luka 6 D1
Banjul 15 B3
Banjuwangi 13 C4
Banks, Islands 19 D-E2
Banks Peninsula 25a G6
Banks Strait 25a E4
Ban Me Thuot 13 B2
Banská Bystrica 4 D3
Bantry 3 A4
Banzare, Coast 27 I2
Baquedano 24 C2
Bar 6 D2
Baranovici 7 C3
Barat Daja, Islands. 13 D4
Barbados 22 E2
Barbastro 5 D1
Barbuda 23 C-D1
Barcaldine 25 C4 25a D2
Barcellona 6 C3
Barcelona (Spain) 5 D2
Barcelona (Venez.) 23 C2
Barcelos 23 C3
Bardaï 16 B2
Bardera 16 E4
Bardiyah 16 C1
Bareilly 11 D3
Barents, Sea 9 B-C2
Bari 6 D2
Barinas 23 B-C2
Barisan Range 13 B4
Barkly West 17 C4
Barletta 6 D2
Barnaul 9 D-E3
Barnstaple 3 B4
Baroda see Vadodara
Barquisimeto 23 B-C2
Barra 23 E4
Barracao do Barreto 23 D3
Barra do Corda 23 E3
Barranquilla 23 B1
Barreiras 23 E4
Barreiro 5 A3
Barrow 20 c5
Barrow Island 25a A2
Barrow, Point 20 b-c5
Barrow, Strait 19 F-G2
Barrow in Furness 3 B-C3
Barsi 11 C4
Barun-Urt 12 D2
Baryn-Bogdo 12 C2
Basankusu 17 B-C1
Basanta 7 G5
Basel: see Basle
Bashi Channel 13 D1
Basilan 13 D3
Basle 4 A-B4
Basoko 16 C4
Basra 10 C2
Basse Terre 23 C-D1
Bass Strait 25 E4
Bassas da India 17 D-E4
Bassein 13 A2
Bass Strait 25a D3
Bastia 5 F2
Bastion, Cape 12 C-D5
Bastuträsk 2 D2
Bata 15 D4

Batan, Island 13 D1
Batangas 13 C-D2
Bathurs Island 25a B1
Bathurst (Austr.) 25a D-E3
Bathurst (Gambia): see Banjul
Bathurst (Canada) 19 K5
Bathurst, Cape 19 C-D2
Bathurst, I. 19 F-G2
Bathurst Inlet 19 F3
Batjan 13 D1
Batna 15 D1
Baton Rouge 20 D-E4
Batouri 15 E4
Battambang 13 B2
Battipaglia 6 C2
Battle Harbour 19 K-L4
Batu, Islands 13 A4
Baturité 23 F3
Bauchi 15 D-E3
Bauld, Cape 19 L4
Bauska 7 B-C2
Bautzen 4 C3
Bawean, 13 C4
Bayanhongor 12 C2
Bayan Kara Shan 11 E2
Bayeux 3 C4
Bay, Islands 21 D3
Bay of Gascox 25a G5
Baykonyr 9 D3
Bayonne 5 C2
Bayram-Ali 9 D4
Bayreuth 4 B-C3
Baza 5 C3
Bazaruto 17 D4
Bear Island 9 B2
Beaufort Sea 19 A-B2
Beaufort West 17 C5
Beaumont 20 D2
Beauvais 3 D4
Beaver 19 F4
Beawar 11 C3
Béchar 15 C1
Be'er Sheva 10 B2
Begicev Island 9 F2
Beira 17 D3
Beirut 10 B2
Béja 6 B3
Bejaïa 15 D1
Béjar 5 B2
Békéscsaba 4 E4
Bekily 17 E4
Bela 11 B3
Belawan 13 A-B3
Belcher Channel 19 G2
Belcher Islands 19 H4
Bel'cy 7 D5
Beled Weyne 16 E4
Belém 23 E3
Belfast 3 B4
Belfort 3 E5
Belgaum 11 C4
Belgium 1 D3
Belgorod 7 F4
Belgrade 6 E1
Belitung 13 B4
Belize 18 M8
Bellary 11 C4
Belle Ile 3 C5
Belle Isle, Strait 19 L4
Bellinzona 4 B4
Belmonte 23 F4
Belmopan 21 D3
Belo 17 E3
Belogorsk 9 G3
Belo Horizonte 24 E1
Belorecensk 7 F-G5
Bel'ov 7 E3
Belovo 9 E3
Beloz'orsk 7 F2
Bel'cy 10 A1
Belyj 7 E3
Benadir 16 E4
Benavente 5 B2
Bender Beila 16 F4
Bendery 7 D5
Benevento 6 C2
Bengal 11 D3
Bengbu 11 D3
Bengazi 16 B-C1
Bengkulu 13 B4
Benguela 17 B3
Béni-Abbès 15 C1
Benin, State 14 C4-5
Benin, City 15 D4
Beni Saf 5 C1
Beni Suef 16 C-D1
Benjamin Constant 23 B-C3
Benoni 17 C4
Benue 15 D4
Berat 6 D2
Berber 16 D3
Berbera 16 E3
Berbérati 16 B4
Berdicev 7 C-D4
Berd'ansk 7 F5
Bereda 16 F3

Berenice 16 D2
Berens 19 G4
Berettyó 4 E4
Berezino 7 D3
Berezovo 9 D2
Bergama 10 A2
Bergamo 6 B1
Bergen 2 A3
Bergerac 5 D1
Berhampur 11 D4
Bering, Sea 9 I-K3
Bering Strait 9 K2
Beringovskij 9 I-K2
Berlevag 2 G1
Berlin 4 C2
Bermejo 24 C2
Bermeo 5 C2
Bermuda 21 F1
Berne 4 A4
Bernburg 4 B3
Bernina 6 B1
Beroroha 17 E4
Ber'oza 7 C3
Bertoua 15 E4
Berwick-upon-Tweed 3 C3
Besançon 3 E5
Bétaré-Oya 15 E4
Betezniki 9 C2-3
Betna 11 D3
Beyla 15 C4
Bezeck 7 F2
Béziers 5 D2
Bhagalpur 11 D3
Bhamo 11 E3
Bhatinda 11 C2
Bhaunagar 11 C3
Bhopal 11 C3
Bhubaneswar 11 D3
Bhutan 8 F4
Biafra 15 D4
Biak 13 E4
Biala Podlaska 4 E3
Bialystok 4 E2
Biarritz 5 C2
Bida 15 D4
Bié 17 B3
Bielefeld 4 B2-3
Biella 6 A1
Bielsko-Biala 4 D-E3
Bighorn 20 C1
Bihac 6 C1
Bihar 11 D3
Bijagós 15 B3
Bijeljina 6 D1
Bijsk 9 E3
Bikaner 11 C3
Bikin 9 G3
Bilaspur 11 D3
Billings 20 C1
Bilma 15 E3
Binacka Morava 6 E2
Binzert 15 D-E1
Bioko 16 B7
Birao 16 C4
Birdum 25a C1
Birjand 10 D-E2
Birlad 6 F1
Birmingham (U.K.) 3 C3
Birmingham (U.S.) 20 E2
Bir Moghreim 15 B2
Birni n'Konni 15 D3
Birobidzhan 9 G3
Birzai 7 C2
Biscay, Bay of 5 C2
Bishiba 4 F4
Biskra 15 D1
Bismarck 20 C1
Bismarck, Archipelago 25 C3
Bissau 15 B3
Bitam 17 B1
Bitola 6 E2
Bitterfontein 17 B5
Biysk 9 E3
Bizerte 15 D1
Björna 2 D3
Black 13 B1
Blackall 25a D2
Blackpool 3 C3
Black Sea 10 A-C1
Black Volta 15 C3-4
Blagoevgrad 6 E2
Blagovescensk 9 G3
Blair Athol 25a D2
Blanca Peak 20 C2
Blanc, Mont 5 E1
Blanco, Cape 20 A1
Blanquilla 23 C1
Blantyre 17 D3
Blenheim 25a G6
Blida 15 D1
Bloemfontein 17 C4-5
Bloemhof 17 C4
Bluefields 21 D3
Blue Nile 16 D3
Bluff 25a F6

Blumenau 24 D-E2
Bo 15 B3
Boa Vista, I. (Cape Vert Islands) 15 A3
Boa Vista (Brazil) 23 C2
Bobo-Dioulasso 15 C3
Bobrujsk 7 D3
Boca do Acre 23 C3
Bochnia 4 D-E3
Bochum 4 A3
Bodajbo 9 F3
Bodélé Depression 16 B3
Boden 2 E2
Bodo 2 C2
Boende 17 B-C2
Boghé 15 B3
Bogor 13 B4
Bogotá 23 B2
Bogucar 7 F-G4
Bohol 13 D3
Boise 20 B1
Bojador, Cape 15 B2
Bojnurd 10 D2
Boké 15 B3
Boksburg 17 C4
Boksitogorsk 7 E2
Bolgrad 7 D5
Bolivar 24 C3
Bolivia 22 D5
Bollnäs 2 C3
Bolmen 2 C4
Bologna 6 B1
Bologoje 7 E2
Bolshevik Island 9 F2
Bolzano 6 B1
Boma 17 B2
Bombala 25 D-E3
Bombay 11 C4
Bomu 16 C4
Bon, Cape 15 E1
Bonaire 23 C1
Bonaparte Archipelago 25a B1
Bonaparte Gulf, Joseph 25a B1
Bondo 16 C4
Bone, Gulf of 13 D4
Bongor 16 B3
Bonifacio, Strait of 6 B2
Bonin Islands 25 C1
Bonn 4 A3
Boothia, Gulf of 19 G-H2
Boothia, Peninsula 19 G2
Bor, (Yugoslavia) 6 E1
Bor, (Sudan) 16 D4
Boras 2 C4
Bordeaux 5 C1
Bordertown 25a D3
Borga 2 F3
Borgefjell 2 C2
Borisoglebsk 7 G4
Borisov 7 D3
Borispol' 7 D4
Borlänge 2 C3
Borneo 13 C3
Bornholm 4 C2
Boroloola 25a C1
Borzja 9 F3
Bosaso 16 E3
Bosna 6 D1
Bosporus 10 A-B1
Bossangoa 16 B4
Bosso 16 E3
Boston 20 F-G1
Botevgrad 6 E2
Bothnia, Gulf of 2 D-E2-3
Botosani 4 F4
Botswana 14 E8
Bouaké 15 C4
Bouar 16 B4
Bouârfa 15 C1
Boudoukou 15 C4
Bougainville 25 C3
Bougouni 15 C3
Boulder 20 C1
Bouna 15 C4
Boundji 17 B2
Bounty Islands 25 D-E5
Bourem 15 C-D3
Bourges 3 D5
Bou Rjeima 15 B3
Bourke 25 C4 25a D3
Bournemouth 3 C4
Boutilimit 15 B3
Bouvet, Island 27 C3
Bow 19 E3
Bowen 25a D1
Brac 6 D2
Brach 16 B2
Bräcke 2 C-D3
Braga 5 A2
Bragança 5 B2
Brahmaputra 11 D3
Branco, Rio 23 C2-3
Brandenburg 4 B-C2
Braniewo 4 D-E2
Br'ansk 7 E3
Brasilia 23 E4

Brasov 6 F1
Bratislava 4 D3
Bratsk 9 E-F3
Braunschweig 4 B2
Brava 17 E1
Bravo, Rio 21 B2
Brazil 22 D-F5
Brazos 20 D2
Breclav 4 D3
Bremen 4 B2
Bremerhaven 4 B2
Brenta 6 B1
Brescia 6 B1
Breslau see (Wroclaw)
Brest, (France) 3 B4
Brest (U.S.S.R.) 7 B-C3
Bria 16 C4
Briançon 5 E1
Bridgetown 23 D1
Brig 4 A4
Brighton 3 C-D4
Brindisi 6 D2
Brisbane 25 C4
Bristol 3 C4
Bristol Bay 20 c7
Bristol, Channel 3 B-C4
British Columbia 19 D-E4
Brive 5 D1
Brjansk 7 E3
Brno 4 D3
Broach 11 C3
Brock Island 19 E2
Brod 6 D1
Brodeur, Peninsula 19 H2
Brody 7 C4
Broken Hill (Zambia): see Kabwe
Broken Hill (Australia) 25 C4 25a C-D3
Bronnoysund 2 B2
Brooks Range 20 C-D6
Broome 25 A-B3 25a B1
Brovary 7 D4
Brownsville 20 D3
Bruck 4 C4
Bruges 3 D4
Brumado 23 E4
Brunei 8 G5
Brunswick 20 E-F2
Brussels 3 E4
Brzeg 4 D3
Bucac 7 C4
Bucaramanga 23 B2
Buchanan 15 B4
Bucharest 6 F1
Budapest 4 D-E4
Budd Coast 27 H2
Budejovice 4 C3
Budogosv 7 E2
Buenaventura 23 B2
Buenos Aires 24 C-D3
Buenos Aires, L. 24 B4
Buffalo 20 F1
Bug 4 E3
Bu Graa 15 B2
Buj 7 G2
Bujumbura 17 C2
Bukacaca 9 F3
Bukama 17 C2
Bukavu 17 C2
Bukhara 9 D3
Bukittinggi 13 A-B3
Bukoba 17 D2
Bulawayo 17 C3-4
Bulgan 12 C2
Bulgaria 1 E4
Bumba 16 C4
Bunbury 25a A3
Bundaberg 25a D-E2
Bunguran 13 B3
Bunguran Islands 13 D3
Buraimi 10 D3
Burao 16 E4
Buraydah 10 C3
Burchun 11 C3
Burdwan 11 E3
Bureya 9 G3
Burgas 6 F-G2
Burgos 5 C2
Burketown 25a C1
Burma 8 F4
Bursa 10 A-B1
Bur Safaga 16 D2
Buru 13 D4
Burundi 14 F6
Bururi 17 C2
Busan 12 E3
Bushehr 10 D3
Buta 16 C4
Butte 20 B1
Button Bay 19 G4
Button Islands 19 K3
Butuan 13 D3
Butung 13 D4
Buzau 6 F1
Buzau, River 6 F1
Buzaymah 16 C2
Byckov 7 D3

Denmark Strait 19 N-O3
Denver 20 C2
Dera 11 B3
Derbent 9 C3
Derby (U.K.) 3 C3
Derby (Austr.) 25 B3 25a B1
Derna 16 C1
Dese 16 D-E3
Deseado, Rio 24 C4
Des Moins, river 20 D1
Desna 7 E3
Desolación, Island 24 B5
Dessau 4 C3
Detroit 20 E1
Deva 6 E1
Devon Island 19 H2
Dezful 10 C2
Dezneva Cape 9 K2
Dhamar 10 C4
Dhanbad 11 D3
Dhaulagiri, Mount 11 D2-3
Dhufar 10 D4
Dhulia 11 C3
Diamantina (Austr.) 25a C-D2
Diamantina (Brazil) 23 E4
Diamantino 23 D4
Dibrugarh 11 D3
Diégo-Suarez 17 E-F3
Diéma 15 C3
Dien Bien Phu 13 B1
Dieppe 3 D4
Digne 5 E1
Dijon 3 E5
Dikson 9 D-E2
Dikwa 15 E3
Dili 13 D4
Dilolo 17 C3
Dinagat 13 D2
Dinar 10 A2
Diourbel 15 B3
Dire Dawa 16 E4
Dirk Hartog Island 25a A2
Dirranbandi 25a D2
Disappointment, Lake 25a B2
Disko, Bay 19 L3
Disko Island 19 L3
Diu 11 C3
Dixon Entrance 19 C4
Diyala 10 C2
Diyarbakir 10 B-C2
Djado 15 E2
Djajapura 25 C3
Djambala 17 B2
Djambi 13 B4
Djanet 15 D2
Djelfa 15 D1
Djenné 15 C3
Djerba 15 E1
Djibouti 16 E3
Djibouti, State 14 G4
Djidjelli 5 E3
Dmitrov 7 F2
Dnepr 7 D3
Dnepropetrovsk 7 E4
Dnestr 7 B-C-D4-5
Dno 7 D2
Dobrus 7 D-E3
Dodecanese 6 F3
Dodoma 17 D2
Doha 10 D3
Dôle 3 E5
Dolinsk 9 H3
Dolores 24 D3
Dolo 16 E4
Dombas 2 B3
Dominica 23 C-D1
Dominican Republic 18 N-O7-8
Don 7 F-G3-4-5
Dona Ana 17 D3
Dondo 17 B2-3
Dondra Head 11 D5
Donets 7 F4
Donetsk 7 F5
Donggala 13 C-D4
Dong Hoi 13 B2
Dongola 16 C-D3
Donna 2 B-C1
Dordogne 5 C-D1
Dori 15 C3
Dortmund 4 A-B3
Dosso 15 D3
Douala 15 D-E4
Douglas 20 C2
Douro 5 A-B2
Dover (U.K.) 3 D4
Dover (U.S.) 20 F2
Dover, Strait of 3 D4
Dovrefjell 2 B3
Dowa 17 D3
Draguignan 5 E2
Drake Passage 27 R-S2
Drakensberg 17 C-D4-5

Dráma 6 E-F2
Drammen 2 B4
Drau 4 C4
Dresden 4 C3
Dreux 3 D4
Drina 6 D1
Drogheda 3 B3
Drogobyc 7 B4
Druja 7 C3
Druzina 9 H2
Drygalski, Islands 27 G2
Duba 10 B3
Dubai 10 D3
Dubawnt Lake 19 F3
Dubbo 25a D-E3
Dublin 3 B3
Dubno 7 C4
Dubuque 20 D1
Ducie 25 G4
Dudinka 9 D-E2
Duero 5 B-C2
Dufferin 19 H4
Dugi, Island 6 C1
Duisburg 4 A3
Dulan 12 B3
Duluth 20 D1
Dumfries 3 B-C3
Dumyat 16 D1
Dunaujváros 4 D4
Duncansby Head 3 C2
Dundaga 7 B2
Dundalk 3 B3
Dundee 3 C2
Dundoo 17 B-C2
Dunedin 25 D5 25a G6
Dungarvan 3 B3
Durango 21 B2
Durazno 24 D3
Durban 17 D4
Durrës 6 D3
D'Urville, Sea 27 I2
Dusanbe 9 D4
Düsseldorf 4 A3
Dvina 9 C2
Dyer, C. 19 L-M3
Dzabhan 12 B2
Dzankoj 7 E5
Dzerzinsk 7 G2
Dzhambul 9 D3
Dzhusaly 9 D3
Dzugdzur Range 9 G3
Dzungaria 11 D1

E

East Cape 25a G5
East Cape: see Dezhneva Cape
East China Sea 12 E3-4
Eastern Ghats 11 C-D4
East Falkland 24 D5
East Germany 1 E3
East London 17 C-D5
East Siberian Sea 9 H1-2
Eberswalde 4 C2
Ebolowa 15 E4
Ebro 5 C-D2
Écija 5 B3
Ecuador 22 C4
Ed-Damer 16 D3
Ed-Debba 16 C-D3
Ed-Dueim 16 C-D3
Edhessa 6 E2
Edinburgh 3 C2-3
Edirne 10 A1
Edjeleh 15 D-E2
Edmonton 19 E4
Edmundston 19 K5
Edsel Ford Range 27 N-O2
Edward VII Peninsula 27 M-N2
Edward, Lake 17 C2
Egadi Islands 6 B-C3
Eger 4 E4
Egersund 2 A4
Egvekinot 9 I2
Egypt 14 E-F3
Eidsvoll 2 B3
Eil 16 F4
Eindhoven 3 E4
Eirunepé 23 B-C3
Eisenach 4 B3
Eisenstadt 4 D3-4
Ejsk 7 F5
El Aaiún 15 B2
El-Asnam 15 C-D1
Elat 10 B3
El-'Atrun 16 C3
Elba, Island 6 B2
Elbe, River 4 B-C2-3
Elbert, Mount 20 C2
Elblag 4 D2
El-Borma 15 D1
Elbrus 10 C1
Elburz, Mountains 10 C-D2

El Djezair: see Algiers
El-Djouf 15 C2
Eldoret 17 D1-2
Eleuthera Island 21 E2
El-Faiyum 16 C-D2
El-Fasher 16 C3
El Ferrol 5 A2
El-Giza 16 C-D1-2
El Goléa 15 D1
Elgon, Mount 17 D1
Elisenvaara 7 D1
Elista 10 C1
Elk 4 E2
Elko 20 B1
Ellesmere I. 19 H-I-K1-2
Ellice Island: see Tuvalu
Ellsworth Land 27 P-Q2
El-Mansura 16 D1
El-Minya 16 C-D1
El-Mreiti 15 C2
El-Muglad 16 C3
El-Obeid 16 C-D3
El-Oued 15 D1
El Paso 20 C2
El Salvador 18 L-M8
El-Turbio 24 B5
Eluru 11 D4
Elvas 5 B3
Ely 3 D3
Em 2 C-D4
Emba 9 C-D3
Embarcación 24 C2
Emden 4 A-B2
Emerald 25a D2
Emi Koussi 16 B3
Emmen 3 E3
Ems 4 A2
Encantada, C.ro de la 21 A1
Encarnación 24 D2
Ende 13 D4
Enderby Land 27 E2
Endere Langar 11 D2
Engels 9 C3
Enggano 13 B4
England 3 C3-4
English Channel 3 B-D4
Eniwetok 25 C-D2
Enna 6 C3
En Nahud 16 C3
Ennedi 16 C3
Enontekiö 2 E-F1
Enschede 3 E3
Ensenada 21 A1
Entebbe 17 D2
Enugu 15 D4
Épernay 3 D4
Épinal 3 E4
Equatorial Guinea 14 C-D5 -
Erfoud 15 C1
Erfurt 4 B3
Erg see Great E.-W. Erg
Erg Iguidi 15 C2
Erhlien 12 D2
Erie 20 F1
Erie, L. 20 E1
Erimo, Cape 12 G2
Eritrea 16 D-E3
Ernakulam 11 C5
Er Rahad 16 C-D3
Erris, Head 3 A3
Er-Roseires 16 C-D3
Erzincan 10 B1
Erzurum 10 C1
Esashi 12 F-G2
Esbjerg 4 A-B2
Ese-Khayya 9 G2
Esfahan 10 C-D2
Eskilstuna 2 D4
Eskimo Point 19 G3
Eskisehir 10 A-B2
Esla, River 5 B2
Esmeraldas 21 D-E4
Esperance 25a B3
Espichel, Cape 5 A3
Espirito Santo 24 E1-2
Esquel 24 B-C4
Essaouira 15 B-C1
Essen 4 A3
Essequibo 23 D2
Estaca de Bares, Cape 5 B2
Estados, I. de los 24 C5
Este, Punta del 24 D3
Estigarribia, Mount 24 C2
Estonia 9 B3
Estremoz 5 A3
Etah 19 I-K2
Ethiopia 14 F-G5
Ethiopian Highlands 16 D-E3-4
Etna 6 C3
Eucla 25a B3
Eugenia, P.ta 21 A2
Euphrates 10 C2
Eureka 20 A1
Europa Island 17 E4

Evansville 20 E2
Evensk 9 H-I2
Everest, Mount 11 D3
Évora 5 B3
Evreux 3 D4
Évvoia 6 E-F3
Eyasi, L. 17 D2
Eyre, L. 25 B2 25a C2
Eyre Peninsula 25a C3

F

Fachi 15 E3
Fada 16 C3
Fada-N'Gourma 15 C-D3
Faeroe Islands 1 B-C2
Fagernes 2 B3
Fair I. 3 C2
Fairbanks 20 D6
Faizabad 11 B-C2
Fakfak 13 E4
Falkland, Islands 24 C-D5
Falköping 2 C4
Falmouth 3 B4
Falster 4 C2
Falticeni 4 F4
Falun 2 C3
Fangak 16 D4
Fanning 25 F2
Farafangana 17 E-F4
Farah 11 B2
Faranah 15 B3
Farasan Islands 10 C4
Farewell, Cape (Austr.) 25a G6
Farewell, Cape (Greenl.) 19 N4
Fargo 20 D1
Faro 5 B3
Farquhar Islands 17 F3
Fars 10 D3
Farsund 2 A4
Fastnet 12 D4
Fastov 7 D4
Fatshan 12 D3
Fauske 2 C-D2
Fdérik 15 B2
Fécamp 3 C-D4
Fehmarn 4 B-C2
Felipe, C. Pto 21 D3
Femund 2 B3
Fenerive 17 E-F3
Fenghsien 12 D3
Fengtai 12 D3
Feodosija 7 E-F5
Fergana 11 D2
Ferkessedougou 15 C4
Fernandopolis 24 D-E2
Ferrara 6 B1
Ferro 23 D4
Fès 15 C1
Fezzan 15 E2
Fianarantsoa 17 E4
Figueira da Foz 5 A2
Figueras 5 D2
Figuig 15 C1
Fiji 25 D3
Filchner Ice Shelf 27 R-S2
Filiatrá 6 E3
Filiasi 4 F4
Finike 10 A-B2
Finisterre, C. 5 A2
Finke 25a C2
Finland 1 F2
Finland, Gulf of 2 E-F5
Finlay 19 D4
Finspang 2 C4
Firat 10 B2
Firth of Forth 3 C2
Fisher Strait 19 H3
Fitzroy 25a B1
Flattery, Cape 25a D1
Flensburg 4 B2
Flers 3 C4
Flinders Island 25a D-E3
Flinders Range 25a C2-3
Flinders Reef 25a D-E1
Flint 20 E1
Flint Island 25 B2
Florence 6 B2
Florencia 23 B2
Flores 13 D4
Flores Sea 13 C-D4
Floriano 23 E3
Florianópolis 24 E2
Florida 20 E3
Florida Strait: 20 E3
Flórina 6 E2
Foca 6 D2
Focsani 6 F1
Foggia 6 C2
Fogo 15 A3
Foix 5 D2
Fontainebleau 3 D4
Foochow 12 D-E4
Forlì 6 B-C1

Formentera 5 D3
Formosa, State: 8 H4
Formosa (Arg.) 24 C-D2
Formosa Strait: 12 D-E4
Ft. Achambault: see Sarh
Fortaleza 23 F3
Forsayth 25a D1
Ft. Charlet: see Djanet
Fort Chimo: 19 I-K4
Fort-Dauphin 17 E4
Ft. Flatters see Zaouiet El-Kabla
Fort Good Hope 19 D3
Fortin Ayacucho 24 C-D2
Ft. Laperrine see Tamanrasset
Fort Liard 19 D-E3
Fort Mc Murray 19 E-F4
Fort Mc. Pherson 19 C3
Fort Myers 20 E3
Fort Nelson 19 D4
Fort Providence 19 E4
Fort Resolution 19 E-F3
Fort Rupert 19 I4
Fort St. John 19 D-E4
Fort-Sevcenko 9 C3
Fort Simpson 19 D3
Fort Smith (Can.) 19 E-F3
Fort Smith (U.S.) 20 D2
Fort Vermilion 19 D-E4
Fort Victoria 17 D4
Fort Wayne 20 E1
Fort William (U.K.) 3 B-C2
Fort William (Can.) see Thunder Bay
Fort Worth 20 D2
Fort Yukon 20 D6
Fougères 3 C4
Fouliang 12 D3-4
Fouta Djallon 15 B3
Foveaux Strait 25a F-G6
Foxe, Basin 19 H13
Foxe Peninsula 19 I3
Foz do Jordao 23 B3
France 1 C-D4
Franceville 17 B2
Francistown 17 C4
Frankfort 20 E2
Frankfurt: 4 C2
Frankfurt am M. 4 B3
Franz Josef Land 9 C-D2
Fraser 19 D4
Fraser or Great Sandy Island 25a E2
Fraserburgh 3 C2
Fredericia 4 B2
Fredericton 19 K5
Frederikshaab 19 L-M3
Frederikshavn 4 B1
Fredrikstad 2 B-C4
Freetown 15 B4
Freiburg 4 A-B3
Fremantle 25a A4
French Guiana 22 E3
Fresco, Rio 23 D3
Fresno 20 B2
Frias 24 C2
Fribourg 4 A4
Friedrichshafen 4 B4
Frisian Islands 3 E3
Froya 5 A-B3
Frunze 9 D3
Fuchow 12 D4
Fuego, Tierra del: 24 C5
Fuerteventura 15 B2
Fujairah 10 D3
Fugi-san 12 F3
Fukien 12 D4
Fukushima 12 F-G3
Fulda 4 B3
Funafuti 25 D-E3
Funchal 15 B1
Fushun 12 E2
Fusin 12 E2
Futuna 25 D-E3
Fuyu 12 E2
Fyn 4 B2

Gajsin 7 D4
Gajvoron 7 D4
Galápagos Islands 22 A-B4
Galati 4 F4
Galka'yo 16 E4
Galle 11 D5
Gallegos, Rio 24 C5
Gallinas, Pta 23 B1
Gallipoli 6 D2
Gällivare 2 E2
Galveston 20 D3
Galway 3 A3
Galway, Bay 3 A3
Gambia 14 A4
Gambia, River 15 B3
Gambier Islands 25 G4
Gamboma 17 B2
Gandhinagar 11 C3
Ganges 11 D3
Ganges Delta 11 D-E3
Gangtok 11 D3
Gao 15 C3
Gao Bang 13 B1
Gaoua 15 C3-4
Gap 5 E1
Garad 16 E-F4
Garanhuns 23 F3
Garda, Lake 6 B1
Gardez 11 B2
Gardner Island 25 E1
Gardo 16 E4
Gargouna 15 D3
Garissa 17 D-E2
Garonne 5 C-D1-2
Garoua 15 E4
Gartok 11 D2
Gary 20 E1
Garzón 23 B2
Gascoyne 25a A2
Gaspé 19 K5
Gata, Cabo de 5 C3
Gatchina 7 D2
Gatooma 17 C3
Gauhati 11 E3
Gávdhos 6 F4
Gävle 2 D3
Gaya (India) 11 D3
Gaya (Niger) 15 D3
Gaza 10 B2
Gaziantep 10 B2
Gbarnga 15 C4
Gdánsk 4 D2
Gdańsk Bay 4 D2
Gdov 7 D2
Gdynia 4 D2
Gedaref 16 D3
Gedi 17 D2
Gediz 6 F3
Gedser 4 C2
Geelong 25a D3
Geiranger 2 A3
Gela 6 C3
Gelendzik 7 F5
Gemena 16 B-C4
Geneina 16 C3
General Acha 24 C3
General Alvear 24 C3
General Pico 24 C3
Geneva 4 A4
Geneva Lake 3 E5
Genicesk 7 E5
Genil 5 B-C3
Genoa 6 B1
Genoa, Gulf of 6 B2
Gent 3 D4
Geographe Bay 25a A3
George 19 K4
Georgetown 23 D2
Georgia (U.S.S.R.) 10 C1
Georgia (U.S.) 20 E2
Georgia, South: see South Georgia
Georgina 25a C2
Georgiu-Dez 7 F-G4
Gera 4 B-C3
Geraldton 23 A4 25a A2
Germany, East 1 E3
Germany, West 1 D3
Gerona 5 D2
Ghadames 15 D-E1
Ghadames 16 A-B1
Ghaghara 11 D3
Ghana 14 B5
Ghanzi 17 C4
Ghardaïa 15 D1
Ghat 16 B2
Ghazikhan 11 B3
Ghazni 11 B2
Gibeon 17 B4
Gibraltar 5 B3
Gibraltar, Strait of 5 B3-4
Gibson Desert 25 B4 25a B2
Gidole 16 D4
Giessen 4 B3
Gifu 12 F3
Giglio, I. of 6 B2
Gijón 5 B2

Jarvis 25 E3
Jask 10 D3
Jasper 19 E4
Jatai 23 D4
Jatobá 23 E3
Java 13 B-C4
Java Sea 13 B-C4
Javari 23 B3
Jedrzejów 4 E3
Jefferson City 20 D2
Jefremov 7 F3
Jèkabpils 7 C2
Jelec 7 F3
Jelenia Góra 4 C-D3
Jelgava 7 B-C2
Jel'n'a 7 E3
Jenisej 9 E2-3
Jenisejsk 9 E3
Jequié 23 E4
Jerbogacon 9 F2
Jérez de la Frontera 5 B3
Jersey 3 C4
Jerusalem 10 B2
Jesenice 6 C1
Jesil 9 D3
Jevpatorija 7 E5
Jhansi 11 C3
Jiddah 10 B3
Jido 11 E3
Jihlava 4 C3
Jima 10 B5
Jiménez 21 B2
Jinja 17 D1
Jinné 12 E1
Jiparaná 23 C3
Jiu 6 E1
Jizan 10 C4
Joao Pessoa 23 F3
Joaquìn V. Gonzalez 24 C2
Jodhpur 11 C3
Joensuu 2 G3
Jogjakarta 13 B-C4
Johannesburg 17 C4
Johnston 25 E2
Johor Baharu 13 B3
Joinville 24 D-E2
Jokkmokk 2 D2
Jolo 13 D3
Jones Sound 19 H2
Jönköping 2 C4
Jordan 8 C4
Jörn 2 E2
Jos 15 D3-4
Juan de Nova, I. 17 E3
Juan Fernández Is. 24 A-B3
Juanjuì 23 B3
Jùazeiro 23 E3
Juba 16 E4
Juba, River: 16 E4
Júcar 5 C3
Juchitàn 21 C3
Juguariaiva 24 E2
Juian 12 D4
Juiz de Fora 24 E2
Juliaca 23 B4
Julianehaab 19 L-M3
Jullundur: 11 C2
Juneau 20 E7
Junìn 24 C3
Jurga 9 E3
Jurmala 2 E4
Juruá 23 C3
Juruena 23 C3
Juruena, River 23 D4
Jutland 4 B1
Jyväskylä 2 F3

K

Kabaena 13 D4
Kabala 15 B4
Kabalo 17 C2
Kabia 13 C-D4
Kabinda 17 C2
Kabul 11 B2
Kabwe 17 C3
Kaduna 15 D3
Kaédi 15 B3
Kafia Kingi 16 C4
Kafue 17 C3
Kagoshima 12 E-F3
Kagul 7 D5
Kai Islands 13 E4
Kaifeng 12 D3
Kaikoura 25a G6
Kaïlas Mountains 11 D2
Kaimana 13 E4
Kairouan 15 D-E1
Kajaani 2 F2
Kajabbi 25a D1
Kajan 13 C3
Kakinada 11 D4

Kalahari Desert 17 C4
Kalamáta 6 E3
Kal'azin 7 F2
Kalémié 17 C2
Kalevala 2 G2
Kalgan 12 D2
Kalgoorlie 25 B4 25a B3
Kalikovici 7 D3
Kalimantan 13 C4
Kalinin 7 E-F2
Kaliningrad 7 B3
Kalispell 20 B1
Kalisz 4 D3
Kallavesi 2 F3
Kalmar 2 C-D4
Kalomo 17 C3
Kamaran, Islands 10 C4
Katrineholm 2 C4
Kamcatka Pen. 9 H-I3
Kamenec-Podol'skij 7 C-D4
Kamenskoje 9 I2
Kamensk-Ural'skij 9 D3
Kamina 17 C2
Kamloops 19 D4
Kampala 17 D1
Kampar 13 B3
Kampot 13 B2
Kampuchea 8 G5
Kamrija 6 E2
Kamysin 9 C3
Kananga 17 C2
Kanazawa 12 F3
Kanchow 12 D4
Kandahar 11 B2
Kandalaksa 9 B2
Kandi 15 D3
Kandy 11 D5
Kane Basin 19 I-K2
Kanev 7 D4
Kangan 10 D3
Kangaroo Island 25a C3
Kangean, Islands 13 C4
Kanggye 12 E2
K'ang-ting 12 B-C3
Kanin, Pen. 9 C2
Kankan 15 C3
Kano 15 D3
Kanpur 11 C3
Kansk 9 E3
Kansu 12 B-C2-3
Kansas 20 C-D2
Kansas City 20 D2
Kantzu 12 B-C3
Kanye 17 C4
Kaohsiung 12 E4
Kaolack 15 B3
Kaoping 12 D3
Kapchagay 9 D3
Kaposvár 4 D4
Kapsukas 7 B3
Kapuas 13 B-C4
Kapuas Range 13 C3
Karachi 11 B3
Karaganda 9 D3
Karaginskij Island 9 I3
Kara-Kalpak 9 C3
Karakoram Ra. 11 C2
Kara Kum 9 C3
Karamai 11 D1
Karamuran Pass 12 A3
Karasburg 17 B4
Kara Sea 9 D2
Kara Shahr 11 D1
Karasjok 2 F1
Kara Tau 9 D3
Karaton 9 C3
Karbala' 10 C2
Kardhitsa 6 E3
Kardzali 6 F2
Karesuando 2 E1
Kargopol' 7 F1
Kariba, Lake 17 C3
Karibib 17 B4
Karima 16 D3
Karimata Islands 13 B4
Karimata, Strait of 13 B4
Karis 2 E3
Karkkila 2 E3
Karl-Marx-Stadt 4 C3
Karlovac 6 C1
Karlshamn 2 C4
Karlskoga 2 C4
Karlskrona 2 C-D4
Karlsruhe 4 A-B3
Karlstad 2 C4
Karmoy 2 A4
Karnataka 11 C4
Kárpathos, Island 6 F4
Karsakpaj 9 D3
Karsi 11 B2
Karymskoje 9 F3
Kasai 17 C2
Kasai, River 17 B-C2
Kasama 17 D3
Kasenga 17 C3
Kasese 17 D1
Kashan 10 D2

Kashgar 11 C2
Kashmir 11 C2
Kasimov 7 G3
Kasira 7 F3
Kaskinen 2 E3
Kaskö 12 E3
Kasongo 17 C2
Kásos 6 F4
Kassala 16 D3
Katangli 9 H3
Katerini 6 E2
Katha 11 E3
Katherine 25a C1
Katihar 11 D3
Katmandu 11 D3
Katowice 4 D3
Kattegat 2 B4
Kauai 25 E-F1
Kaunas 7 B-C3
Kaura Namoda 15 D3
Kavála 6 F2
Kavalerovo 9 G3
Kavaratti 11 C4
Kawthaung 13 A2
Kaya 15 C3
Kayes 15 B3
Kayseri 10 B2
Kazacje 9 G-H2
Kazakhstan 9 C-D3
Kazan: see Volcano Is.
Kazan (U.S.S.R.) 9 C3
Kazanlâk 6 F2
Kazatin 7 D4
Kazerun 10 D3
Kéa 6 F3
Kecskemét 4 D-E4
Kedainiai 7 B3
Kediri 13 C4
Kédougou 15 B3
Keetmanshoop 17 B-C4
Kefallinìa 6 E3
Kelago 16 E4
Kelang 13 B3
Kelloselkä 2 G2
Kem 9 B2
Ké Macina 15 C3
Kemerovo 9 E3
Kemi 2 F2
Kemijärvi 2 F2
Kmpsey 25a E3
Kempten 4 B4
Kenai Pen. 20 C-D7
Kendari 13 D4
Keng Tung 13 A-B1
Kenho 12 E1
Kénitra 15 C1
Kenora 19 G5
Kent, Peninsula 19 F3
Kentucky 20 E2
Kenya 14 F5
Kenya, Mount. 17 D2
Kerala 11 C4-5
Kerc' 7 E-F5
Kerintji 13 B4
Kerkenna 15 E1
Kerki 9 D4
Kérkira, City 6 D3
Kérkira Island 6 D3
Kerman 10 D2
Kermanshah 10 C2
Kerme, G. of 6 F-G3
Kerulen 12 D2
Kesténga 2 G2
Keta 15 D4
Ketapang 13 C4
Ketrzyn 4 E2
Key West 20 E3
Kezma 9 E-F3
Khabarovsk 9 G-H3
Khairpur 11 B3
Khalkis 6 E3
Khanaqin 10 C2
Khandwa 11 C3
Khaniá 6 E4
Khanka, Lake 9 G3
Kharagpur 11 D3
Khara Khoto (Heicheng) 12 B-C2
Kharkov 7 F4
Khartoum 16 D3
Khash 10 E3
Khaybar 10 B-C3
Khemis Miliana 16 D3
Kheta 9 E2
Khilok 12 D1
Khingan Mountains, Great 12 D-E1-2
Khingan Mountains, Little 12 E1-2
Khios 6 F3
Khiuma 7 B2
Khiva 9 C-D3
Khodzheyli 11 A1

Kholmsk 9 G-H3
Khong 13 B2
Khon Kaen 13 B2
Khoper, River 7 G4
Khorasan 10 D2
Khorog 9 D4
Khorramabad 10 C-D2
Khotan 11 C-D2
Khotin 7 C4
Khulna 11 E3
Kiamusze 12 E-F2
Kian 12 D4
Kiangsi 12 D4
Kiangsu 12 D-E3
Kiantajärvi 2 F-G2
Kiaohsien 12 D3
Kichcik 9 H3
Kidal 15 D3
Kiel 4 B2
Kielce 4 E3
Kienshui 12 C4
Kiev 7 D4
Kiffa 15 B3
Kigali 17 D2
Kigoma 17 D2
Kikwit 17 B2
Kilchu 12 E2
Kili Bulak 12 B3
Kilimanjaro 17 D2
Kilkenny 3 B3
Kilkis 6 E2
Kimberley (Austr.) 25a B1
Kimberley (S. Africa) 17 C4
Kimchaek 12 E-F2
Kimry 7 F2
Kinabalu 13 C3
Kindia 15 B3
Kindu 17 C2
Kinesma 7 G2
King Christian IX Land 19 N-O3
King Christian X Land 26 N2
King Frederik VI Land 19 M3
King Frederik VIII Land 26 O-N2
Kingisepp (Estonia) 7 B2
Kingisepp (Russia Fed.) 7 D2
King Island 25a D3
King Leopold Range 25a B1
Kingoonya 25a C3
King's Lynn 3 D3
King Sound 25a B1
Kingston (Austr.) 25a F6
Kingston (Canada) 19 I5
Kingston (Jamaica) 21 E3
Kingston-upon-Hull 3 C-D3
King William Island 19 G3
King William's Town 17 C-D5
Kingyang 12 C3
Kinhwa 12 D4
Kinnula 2 E-F3
Kinshasa 17 B2
Kipembawe 17 D2
Kirensk 9 F3
Kirgiziya 9 D3
Kiribati 25 D2-3
Kirin 12 E2
Kirkcaldy 3 C2
Kirkenes 2 G1
Kirkpatrick, Mount 27 K1
Kirkuk 10 C2
Kirov 7 E3
Kirovograd 7 D-E4
Kirovsk 9 B-C2
Kirovskij 9 H3
Kirsanov 7 G3
Kiruna 2 D2
Kisangani 17 C1
Kiselevsk 9 E3
Kisii (Kenya) 12 F2
Kishinev 7 D5
Kiskunfélegyháza 4 D-E4
Kismayu 17 E2
Kissidougou 15 B-C4
Kisumu 17 D2
Kita 15 C3
Kitakyushu 12 E-F3
Kitale 17 D1
Kitgum 16 D4
Kithira 6 E3
Kithnos 6 E-F3
Kittilä 2 F2
Kitwe 17 C3
Kiuchuan 12 B-C2-3
Kiungchow Strait 12 D4
Kivu, L. 17 C2
Kizema 7 H1
Kizilirmak 10 B1
Kizyl-Arvat 9 C3
Kjustendil 6 E2
Klabat 13 D3
Kladno 4 C3
Klagenfurt 4 C4

Klaipéda 7 A-B3
Klar 2 C3
Klicev 7 D3
Klin 7 F2
Klincy 7 D-E3
Klodzko 4 D3
Knin 6 D1
Knittelfeld 4 C4
Knox, Coast 27 H2
Knoxville 20 E2
Knud Rasmussens Land 19 K-L2
Kobe 12 F3
Koblenz 4 A3
Kobriu 7 C3
Kobuk 20 B-C6
Kodiak 20 C7
Kodiak Island 20 C-D7
Kodok 16 D3
Kohima 11 E3
Kohtla-Järve 7 C-D2
Kokand 9 D3
Kokiu 12 C4
Kokkoka 2 E-F3
Kola Peninsula 9 B2
Kolar Gold Fields 11 C4
Kolda 15 B3
Kolding 4 B2
Kolgujev I. 9 B-C2
Kolhapur 11 C4
Kolìn 4 C3
Kolobrzeg 4 C2
Kolokani 15 C3
Kolomna 7 F3
Kolomyja 7 C4
Kolpasevo 9 D-E3
Kolwezi 17 C3
Kolyma 9 H2
Kolyma Plain 9 H2
Kolyma Range 9 H2
Kolyma Range 9 H2
Komandorskije Islands 9 I3
Komárno 4 D4
Komotini 6 F2
Kompong 13 B2
Kompong Som (Sihanoukville) 13 B2
Komrat 7 D5
Komsomolets, Island 9 F1
Komsomolsk 9 G3
Kondoa 17 D2
Kongolo 17 C2
Kongsberg 2 B4
Kongsvinger 2 B-C3
Konin 4 D2
Konosha 7 G1
Konotop 7 E4
Kontagora 15 D3
Kontum 13 B2
Konya 10 B2
Köping 2 C4
Korçë 6 E2
Korcula 6 D2
Kordofan 16 C-D3
Korea, North 8 H3-4
Korea, South 8 H4
Korea, Strait of 12 E-F3
Korf 9 I2
Korhogo 15 C4
Koriyama 12 G3
Korja 11 D1
Korosten 7 D4
Korsakov 12 G2
Korsun'-Sevcenkovsky 7 D-E4
Korsor 4 B2
Korti 16 D3
Koryak Range 9 I2
Koscierusko, Mount 25 C4 25a D-E
Kosice 4 E3
Kosti 16 D3
Kostroma 7 F-G2
Kostrzyn 4 C2
Kost'ukovici 7 E3
Koszalin (Koslin) 4 D2
Kota 11 C3
Kota Baharu 13 B3
Kotabaru (Borneo) 13 C4
Kota Kinabalu 13 C3
Kotelny I. 9 G-H2
Kotka 2 F3
Kotlas 7 H2
Kotor 6 D2
Kotovsk 7 D5
Kotri 11 B3
Kotuj 9 F2
Kotzebue Sound 20 B6
Koudougou 15 C3
Kouvola 2 F3
Kovdor 9 B2
Kovel 7 C4
Kovrov 7 G2
Kowloon 12 D4

Kragero 2 B4
Kragujevac 6 D-E1
Kraków 4 D3
Kramfors 2 D3
Krasino 9 C2
Kraskino 12 F2
Krasnodar 7 F5
Krasnograd 7 E4
Krasnojarsk 9 E3
Krasnoslobodsk 7 G-H3
Krasnovodsk 9 C3
Krasnyj Jar 9 C3
Krasnyj-Luc 7 F4
Krasnystaw 4 E3
Kratié 13 B2
Krefeld 4 A3
Kremencug 7 E4
Kremenec 7 C4
Krems 4 C-D3
Kribi 15 E4
Kricov 7 D3
Krishna 11 C4
Kristiansand 2 A4
Kristianstad 2 C4
Kristiansund 2 A3
Kristinehamn 2 C4
Kristinestad 2 E3
Krivoy Rog 7 E4
Krk 6 C1
Kronshtadt 7 D1-2
Kroonstad 17 C4
Kropotkin 7 G5
Krugersdorp 17 C4
Krusevac 6 E2
Ksar el Boukhari 5 D4
Kuala 15 B3
Kuala Lumpur 13 B3
Kuantan 13 B3
Kuban 7 F5
Kucha 11 D1
Kuching 13 B-C3
Kudat 13 C3
Kufra Oasis 16 C2
Kuhak 10 E3
Kuldiga 7 B2
Kuloj 7 G1
Kul'sary 9 C3
Kulunda 9 D-E3
Kulyab 9 D4
Kuma 10 C1
Kumamoto 12 F3
Kumanovo 6 E2
Kumasi 15 C-D4
Kumbakonam 11 D4
Kumbo 15 E4
Kumo 15 E3-4
Kunashir 9 H3
Kunasir 9 H3
Kunduz 11 B2
Kungrad 9 C-D3
Kungur 11 C2
Kunlun Shan 12 A-B3
Kunming 12 C4
Kuopio 2 F-G3
Kupang 13 D5
Kupstein 4 C4
Kurdistan 10 C2
Kurgan 9 D3
Kuria Muria Islands 10 D4
Kuril Island 9 H3
Kurnod 11 C4
Kursk 7 F4
Kuruk Tagh 11 D-E1
Kusaie 25 D2
Kushiro 12 G2
Kushka 9 D4
Kuskokwim 20 B-C6
Kusmurun 9 D3
Kustanay 9 D3
Kutaisi 10 C1
Kutch 11 B3
Kutno 4 D2
Kutsing 12 C4
Kuusamo 2 F-G2
Kuvsinovo 7 E2
Kuwait, State 8 D4
Kuwait, City 10 C3
Kwajalein 25 D2
Kwangneung 12 E-F3
Kwango 17 B2
Kwangsi-Chuang 12 C-D4
Kwangtung 12 D4
Kwangyuan 12 C3
Kweichow 12 C4
Kweilin 12 C-D4
Kweiting 12 C4
Kweiyang 12 C4
Kwilu 17 B2
Kyakhta 12 C1
Kyaukpyu 11 E4
Kyoto 12 F3
Kyushu 12 E3
Kyzyl 9 E3
Kyzylkum 9 D3
Kzyl-Orda 9 D3

L

Labe 4 C3
Labé 15 B3
Labrador 19 I-K4
Labrador City 19 I-K4
Lábrea 23 C3
Laccadive Islands 11 C4-5
La Coronilla 24 D3
La Coruña 5 A2
La Crosse 20 D1
Ladysmith 17 D4
Laeso 4 B1
Lafia 15 D4
Lagen 2 B3
Laghouat 15 D1
Lagos 15 D4
La Grand'-Combe 5 E1
La Grande 10 I4
La Guaira 23 C1
Laguna 24 E2
Lahore 11 C2
Lahti 2 F3
L'Aia 3 E3
Laila 10 C4
Laisvall 2 D2
Lakeland 20 E-F3
Lakse Fjord 2 F1
Lakselv 2 F1
Lakshadweep 11 C5
Lambaréné 17 B2
Lambton, Cape 19 D2
Lamia 6 E3
Lampang 13 A-B2
Lampedusa, Island 6 C4
Lamu 17 E2
Lancaster Sound 19 H2
Lanchow 12 C3
Land's End 3 B4
Landskrona 2 C5
Langöy 2 C1
Langsa 13 A3
Lang Son 12 C4
Lan Yu 12 E4
Lansing 20 E1
Lanzarote 15 B2
Laoag 13 C-D2
Lao Cai 13 B1
Laon 3 D-E4
La Oroya 23 B4
Laos 8 G4-5
La Palma 15 B2
La Palma (Pan.) 21 E4
La Paz (Mexico) 21 A2
La Paz (Bolivia) 23 C4
Lapeenranta 2 F3
La Pérouse, Strait of 12 G2
Lapinlahti 2 F-G3
La Plata 24 D3
Lappland 2 E-G1
Laptev Sea 9 F-G2
L'Aquila 6 C2
Lar 10 D3
Larache 5 B4
Laredo 20 D3
Larestan 10 D3
Largeau 16 B-C3
La Rioja 24 C2
Lárisa 6 E3
Larkana 11 B3
Larne 3 B3
La Roche-s-Yon 3 C5
La Rochelle 5 C1
Larsen Ice Shelf 27 R2
Las Anod 16 E4
La Serena 24 B2
Lashio 13 A1
Las Palmas (Canary Is.) 15 B2
La Spézia 6 B1
Las Plumas 24 C4
Lastoursville 17 B2
Las Vegas 20 B2
Latacunga 23 B3
Latina 6 C2
Latvia 9 B3
Lau Islands 25 E3
Lauceston 25a D4
Laudeck 4 B4
Laudshut 4 B-C3
Launceston 25 C5
La Unión 21 D3
Lausanne 4 A4
Laut 13 C4
Laval 3 C5
Lavéra 5 E2
Laverton 25a B2
Lavinia, Mt. 11 C5
Laysan 25 E1
Leaf 19 I4
Lebanon 8 C4
Lebedin 7 E4
Lebesby 2 F1
Lebork 4 D2
Lebu 24 B3
Lecce 6 D2
Le Creusot 3 D-E5
Ledesma 24 C2

Leeds 3 C3
Leeuwarden 3 E3
Legaspi 13 D2
Leghorn 6 B2
Legnica 4 C-D3
Leh 11 C2
Le Havre 3 D4
Leibnitz 4 C4
Leicester 3 C3
Leigh Creek 25a C-D3
Leikanger 2 A3
Leipzig 4 C3
Lejes 23 F3
Le Mans 3 D5
Lena 9 F-G2-3
Leninakan 10 C1
Leningrad 7 D1-2
Leninsk-Kuznekij 9 E3
Léo 15 C3
Leoben 4 C4
León, (Sp.) 5 B2
León, (Mexico) 21 B2
León, (Nicar.) 21 D3
Leonora 25a B2
Lepel' 7 D3
Lepsy 9 D-E3
Le Puy 5 D1
Lérida 5 D2
Lerma 21 B2
Lesina 6 D2
Leskovac 6 E2
Lesotho 14 E9
Lesozavodsk 9 G3
Les Sables d'Olonne 3 C5
Lesser Antilles 23 C1
Lésvos 6 F3
Leszno 4 D3
Lethbridge 19 E5
Leti Islands 13 D4
Leticia 23 B-C3
Levádhia 6 E3
Levanger 2 B3
Levick, Mount 27 L2
Levkás 6 E3
Lewis 3 B2
Lexington 20 E2
Leyte 13 D2
L'gov 7 E4
Lhasa 11 E3
Lhatse 11 D3
Liaoning 12 D-E2
Liaoyuan 12 E2
Liard 19 D3
Libenge 17 B1
Liberec 4 C3
Liberia 14 A-B5
Libourne 5 C1
Libreville 17 A1
Libya 14 D-E3
Libyan Desert 16 C2
Licata 6 C3
Lichoslavl' 7 E2
Lida 7 C3
Lidköping 2 C4
Lienyunkang 12 D-E3
Lienz 4 C4
Liepaja 7 A-B2
Lieksa 2 G3
Liège 3 E4
Liechtenstein 1 D-E4
Lihou Reef and Cays 25a E1
Likasi 17 C3
Likiang 12 C4
Lille 3 D4
Lille Baelt 4 B2
Lillehammer 2 B3
Lillesand 2 B4
Lilongwe 17 D3
Lim 6 D2
Lima 23 B4
Limassol 10 B2
Limerick 3 A3
Limnos 6 F3
Limoges 5 D1
Limón 21 D3
Linachamari 2 G-H1
Linares (Sp.) 5 C3
Linares (Chile) 24 B3
Lincoln (U.K.) 3 C3
Lincoln (U.S.) 20 D1
La Unión 21 D3
Lindesnes 2 A4
Lindi 17 C1
Line Islands 25 E-F2-3
Linfen 12 D3
Lingayen 13 C-D2
Lingga Islands 13 B4
Linguère 15 B3
Linhai 12 E4
Linkiang 12 E2
Linköping 2 C-D4
Linkow 12 E-F2
Linoli 17 D-E2
Linosa, Island 6 C4
Linsia 12 C3
Linz 4 C3
Lipari Islands 6 C3

Lipeck 7 F-G3
Lira 16 D4
Liri 6 C2
Lisala 16 C4
Lisbon 5 A3
Lisburne, Cape 20 a-b 6
Lishui 12 E3
Lisicansk 7 F4
Listowel 3 A3
Litang 12 C4
Lithinon, Cape 6 F4
Lithuania 9 B3
Little Andaman 11 E4
Little Cayman 21 D2
Little Khingan Mountains 12 E1-2
Little Minch 3 B2
Little Rock 20 D2
Liuchow 12 C-D4
Livingstone: see Maramba
Livny 7 F3
Livramento 24 D3
Liwale 17 D2
Lizard, Point 3 B4
Ljahov, Is. 9 G-H2
Ljovova, Is. 9 G-H2
Ljungan 2 C-D3
Ljusdal 2 C3
Ljusnan 2 C3
Llan 12 E2
Llanes 5 B2
Lliang 12 C4
Lligan 13 D3
Llinski 12 G2
Llullaillaco 24 C2
Loange 17 B-C2
Loango Buele 17 B2
Lobatsi 17 C4
Lobito 17 B3
Lodejnoje Polje 7 E1
Lodja 17 C2
Lodwar 16 D4
Lódz 4 D-E3
Lofoten, Islands 2 C1
Logan, Mt. 20 D-E6
Logroño 5 C2
Loho 12 D3
Lohtaja 2 E2
Loikaw 13 A1-2
Loire 3 C-D5
Loja (Sp.) 5 B3
Loja (Ecuad.) 23 B3
Lolland 4 B2
Lom (Norv.) 2 A-B3
Lom (Bulg.) 6 E2
Lomami 17 C1
Lomblen 13 D4
Lombok 13 C4
Lomela 17 C2
Lomela, River 17 C2
Lomonosov 7 D2
Lomza 4 E2
London (U.K.) 3 C-D4
London (Can.) 19 H5
Londonderry 3 A-B3
Longford 3 B3
Long Island 21 E2
Longreach 25a D2
Long Xuyen 13 B2-3
Lonsdal 2 C2
Lopatka, Cape 9 H-I3
Lopez, Cape 17 A2
Lop Nor 11 E1
Lorca 5 C3
Lorica 23 B2
Lorient 3 B-C5
Los Angeles (U.S.) 20 A-B2
Los Angeles (Chile) 24 B3
Loshan 12 C4
Los Roques, Island 23 C1
Lot 5 D1
Lotta 2 G1
Loudéac 3 C4
Louga 15 B3
Louisiana 20 D2
Louisville 20 E2
Lourenço Marques (Maputo) 17 D4
Lovec 6 F2
Lowa 17 C2
Lowicz 4 D-E2
Loyalty Islands 25 D4
Loyang 12 D3
Lozovaja 7 E-F4
Lualaba 17 C2
Luanda 17 B2
Luang Prabang 13 B1
Lua Nova 23 D3
Luanshya 17 C3
Luapula 17 C2
Luarca 5 B2
Luau 17 C3
Lubango 17 B3
Lübeck 4 B2
Lübeck Bay 4 B2
Lublin 4 E3
Lubny 7 E4

L'ubotin 7 E4
Lubumbashi 17 C3
Lucca 6 B2
Lucenec 4 D-E3
Lucerne 4 B4
Luchow 12 C4
Luck 7 C4
Lucknow 11 D3
Lüderitz 17 B4
Ludhiana 11 C2
Ludl2 2 C3
Ludvika 2 C3
Ludwigshafen 4 A-B3
Luebo 17 C2
Luga 7 D2
Lugano 4 B4
Lugenda 17 D3
Lugh Ganane 16 E4
Lugo 5 B2
Lugoj 6 E1
Luichow Peninsula 12 C-D4
Lukenie 17 C2
Lule 2 E2
Lulea 2 E2
Lülua 17 C2
Lüleburgaz 10 A1
Lulua 17 C2
Lund 2 C5
Lunda 17 B-C2
Lüneberg 4 B2
Lungsi 12 C3
Luni 11 C3
Luninec 7 C3
Luq 16 E4
Lusaka 17 C3
Lusambo 17 C2
Lushoto 17 D2
Lushun 17 C3
Lüta (Dairen) 12 E3
Lutong 13 C3
Lützow-Holm B. 27 D-E2
Luxor 16 D2
Luzon 13 C-D2
Luzon, Strait of 13 D1-2
L'vov 7 C4
Lyallpur 11 C2
Lycksele 2 D2
Lydenburg 17 D4
Lynchburg 20 E-F2
Lynn Lake 19 F-G4
Lyon 5 E1
Lyon, Gulf of 5 D2

M

Ma'an 10 B2
Maarianhamina 2 D-E3
Maas 3 D4
Maastricht 3 E4
Macaé 24 E2
Macao 8 G4
Macapá 23 D2
Macau 23 F3
Macdonnell Range 25a C2
Macerata 6 C2
Maceió 23 F3
Macenta 15 C4
Machu Picchu 23 B4
Mackay 25 C4 25a D2
Mackay, Lake 25a B2
Mackenzie 19 C-D3
Mackenzie, Bay 19 C2
Mackenzie King, I. 19 D-E2
Mâcon 3 E5
Macon 20 E2
Macquarie Islands 27 K3
MacRobertson Land 27 E-F2
Madagascar 14 G7-8
Madang 25 C3
Madeira 15 B1
Madeira Archipelago 15 B1
Madeira, R. 23 C-D3
Madhya Pradesh 11 C-D3
Madina do Boé 15 B3
Madinat ash-Sha'b 10 C4
Madir 20 D4
Madison 20 D-E1
Madiun 13 C4
Madjene 13 C4
Madras 17 D4
Madre de Dios, I. 24 B4
Madre de Dios, R. 23 B-C4
Madrid 5 C2
Madura 13 C4
Madurai 11 C5
Mae Sariang 13 A-B2
Mafeking 17 C4
Mafia 17 E2
Magadan 9 H3
Magadi 17 D2
Magdagaci 9 G3
Magdalena (Bolivia) 23 C4
Magdalena (Arg.) 24 D3
Magdalena, R. 23 B2
Magdeburg 4 B-C2-3

Magelang 13 B-C4
Magellan, Strait of 24 B-C5
Mageroy 2 E-F1
Maggiore, L. 6 B1
Maghiana 11 C2
Magnitogorsk 9 D3
Mahabad 10 C2
Mahakam 13 C3-4
Mahalapye 17 C4
Maharashtra 11 C4
Mahdia 6 B4
Mahé 17 F2
Mahenge 17 D2
Mahón 5 E3
Maiduguri 15 E3
Maimana 11 B2
Mai-Ndombe, L. 17 B-C2
Main 4 B3
Maine 20 F-G1
Mainland (Orkney) 3 B-C2
Mainland (Shetland Is.) 3 C1
Maintirano 17 E3
Mainz 4 A-B3
Maja 9 G2
Maji 10 B5
Majkop 7 G5
Majoli 23 D2
Majorca 5 D3
Majunga 17 E3
Makale 16 D-E2
Makarikari 17 C4
Makarjev 7 G2
Makarov 9 H3
Makasar 13 C4
Makassar, Str. of 13 C4
Makat 9 C3
Makejevka 10 B-C1
Makhachkala 10 C1
Makin 25 D2
Maklakovo 9 E3
Makokou 17 B1
Makoua 17 B1
Makran 10 D-E3
Maksaticha 7 E-F2
Makurdi 15 D4
Malabo 15 D4
Malacca, Str. of 13 A-B3
Málaga 5 B3
Malaja-Visera 7 E2
Malang 13 C4
Malanje 17 B2
Malargüe 24 C3
Malatya 10 B2
Malawi 14 F7
Malawi, Lake 17 D3
Malay Peninsula 13 A-B3
Malaysia 8 G5
Malbork 4 D2
Malden 25 F3
Maldives 8 E5
Male 11 C5
Maléa, Cape 6 E3
Malegaon 11 C3
Mali 14 B-C4
Malin 7 D4
Malin Head 3 A-B3
Malindi 17 E2
Malko Tarnovo 6 F-G2
Mallaig 3 B2
Mallawi 16 D2
Maloy 2 A3
Malpelo, I. (Col.) 23 A2
Malselv 2 D1
Malta 1 E5
Malvinas: see Falkland Islands
Mambone 17 D4
Mamoré, R. 23 C4
Mamou 15 B3
Man 15 C4
Man, I. of 3 B3
Mana 23 D2
Manacapuru 23 C3
Manacor 5 D3
Manado 17 E4
Managua 21 D3
Manakara 17 E4
Manano Machado 17 B3
Manass 11 D1
Manaus 23 C-D3
Manchester 3 C3
Manchouli 12 D-E2
Manchuria 12 E2
Manda 17 D3
Mandal 2 A4
Mandalay 13 A1
Mandalgov' 12 C2
Manfredonia 6 C-D2
Mangalore 11 C4
Mango 15 D3
Mangole 13 D4
Mangueira, L. 24 D3
Mangyai 12 B3
Mani 11 D2

Manicoré 23 C-D3
Manicouagan 19 K4
Manihiki 25 E3
Manila 13 C-D2
Manipur 11 E3
Manisa 10 A2
Manitoba 19 G4
Manitoba, L. 19 F-G4
Manizales 23 B2
Mankoya 17 C3
Mannar, G. of 11 C5
Mannar 11 C-D5
Mannheim 4 B3
Manokwari 13 E4
Manono 17 C2
Manresa 5 D2
Mansel, I. 19 H3
Manturovo 7 G-H2
Manwakh 10 C4
Manzanillo (Mexico) 21 B3
Manzanillo (Cuba) 21 E2
Mao 16 B3
Mapuera 23 D3
Maputo (Lourenço Marques) 17 D4
Maquinchao 24 C4
Marabá 23 D-E3
Maracá, I. 23 D-E2
Maracaibo 23 B1
Maracaibo, Lake 23 B1-2
Maracaju 24 D2
Maracay 23 C1
Maradi 15 D3
Marajó, Bay 23 E2-3
Marajó I. 23 D-E3
Maramba 17 C3
Maranhao 23 E3
Marañón 23 B3
Maradi 17 B2
Marari 23 C3
Marburg a.d.L. 4 B3
Marcelino 23 C3
Mar Chiquita, Lake 24 C3
Mardan 11 C2
Mar del Plata 24 D3
Margarita 23 C1
Mari 9 C3
Maria Islands 25 F4
Maria van Diemen, Cape 25a F-G5
Mariana Islands 25 C2
Ma'rib 10 C4
Maribo 4 B2
Maribor 6 C1
Marica 6 F2
Maridi 16 C-D4
Mariehamn 2 D3
Marie Louise 17 F2
Mariental 17 B4
Mariestad 2 C4
Marion Reef 25a E1
Markham Mount. 27 I-K1
Markovo 9 I2
Marmara, Sea of 6 F-G2
Marmaris 10 A2
Marmolada 6 B-C1
Marne 3 D4
Maroantsetra 17 E-F3
Maroni 23 D2
Maroua 15 E3
Marovoay 17 E3
Marquesas, Islands 25 G3
Marrakech 15 C1
Marree 25a C2
Marrupa 17 D3
Marsabit 16 D4
Marsala 6 C3
Marseille 5 E2
Marshall Hay 25a C2
Marshall Islands 25 D2
Martaban, G. of 13 A2
Martapura 13 B4
Martinique 23 C-D1
Martin Vaz, I. 24 F-G1-2
Martre, L. la 19 D-E3
Maryborough 25a E2
Maryland 20 F2
Masaka 17 D2
Masasi 17 D3
Masbate 13 D2
Mascara 5 D4
Maseru 17 C4
Mashhad 10 D-E2
Masinloc 13 C2
Masirah 10 E3
Masoala, C. 17 F3
Massachusetts 20 F1
Massangena 17 D4
Massénya 16 B3
Massif Central 5 D1
Matagalpa 21 D3
Matamoros 21 C2
Matanzas 21 D2
Matapán C. 6 E3
Matara 11 C-D5
Mataram 13 C4
Matehuala 21 B2
Matera 6 D2

Mateur 6 B3
Mathura 11 C3
Matockin Sar 9 C-D2
Mato Grosso 23 D4
Matruh 16 C1
Matsue 12 E3
Matsuo 12 G2
Matsuyama 12 F3
Maturin 23 C2
Mau-é-ele 17 D4
Maun 17 C4
Mauna Kea 25 F2
Mauritania 14 A-B4
Mauritius 14 A9
Mayaguana 21 E2
Mayaguez 21 F3
Mayotte 17 E3
Mazar-i-Sharif 11 B2
Mazatlán 21 B2
Mazeikiai 7 B2
Mbabane 17 D4
Mbaïki 16 B4
Mbala 17 D2
Mbale 17 D1
Mbanza Congo 17 B2
Mbeya 17 D3
Mbout 15 B3
Mbuji-Mayi 17 C2
Mcensk 7 F3
McKinley, Mount 20 C-D6
M'Clintock Channel 19 F2
M'Clure Strait 19 D-E2
Mecca 10 B3
Medan 13 A3
Medellin 23 B2
Medford 20 A1
Medgidia 6 G1
Medicine Hat 19 E-F4-5
Medina 10 B3
Mediterranean Sea 1 D-F5
Medvezjegorsk 9 B-C2
Meekatharra 25a A2
Meerut 11 C3
Megerda 15 D1
Megion 9 D2-3
Meighen I. 19 F-G1
Meiktila 13 A1
Meissen 4 C3
Mejillones 24 B2
Meknès 15 C1
Melaka 13 B3
Melanesia 25 C-D2-3
Melbourne 25 C4 25a D3
Melfi 16 B3
Melilla 5 C4
Melitopol' 7 E5
Mellerud 2 B-C4
Melo 24 D3
Melrhir 15 D1
Melun 3 D4
Melville Bay 19 K2
Melville, I. (Canada) 19 E-F2
Melville, I. (Austr.) 25 B3 25a B-C1
Melville Pen. 19 H2
Memmingen 4 B3
Memphis 20 E2
Mena 7 E4
Ménaka 15 D3
Menam 13 B2
Mende 5 D1
Menderes 10 A2
Mendocino, C. 20 A1
Mendoza 24 C3
Menfi 16 C-D2
Mengtsz 12 C4
Menongue 17 B3
Mentawai Islands 13 A-B3-4
Mentawai Strait 13 A-B3-4
Meraker 2 B3
Merano 6 B1
Merauke 25 B3
Merca 17 E1
Mercedes (Arg.) 24 C3
Mercedes (Arg.) 24 C-D3
Mercedes (Arg.) 24 D2
Mercedes (Uruguay) 24 D3
Meregh 16 E4
Mergui 13 A2
Mergui, Archipelago 13 A2
Mérida (Sp.) 5 B3
Mérida (Mexico) 21 C-D2
Mérida (Venez.) 23 B2
Meridian 20 E2
Merir 13 E3
Merowe 16 D4
Merredin 25a A3
Merseburg 4 B3
Mesewa 16 D3
Meshra er Req. 16 C-D4
Mesolóngion 6 E3
Mesopotamia 10 C2
Messina (Italy) 6 C3
Messina (South Africa) 17 C-D4
Messina, Str. of 6 C3

Meta 23 B-C2
Metz 3 E4
Mexiana, I. 23 E2-3
Mexicali 21 A1
Mexico, State 18 K-L7-8
Mexico, City 21 B-C3
Mexico, Gulf of 21 C-D2
Mezen 9 C4
Miami 20 E2
Michajlovka 7 G4
Michigan 20 E1
Michigan, Lake 20 E1
Micronesia 25 C-D2
Micurinsk 7 F-G3
Middlesbrough (Teesside) 3 C3
Midway I. 25 E1
Mienyang 12 C3
Mieres 5 B2
Mihajlovgrad 6 E-F2
Mikkeli 2 F3
Milan 6 B1
Mildura 25a D3
Milford Sound 25a F6
Milk 20 C1
Millau 5 D1
Millerovo 7 G4
Millicent 25a C3
Milos 6 F3
Milwaukee 20 E1
Minahassa, Pén. 13 D3
Minas 24 D3
Minas Gerais 24 E1-2
Minch, North 3 B2
Mindanao 13 D3
Mindanao Sea 13 D3
Mindoro 13 C-D2
Minicoy 11 C5
Minna 15 D3-4
Minneapolis 20 D1
Minnesota 20 D1
Miño 5 A-B2
Minorca 5 D-E2-3
Minot 20 C1
Minsk 7 C3
Minusinsk 9 E3
Miquelon 19 L5
Miraflores 23 B2
Miraj 11 C4
Mirbat 10 D4
Mirim, L. 24 D3
Mirnyy 9 F2
Mirpur Khas 11 B-C3
Mirzapur 11 D3
Miskolc 4 E3
Misool 13 D4
Mississippi 20 D-E2
Mississippi, River 20 D1-2
Missoula 20 B1
Missouri 20 D2
Missouri, River 20 B-C1
Mistassini, L. 19 I4
Mitilíni 6 F3
Mitrovica 6 D-E2
Mitú 23 B-C2
Mitzic 17 B1
Miyako 12 G3
Miyakonojo 12 F3
Miyaneh 10 C2
Miyazaki 12 F3
Mizen Head 3 A4
Mjosa 2 B3
Mlawa 4 E2
Mljet 6 D2
Motril 5 C3
Mocha 16 E4
Mobile 20 E2
Moçambique 14 F7-8
Mochudi 17 C4
Mocoa 23 B2
Mocuba 17 D3
Mogadishu 16 E4
Mogil'ov 7 D3
Mogil'ov-Podol'skij 7 C-D4
Mogoca 9 F3
Mogpo 12 E3
Moheli 17 E3
Moho 12 E1
Moi Rana 2 C2
Moisaküla 7 C2
Moldavia 7 C-D4-5
Molde 2 A3
Molepolai 17 C4
Mollendo 23 B4
Molodecno 7 C3
Moluccas 13 D3-4
Molucca Sea 13 D3-4
Momao 23 B2
Mombasa 17 D-E2
Mombetsu 12 G2
Mompós 23 B2
Mon 4 C2
Moncegorsk 2 G-H1
Monforte de Lemos 5 B2
Mongalla 16 D4
Mongo 16 B3

Mongolia 8 F-G3
Mongororo 16 C3
Mongu 17 C3
Monrovia 15 B4
Mons 3 D4
Montague Island 20 D7
Montana 20 B-C1
Montauban 5 D1
Mont-de-Marsan 5 C2
Monteagudo 24 C1
Monte Caseros 24 C-D3
Montego Bay 21 D-E3
Montélimar 5 E1
Monte Lindo, R. 24 C-D2
Monteria 23 B2
Monterrey 21 B-C2
Montes Claros 23 E4
Montevideo 24 D3
Montgomery 20 E2
Montilla 5 B3
Montluçon 3 D5
Montpelier 20 F1
Montpellier 5 D2
Montreal 19 I5
Montreux 4 A4
Montrose 3 C2
Montserrat 23 E1
Moora 25a A3
Moose Jaw 19 F4
Moosonee 19 H4
Mopti 15 C3
Moquegua 23 B4
Mora 2 C3
Moradabad 11 C3
Morava, Riv. (Czechosl.) 4 D3
Morava, Riv. (Yugosl.) 6 E1
Moray Firth 3 C2
Moree 25a E2
Morelia 21 B3
Morella 5 C2
Moresul 6 E1
Morioka 12 G3
Morlaix 3 C4
Morocco 14 A-B2-3
Moro, G. de 13 D3
Morogoro 17 D2
Morombe 17 E4
Morondava 17 E4
Moroni 17 E3
Morotai 13 D3
Moroto 16 D4
Morozovsk 7 G4
Morris Jesup, Cape 26 N1
Morsansk 7 G3
Mortes, R. das 23 D4
Morvi 11 C3
Moscow 7 F3
Moselle 3 E4
Moshi 17 D2
Mosjoen 2 C2
Mosquitos, Gulf of 21 D3-4
Moss 2 B4
Mossâmedes 17 B3
Mossel Bay 17 C5
Mossendjo 17 B2
Mossman 25a D1
Mossoró 23 F3
Mossuril 17 E3
Most 4 C3
Mostaganem 15 D1
Mostar 6 D2
Mosul 10 C2
Motala 2 C4
Motril 5 C3
Mouila 17 B2
Moulmein 13 A2
Moundou 16 B4
Mount Gambier 25a C-D3
Mount Isa 25a C2
Mount Magnet 25a A-B2
Mount Morgan 25a D-E2
Moura (Port.) 5 B3
Moura (Brazil) 23 C3
Moussoro 16 B3
Moyale 16 D4
Moyobamba 23 B3
Mozambique, Channel 17 E3-4
Mozyr 7 D4
Mpanda 17 D2
Mpika 17 D3
Msaken 6 B4
Mstislavl' 7 D3
Mtwara 17 E3
Muang Ubon 13 B2
Muaraenim 13 B4
Mufulira 17 C3
Mukacevo 7 B-C4
Mukden 12 E2
Mulhacén 5 C3
Mulhouse 3 E5
Mull 3 B2
Mullewa 25a A2
Mullingar 3 B3
Mulobezi 17 C3
Multan 11 C2
Muna 13 D4

Mongolia 8 F-G3
Mundo Novo 23 E4
Mundubbera 25a D-E2
Munich 4 B3
Munku-Sardyk 12 B1
Muonio 2 E2
Muonio 2 E2
Mur 4 C4
Murchison 25a A2
Murcia 5 C3
Muren 12 C2
Mures 6 E1
Murmansk 9 B-C2
Murmasi 2 G-H1
Murom 7 G3
Muroran 12 G2
Murray 25 B-C4
Murray Bridge 25a C-D3
Murray, River 25a C-D3
Murud 13 C3
Murzuq 16 B2
Musala 6 E2
Muscat 10 D3
Musgrave Range 25a C2
Musoma 17 D2
Mutankiang 12 E2
Mutsu 12 G2
Muyinga 17 D2
Muynak 11 A1
Muzaffarpur 11 D3
Mvolo 16 D4
Mvuma, L. 17 C-D2
Mwanza 17 D2
Mweru, L. 17 C-D2
Mwinilunga 17 C3
Myitkyina 11 E3
Myngyan 13 A1
Mysore, State: see Karnataka
Mysore, Town 11 C4
My-tho 13 B2-3

N

Nabeul 6 B3
Nachicevan 10 C2
Nadia 11 C3
Nador 5 C5
Nadvornaja 7 B-C4
Nafud Desert 10 B-C3
Naga 13 D2
Nagaland 11 E3
Nagaoka 12 F3
Nagappattinam 11 D4
Nagasaki 12 E3
Nagchu 11 E2
Nagercoil 11 C5
Nagornyj 9 G3
Nagoya 12 F3
Nagpur 11 C-D3
Nagykanizsa 4 D4
Naha 12 E4
Nain 19 K4
Nairobi 17 D2
Najin 12 F2
Najran 10 C4
Nak'amet 16 D4
Nakhl 10 B3
Nakhodka 9 G3
Nakhon 13 B2
Nakhon Pathom 13 A-B2
Nakhon Phanon 13 B2
Nakhon Ratchasima 13 B2
Nakhon Sawan 13 B2
Nakhon Si Thammarat 13 A-B3
Nakuru 17 D2
Nalayh 9 F3
Nalcik 10 C1
Namapa 17 D-E3
Nambour 25a E2
Namcha Barwa 11 E3
Nam Dinh 13 B1
Namib Desert 17 B4
Namibia: see South West Africa
Nampo 12 E3
Nampula 17 D3
Namsos 2 B2
Namsskogan 2 C2
Namtu 11 E3
Nanaimo 19 D5
Nanchang 12 D4
Nanchung 12 C3
Nancy 3 E4
Nanga Parbat 11 C2
Nanking 12 D3
Nanning 12 C4
Nanping 12 D4
Nansha Islands 13 C2
Nan Shan 12 B3
Nantes 3 C5
Nantung 12 E3
Nanumea 25 D3
Nanyang 12 D3
Nanyuki 17 D1
Nao, C. de la 5 D3

Napier 25a G5
Naples 6 C2
Naples, G. of 6 C2
Napo 23 B3
Naqub 10 C4
Narayanganj 11 D3
Narbonne 5 D2
Narew 4 E2
Narian-Mar 9 C-D2
Narmada 11 C-D2
Narodnaja 9 D2
Naro-Forminsk 7 E-F3
Narrandera 25a D3
Narrogin 25a A3
Narssarssuaq 19 M3
Narva 7 C-D2
Naryn 9 D3
Nase 12 E-F4
Nashville 20 E2
Näsijarvi 2 E-F3
Nasik 11 C4
Nasirabad 11 E3
Nassau 21 E2
Nasser, L. 16 D2
Nässjö 2 C4
Nata 17 C4
Natal (South Afr.) 17 D4
Natal (Brazil) 23 F3
Naturaliste, Cape 25a A3
Nauru 25 D3
Nauta 23 B3
Navarino, C. 9 I-K2
Navl'a 7 E3
Nawabshah 11 B3
Nawchi 13 A2
Náxos 6 F3
Nazaré 23 F4
Nazareth 10 B2
Nazija 7 D-E2
Nazwa 10 D3
Nazyvajevsk 9 D3
Ndalatando 17 B2
Ndélé 16 C4
N'Djamena 15 E3
Ndjolé 17 B1-2
Ndola 17 C3
Near Islands 9 I3
Nebit-Dag 9 C4
Nebolci 7 E2
Nebraska 20 C-D1
Neckar 4 B3
Necker 25 E1
Necochea 24 D3
Needles 20 B2
Negele 16 D4
Negombo 11 C5
Negra, P.ta 23 A3
Negrais, Cape 13 A2
Negro, Rio (Arg.) 24 C3-4
Negro, Rio (Brazil) 23 C2-3
Negros 13 D3
Nehbandan 10 D-E2
Neikiang 12 C4
Neisse 4 C3
Neiva 23 B2
Nejd 10 C3
Nekemte 16 D4
Nelidovo 7 E2
Nellore 11 D4
Nelma 12 F2
Nelson (Austr.) 25a G6
Nelson (Canada) 19 E5
Nelson, River 19 G4
Néma 15 C3
Neman 7 B3
Nemuro 12 H2
Nenagh 3 B3
Nenana 20 D6
Nepal 8 F4
Nercinsk 9 F3
Neretva 6 D2
Nerva 5 B3
Néstos 6 F2
Nesviz 7 C3
Netherlands 1 D3
Neubrandenburg 4 B-C2
Neuchâtel 4 A4
Neumünster 4 B2
Neuquen 24 C3
Neuruppin 4 C2
Neustrelitz 4 C2
Nevel' 7 D2
Nevelsk 9 H3
Nevers 3 D5
Nevis 21 F3
New Amsterdam 23 D2
New Britain 25 C3
New Brunswick 19 K5
New Caledonia 25 D4
Newcastle 25a E3
Newcastle (S. Africa) 17 C-D4
Newcastle u. Tyne 3 C3
Newcastle Waters 25 B3
New Delhi 11 C3
Newenham, Cape 20 b7
Newfoundland, State 19 K-L4-5

Newfoundland, Islands 19 L5
New Guinea 25 B-C3
New Hampshire 20 F1
New Haven 20 F1
New Hebrides see Vanuatu
New Ireland 25 C3
New Jersey 20 F2
New Mexico 20 C2
New Norfolk 25a D4
New Orleans 20 E3
New Plymouth 25 D4 25a G5
Newport News 20 F2
New Providence 21 E2
New Siberia Island 9 H2
New Siberian Islands 9 H1-2
New South Wales 25 C4 25a D-E3
New Westminster 19 D-E5
New York, City 20 F1-2
New York, State 20 F1
New Zealand 25 D4-5
Nezin 7 D-E4
Ngaundéré 15 E4
Ngok Linh 13 B2
Ngorongoro 17 D2
Nguru 15 E3
Ngwane 14 F8
Nhamundà 23 D3
Nha Trang 13 B-C2
Niafounké 15 C3
Niagara Falls 19 H5
Niamey 15 D3
Niangara 16 C4
Nias 13 A3
Nicaragua 18 M8
Nicaragua, L. 21 D3
Nicastro 6 D3
Nice 5 E2
Nicobar Islands 11 E5
Nicosia 10 B2
Nicoya Peninsula 21 D4
Nieuw Nickerie 23 D2
Niger 15 C-D4
Niger, River 15 C-D3-4
Nigeria 14 C-D4
Niigata 12 F3
Nijmegen 3 E4
Nikel 9 B2
Nikolajev 7 D5
Nikolajevsk-na-Amure 9 H3
Nikol'sk 7 H2
Nikopol' 7 E5
Niksić 6 D2
Nile 16 D3
Nile, Blue 16 D3
Nile, White 16 D4
Nîmes 5 E2
Nineveh 10 C2
Ningan 12 E-F2
Ningpo 12 E4
Ning Ting Shan 12 B3
Ningwu 12 D3
Niobrara 20 C1
Nioro 15 C3
Niort 3 C5
Nipigon, L. 19 H5
Nis 6 E2
Niteról 24 E2
Nitra 4 D3
Niue 25 E3
Nizamabad 11 C4
Niz-Lomov 7 G-H3
Nizneangarsk 9 F3
Nizneudinsk 9 E3
Niz. Tagil 9 D3
Njandoma 9 B-C2
Nkongsamba 15 D-E4
Noatak 20 B-C6
Nobeoka 12 F3
Nogales 21 A1
Noginski 9 E2
Noirmoutier, I. de 3 C5
Nokia 2 E3
Nome 20 B6
Nomoi Is. 25 C2
Nong Khai 13 B2
Nordfjorden 2 A3
Nordfold 2 C-D2
Nordreisa 2 E1
Nordvik 9 F2
Norfolk 20 F2
Norfolk, Islands 25 D4
Norilsk 9 E2
Normanton 25 C3 25a D1
Norman Wells 19 C-D3
Norquinco 24 C4
Norrköping 2 D4
Norrland 2 C-D2
Norseman 25a B3
North Andaman 11 E4
Norte, C. 23 E2
Northam 25a A3
Northampton (Austr.) 25a A2
Northampton (U.K.) 3 C3

123

North Battleford 19 E-F4
North Cape (Austr.) 25a G5
North Cape (Norway) 2 F1
North Channel 3 B3
North Carolina 20 E-F2
Northern Ireland 3 B3
Northern Territory 25 B3-4 25a C1-2
North Frisian Islands 3 E3
North Island 25 D-E4 25a G5
North Platte 20 C-D1
North Saskatchewan 19 E-F4
North Sea 3 D-E2-3
North West Cape 25 A4 25a A2
North West Territories 19 D-I3
Norton Sound 20 b6
Norway 1 D-E-F3
Norwegian Sea 2 A-B1-2
Norwich 3 D3
Nota 2 G1
Noteć 4 D2
Noto 6 C3
Notodden 2 B4
Notre Dame, Bay 19 L4
Nottingham 3 C3
Nottingham, Island 19 I3
Nouadhibou 15 B2
Nouakchott 15 B3
Nouméa 25 D4
Nova Chaves 17 B-C3
Nova Freixo 17 D3
Novaja Zemlya 9 C-D2
Nova Lisboa: see Huambo
Nova Scotia 19 K5
Novgorod 7 D2
Novi Pazar 6 E2
Novi Sad 6 D1
Novoanninskij 7 G4
Novocerkassk 7 F-G5
Novograd-Volynskij 7 C4
Novogroudok 7 C3
Novokazalinsk 9 D3
Novokuznetk 9 E3
Novomoskovsk 7 F-G3
Novo Redondo 17 B3
Novorossijsk 7 F5
Novorzev 7 D2
Novosakhtinsk 7 F-G5
Novosibirsk 9 D-E3
Novosohol'niki 7 D2
Novozybkov 7 E3
Novyi-Oskol 7 F4
Novyj-Port 9 D2
Nowy Sacz 4 D-E3
Nowy Targ: see Las
Nubian Desert 16 D2
Nuevitas 21 E3
Nuku'alofa 25 E4
Nuku-Hiva 25 F3
Nukus 9 C3
Nulato 20 C6
Nullagine 25a B2
Nullarbor Plain 25a B-C3
Nunivak I. 20 B6
Nunkiang 12 E2
Nuoro 6 B2
Nurmes 2 G3
Nuremberg 4 B-C3
Nutsin 12 E3
Nyasa, Lake: see Malawi
Nyborg 4 B2
Nyíregyháza 4 E4
Nyköping 2 D4
Nylstroom 17 C4
Nyngan 25a D3
Nysa 4 D3
Nzérékoré 15 B-C4

O

Oahu 25 E-F1
Oakland 20 A2
Oamaru 25a G6
Oates Coast 27 K2
Oaxaca 21 C3
Ob 9 D-E2-3
Ob, Gulf of 9 D2
Oban 3 B2
Obbia 16 E-F4
Obi 13 D4
Obidos 23 D3
Obihiro 12 G2
Oblucje 9 G3
Obninsk 7 E-F3
Obo 16 C4
Obojan 7 F4
Ocean Island 25 D3
Ocha 9 H3
October Revolution Island 9 E2
Ocussi 13 D4

Odda 2 A3
Odemira 5 A3
Odense 4 B2
Oder 4 C-D3-2
Odessa 7 D5
Odienné 15 C4
Offenbach 4 B3
Ofira 10 B3
Ogaden 16 B4
Ogasawara: see Bonin Islands
Ogbomosho 15 D4
Ogooué 17 D2
Ohanet 15 D2
Ohio 20 E1
Ohrid 6 E2
Ohrid, Lake 6 D-E2
Oise 3 D4
Oita 12 F3
Ojos del Salado 24 C2
Oka 7 F-G3
Okahandja 17 B4
Okavango Swamp 17 B-C3
Okhotsk 9 H3
Okhotsk, Sea of 9 H3
Oki Is. 12 F3
Okinawa 12 E4
Okino: see Parece Vela
Oklahoma 20 D2
Oklahoma City 20 D2
Oktjabrskij 9 H3
Oktyabrskoye 9 D2
Öland 2 D4
Olavarria 24 C3
Olbia 6 B2
Oldenburg 4 A-B2
Olekma 9 G3
Olekminsk 9 G2
Olenegorsk 2 G-H1
Olenëk 9 F2
Olenëk, River 9 F2
Olenino 7 E2
Oléron, île d' 5 C1
Oleśnica 4 D3
Olgiy 12 A-B2
Olifants 17 D4
Oljutorskij 9 I2
Oljutorskij, Cape 9 I3
Olomouc 4 D3
Olonec 7 E1
Olsztyn (Allenstein) 4 E2
Oltre Giuba 17 E1-2
Oluan Pi Cape 12 D-E4
Olympia 20 A1
Olympus 6 E3
Oman 8 D4-5
Oman, Gulf of 8 D-E4
Omdurman 16 C-D3
Omolon 9 H-I2
Omsk 9 D3
Omu 12 G2
Onaha 20 D1
Ondangua 17 B3
Onega 9 B-C2
Onega L. 7 E-F1
Onekotan 9 H3
Ongole 11 D4
Onitsha 15 D4
Onon 9 F3
Onslow 25 A4 25a A2
Ontario 19 H4-5
Ontario, L. 20 F1
Oodnadatta 25 B4 25a C2
Oos Londen: see East London
Opava 4 D3
Opocka 7 D2
Opole 4 D3
Opua 25a G5
Oradea 4 E4
Oran (Algeria) 15 C1
Orán (Arg.) 24 C2
Orange Free State 17 C4
Orange, Cape 23 D2
Orange, River 17 B-C4-5
Orango 15 B3
Oranjemund 17 B4
Ordynskiy 12 C1
Ordos Plateau 12 C2-3
Ordzonikidze 10 C1
Örebro 2 C4
Orechovo-Zujevo 7 F3
Oregon 20 A-B1
Orellana 23 B3
Orense 5 B2
Orgejev 7 D5
Orinoco 23 C2
Orissa 11 D3-4
Oristano 6 B3
Orizaba 21 C3
Orkanger 2 B3
Orkney Islands 3 C2
Orléans 3 D5
Orlovskij 7 G5
Ormoc 13 D4
Örnsköldsvik 2 D3

Or'ol 7 F3
Orosei 6 B2
Orotukan 9 H2
Orsa 7 D3
Orsk 9 C-D3
Oruro 23 C4
Os 9 D3
Osaka 12 F3
Oshogbo 15 D4
Osijek 6 D1
Osipovici 7 C-D3
Oskarshamn 2 D4
Oslo 2 C4
Osmarino 9 E2
Osnabrück 4 A-B2
Osorio 24 E2
Osorno 24 B2
Ossa, Mount 25a D4
Ostaskov 7 D-E2
Ostende 3 D4
Österdal 2 C3
Östersund 2 C3
Ostrawa 4 D3
Ostrov 7 D2
Ostrów 4 E2
Ostrów Wielkopolski 4 D3
Osumi Islands 12 E-F3
Osumi Str. 12 F3
Otaru 12 F-G2
Otavi 17 B3
Otjiwarongo 17 B4
Otra 2 A4
Otranto 6 D2
Otranto, Strait of 6 D2-3
Otta 2 B3
Ottawa 19 I5
Otway, Cape 25a D3
Ouadaï 16 B3
Ouadda 16 C4
Ouagadougou 15 C-D3
Oualata 15 C3
Oudtshoorn 17 C5
Ouessant, I. d' 3 B4
Ouesso 17 D3
Oujda 15 C1
Oulainen 2 F2
Oulu 2 F2
Oulu, River 2 F2
Oulujärvi 2 F2
Ouricuri 23 E-F3
Ouse 3 C3
Outardes 19 K4
Outer Herbrides 3 B2
Outjo 17 B4
Outokumpu 2 G3
Ovalle 24 B3
Ovamboland 17 B3
Oviedo 5 B2
Ovruc 7 D4
Oxford 3 C4
Oyapock 23 D2
Oyem 17 B1
Oyo 15 D4
Ozamiz 13 D3
Ozernovskij 9 H3
Ozieri 6 B2

P

Paarl 17 B5
Pabianice 4 D3
Pacasmayo 23 A-B3
Pacific Ocean 25 B-G1-4 25a G5-6
Pachuca 21 C2
Padang 13 B4
Paderborn 4 B3
Padua 6 B1
Padun 2 G-H1
Pag 6 C1
Pagadian 13 D3
Pagai Islands 13 A-B4
Pagalu 17 A2
Paicheng 12 E2
Päijänne 2 F3
Paimpol 3 C4
Paita 23 A3
Pajala 2 E2
Pakistan 8 E4
Pakse 13 B2
Pala 16 B4
Palana 9 H3
Palanga 7 B2-3
Palangka Raya 13 C4
Palapye 17 C4
Palau 6 B2
Palau Islands 25 B2
Palawan 13 C2-3
Paldiski 7 B2
Palembang 13 B4
Palencia 5 B2
Palermo 6 C3
Palimé 15 D4
Palliser, Cape 25a G6
Palma 5 D3
Palmas, C. 15 C4

Palmer Archipelago 27 R2
Palmerston 25 E3 25a G6
Palmira (Syria) 10 B2
Palmira (Colom.) 23 B2
Palmyra 25 F3
Palopo 13 C-D4
Palos, G. de 5 C3
Pamir 11 C2
Pampas 24 C3
Pamplona 5 C2
Panamá 18 M-N9
Panamá G. of 21 E4
Panay 13 D2
Pancevo 6 E1
Pangilov 9 D-E3
Pangkalanberandan 13 A3
Pangkalpinang 13 B4
Panjgur 11 B3
Panjim 11 C4
Pantelleria, Island 6 C3
Paoki 12 C3
Paoshan 12 B4
Paoting 12 D3
Paotow 12 C2
Papeete 25 F3
Papua New Guinea 25 C3
Paracel Is. 13 C2
Paraiba 23 E3
Paraguai River 23 D4
Paraguaná Peninsula 23 C1
Paraguay 22 D-E6
Paraguay, River 24 D2
Parakhino-Poddubje 7 E2
Paramaribo 23 D2
Paramonga 23 A-B4
Paramusir 9 H3
Parana (Brazil) 23 E4
Parana (Arg.) 24 C-D3
Parana, R. (Brazil) 23 E4
Parana, R. (Arg.) 24 C-D2-3
Paranaguá 24 E2
Paranaiba, R. 23 D-E4
Paranapanema 24 D2
Parcel Vela 25 B1
Parepare 13 C4
Pariaman 13 A-B4
Pariñas, Pta 23 A3
Parintins 23 D3
Paris 3 D4
Parkano 2 E3
Parma 6 B1
Parnaiba 23 E3
Parnaiba, R. 23 E3
Parnassós 6 E3
Pärnu 7 B-C2
Paroo 25a D2
Parral 24 B3
Parry Is. 19 E-F2
Paru 23 D3
Paru de Oeste 23 D2-3
Pasau 4 C3
Pasni 11 B3
Paso de Indios 24 B-C4
Passero, C. 6 C3
Passo Fundo 24 D2
Pastaza 23 B3
Patagonia 24 B-C4
Patan 11 C3
Patiala 11 C2
Patna 11 D3
Patos 23 F3
Patos, Lagoa dos 24 D-E3
Patras 6 E3
Patrocínio 23 E4
Pattani 13 B3
Pau 5 C2
Paulistana 23 E3
Paulo Afonso 23 E-F3
Pavia 6 B1
Pavlodar 9 D3
Pavlovo 7 G2
Pavlovskaja 7 F-G5
Paysandú 24 D3
Peace 19 E4
Peace River 19 E4
Peak Hill 25a A-B2
Peč 6 E2
Pecenga 9 B2
Pecora 9 C2
Pecora, River 9 C2
Pecory 7 C-D2
Pecos 20 C2
Pécs 4 D4
Pegu 13 A2
Pehan 12 E2
Pehpei 12 C3
Pei Shan 12 B2
Peixe 23 E4
Pekalongan 13 B-C4
Pekin 12 D2
Peleduy 9 F3
Peleng 13 D4
Pelkosenniemi 2 F2
Pello 23 E1
Pelly 19 C3
Peloponnesus 6 E3

Pelotas 24 D3
Pematangsiantar 13 A3
Pemba 17 E2
Pembroke 3 B4
Peñarroya-Pueblonuevo 5 B3
Penas, G. of 24 B4
Pendleton 20 B1
Pengpu 12 D3
Penki 12 E2
Pennsylvania 20 F1
Peno 7 E2
Pensacola 20 E2
Penza 9 C3
Penzance 3 B4
Peoria 20 D-E1
Percival Lakes 25a B2
Pereslavl'-Zalesskij 7 F-G2
Pergamino 24 C3
Périgeux 5 D1
Perm 9 C3
Pernambuco 23 E-F3
Pernik 6 E2
Perpignan 5 D2
Persepolis 10 D2-3
Persian Gulf 10 C-D3
Perth (U.K.) 3 B-C2
Perth (Austr.) 25 A4 25a A3
Peru 22 C4-5
Perugia 6 C2
Pervomajsk 7 D4-5
Pervoural'sk 9 C3
Pesaro 6 C2
Pescara 6 C2
Peshawar 11 B-C2
Peshkopi 6 E2
Peshovo 7 E2
Peter I. 27 Q2
Peterborough 25a C-D3
Peterhead 3 C2
Petermann Peak 26 N2
Peter Pond, L. 19 E-F4
Peterson, Mt 27 Q2
Pétionville 21 F2
Petric 6 E2
Petrikov 7 D3
Petropavlovsk 9 D3
Petropavlovsk-Kamcatskij 9 H-I3
Petrópolis 24 E2
Petrosani 6 E-F1
Petrovsk 12 C1
Petrozavodsk 7 E1
Pevek 9 I2
Phan Rang 13 B-C2
Philadelphia 20 F2
Philippines 8 H5
Phitsanulok 13 B2
Phnom Penh 13 B2
Phoenix Islands 25 E3
Phuket 13 A3
Piacenza 6 B1
Pianosa 6 B2
Piaui 23 E3
Pidurutalagala 11 D5
Piedras Negras 21 B2
Pierre 20 C1
Pietermaritzburg 17 D4
Pietersburg 17 C4
Pietra Neamt 4 F4
Pietrosu 4 F4
Pihtipudas 2 F3
Pila 4 D2
Pilcomayo 24 C2
Pilica 4 D3
Pilsen 4 C3
Pinang 13 A-B3
Pinar del Rio 21 D2
Pine Creek 25a B-C1
Pines, Isle of 21 D2
Pingliang 12 C3
Pinsk 7 C3
Pintados 24 B2
Piombino 6 B2
Piotrków Trybunalski 4 D3
Piraeus 6 E3
Pirapora 23 E4
Pires do Rio 23 E4
Pirgos 6 E3
Piripiri 23 E3
Pirot 6 E2
Pisa 6 B2
Pisagua 24 B1
Pisco 23 B4
Pisek 4 C3
Pistoia 6 B1-2
Pisuerga 5 B2
Pitcairn Island 25 G4
Pite 2 D2
Pitea 2 E2
Pitesti 6 F2
Pitkäranta 7 D-E1
Pittsburgh 20 E-F1
Piura 23 A-B3
Planen 4 C3
Plasencia 5 B2
Plata, Rio de la 24 D3

Platte I. 17 F2
Platte, R. 20 C-D1
Platte, North 20 C1
Platte, South 20 C1
Pleiku 13 B2
Plescenicy 7 C-D3
Pleven 6 F2
Ploce 6 D2
Plock 4 D-E2
Ploiesti 6 F1
Plovdiv 6 F2
Plumas, Las: see Las Plumas
Plymouth 3 B4
Plzen 4 C3
Po 6 A-B1
Pocatello 20 B1
Pocep 7 E3
Pocinok 7 E3
Podkamennaja Tunguska 9 E2
Podol'sk 7 F3
Podporozje 7 E1
Poinsett, C. 27 H2
Pointe Noire 17 A-B2
Pokka 2 F1
Pokrovsk 9 G2
Pola: see Pula
Poland 1 E-F3
Pol'arnyj 2 H1
Poliyiros 6 E2
Polock 7 D3
Poltava 7 E4
Polten 4 C3
Polynesia 25 E-F2-4
Pombal 5 A3
Ponce 21 F2
Ponder 20 C1
Pondicherry 11 D4
Pond Inlet 19 I2
Ponferrada 5 B2
Ponta Grossa 24 D2
Ponta Pora 24 D2
Ponte Nova 24 E1
Pontevedra 5 A2
Pontianak 13 B4
Pontine Mountains 10 B1
Ponziane Islands 6 C2
Poona 11 C4
Poopó L. 23 C4
Popayán 23 B2
Popocatépetl 21 C3
Porbandar 11 B3
Porchov 7 D2
Porcupine 20 d-e6
Pordenone 6 B-C1
Pori 2 E3
Porjus 2 D2
Porkkala 2 F5
Poronajsk 9 H3
Porsanger Fjord 2 F1
Portadown 3 B3
Portage la Prairie 19 F-G4-5
Portalegre 5 B3
Port Arthur: see Thunder Bay
Port Augusta 25 B4 25a C-D3
Port-au-Prince 21 E3
Port-aux-Basques 19 L5
Port Blair 11 E4
Port Cartier 19 K5
Port Douglas 25a D1
Port Elizabeth 17 C5
Port Gentil 17 A2
Port Harcourt 15 D4
Port Hedland 25a A-B2
Portimao 5 A3
Portland (Oregon) 20 A1
Portland (Maine) 20 G1
Port Louis 17 F4
Port Moresby 25 C3
Port Natal: see Durban
Port Nolloth 17 B4
Pôrto 5 A2
Pôrto Alegre 24 D-E3
Pôrto Alexandre 17 B3
Pôrto Casado 24 D2
Pôrto de Moz 23 D3
Pôrto Esperança 24 D1
Pôrto Mendes 24 D2
Pôrto Murtinho 24 D2
Pôrto Nacional 23 E4
Porto Novo 15 D4
Port of Spain 23 C-D1
Porto Torres 6 A-B2
Porto Vecchio 5 F2
Porto Velho 23 C3
Portoviejo 23 A3
Port Pirie 25a C-D3
Port Said 16 D1
Port Shepstone 17 C5
Port St. Johns: see Umzimvubu
Port Sudan 16 D2-3
Portsmouth 3 C4
Portugália: see Dundo
Port Vladimir 2 H1

124

Portugal 1 C4-5
Posadas 24 D2
Poseh 12 C4
Posio 2 F-G2
Poso 13 D4
Postavy 7 C3
Poste M. Cortier 15 C-D2
Poste Weygand 15 C-D2
Potchefstroom 17 C4
Potenza 6 C-D2
Potiskum 15 D-E3
Potosi 24 C1
Potow 12 D3
Potsdam 4 C2
Povorino 7 G4
Powell, L. 20 B-C2
Poyang Lake 12 D4
Pozarevac 6 E1
Poznan 4 D2
Prague 4 C3
Prahovo 6 E1
Praia 15 A3
Prenzlau 4 C2
Pres. Epitácio 24 D2
Presov 4 E3
Prespa, Lake 6 E2
Preston 3 C3
Prêto 24 E2
Pretoria 17 C4
Préveza 6 E3
Pribilof, Is. 20 B7
Prieska 17 C4
Prijedor 6 D1
Prilep 6 E2
Priluki 7 E4
Primorsk 7 D1
Primorsko-Achtarsk 7 F5
Prince Albert 19 F4
Prince Charles Island 19 I3
Prince Edward Island
  (Can.) 19 K5
Prince Edward I. (South
  Afr.) 27 D3
Prince Harald Coast 27
  D-E2
Prince Leopold Coast 27
  A-B2
Prince of Wales Island 19
  F-G2
Prince of Wales, Cape 20 b6
Pr. Patrick I. 19 D-E2
Prince Rupert 19 D4
Princess Astrid Coast 27 C2
Princess Martha Coast 27
  B2
Prince Williams Sound 20
  d6-7
Principe 15 D4
Principe da Beira 23 C4
Prinzapolca 21 D3
Prioz'orsk 7 D1
Pristina 6 E2
Proddatur 11 C4
Progreso 21 C-D2
Prokopjevsk 9 E3
Prome 13 A2
Propriá 23 F4
Prostejov 4 D3
Providence Islands 17 F2
Providence 20 F1
Providencia Is. (Col.) 21
  D-E3
Providenija 9 K2
Provo 20 B1
Prut 7 C5
Pruzany 7 B-C3
Przemyśl 4 E3
Przeval'sk 11 C1
Pskov 7 D2
Pucallpa 23 B3
Pucheng 12 D4
Puebla 21 C3
Pueblo 20 C2
Pueblo Hundido 24 C2
Puerto Aisen 24 B4
Puerto Armuelles 21 D4
Puerto Ayacucho 23 C2
P.to Barrios 21 D3
Puerto Berrio 23 B2
Puerto Cortés (Costa Rica)
  21 D4
Puerto Cortés (Hond.) 21
  D3
Puerto Deseado 24 C4
Puerto Esperanza 23 B3-4
Puerto Madryn 24 C4
Puerto Maldonado 23 B-C4
Puerto Montt 24 B4
Puerto Natales 24 B5
Puerto Pinasco 24 D2
Puerto Plata 21 E-F2
Puerto Princesa 13 C3
Puerto Rico 18 O8
Pula 6 C1
Pulo Anna 13 E3
Puna I. 23 A3
Punakha 11 E3

Pungenskoye 9 C-D2
Punjab 11 B-C2
Puno 23 B4
Punta Arenas 29 B5
Puntak Chain 25 D2
Puntarenas 21 D4
Puntjak Djaja 13 E4
Puri 11 D4
Pursat 13 B2
Purus 23 C3
Puskin 7 D2
Pustoska 7 D2
Putao 11 E3
Putehachi 12 D-E2
Putorana 4 B2
Putumayo 23 B3
Pyinmana 13 A2
Pyongyang 12 E3
Pyrenees 5 C-D2
Pyrgos 6 E3

Q

Qala-i-Kang 11 B2
Qala Nau 11 B2
Qalat 11 B2-3
Qal'at Bishah 10 C3
Qasr al-Burayqah 16 B1-2
Qatar 8 D4
Qazvin 10 C2
Qena 16 D2
Qeshm I. 10 D3
Qom 10 D2
Quan Long 13 B3
Quang Ngai 13 B-C2
Quang Tri 13 B2
Qu'Appelle 19 F4
Quebec, State 19 I4
Quebec, City 19 I5
Queen Adelaide Arch. 24
  B5
Queen Charlotte Islands 19
  C4
Queen Charlotte Strait 19
  C-D4
Queen Elizabeth Islands 19
  D-H1-2
Queen Mary Coast 27 G2
Queen Maud Land 27 C-D2
Queen Maud Ra 27 L-O1
Queensland 25 C3-4 25a
  D2
Queenstown 17 C5
Quelimane 17 D3
Quemoy, Is. 12 D4
Que Que 17 C3
Querétaro 21 B-C2
Quetta 11 B2
Quezaltenango 21 C3
Quezon City 13 D2
Quiaca, La 24 C2
Quifuma 17 B2
Quilpie 25a D2
Quimper 3 B5
Quincy 20 D2
Quines 24 C3
Qui Nhon 13 B-C2
Quito 23 B3
Quiseir 16 D2

R

Raahe 2 E-F2
Rabat 15 C1
Rabaul 25 C3
Radom 4 E3
Radomysl 7 C-D4
Rafaela 24 C3
Rafha 10 C3
Rafsanjan 10 D2
Ragusa 6 C3
Raichur 11 C4
Rainier Mt. 20 A1
Raipur 11 D3
Rajahmundry 11 D4
Rajang 13 C2
Rajasthan 11 C3
Rajcikhinsk 12 E-F1
Rajkot 11 C3
Rajshahi 11 D3
Rakops 17 C4
Rakvere 7 C2
Raleigh 20 F2
Ralik Chain 25 D2
Rampur 11 C-D3
Rancagua 24 B3
Randers 4 B1
Rangoon 13 A2
Rantekombola 13 C-D4
Rapa Iti 25 F4
Ras-al-Khaimah 10 D3
Ras Dashan 16 D3
Ras Hafun 16 F3

Rasht 10 C2
Ras Madra Kah 10 D4
Ras Tannurah 10 D3
Ratak Chain 25 D2
Rathenow 4 C2
Ratlam 11 C3
Rauchi 11 D3
Rauma 2 E3
Raurkela 11 D3
Rava-Russkaja 7 B-C4
Ravenna 6 C1
Rawalpindi 11 C2
Rawson 24 C4
R'azan 7 F3
Razgrad 6 F2
R'azsk 7 G3
Ré, Ile de 3 C5
Reading 3 C4
Recherche, Archipelago of
  the 25a B3
Recica 7 D3
Recife 23 F3
Rockhampton 25a E2
Reconquista 24 C2
Red Deer 19 E4
Red Lake 19 G4
Red River (Vietnam) 13 B1
Red River (U.S.) 20 D1-2
Red Sea 16 D-E2-3
Regensburg 4 B-C3
Reggane 15 D2
Reggio Calabria 6 C-D3
Reggio nell'Emilia 6 B1
Regina 19 F4
Rehoboth 17 B4
Reims 3 E4
Reindeer Lake 19 F4
Reinosa 5 B2
Reka Devnja 6 F-G2
Remanso 23 E3
Remscheid 4 A3
Rena 2 B3
Rendsburg 4 B2
Rengat 13 B3-4
Reni 7 D5
Rennes 3 C4
Reno, River 6 B1
Reno (U.S.) 20 B2
Republican 20 C-D1-2
Requena 5 C3
Resita 6 E1
Resistencia 24 C-D2
Resolution, Islands 19 K3
Réthimnon 6 F4
Réunion 17 F4
Revilla Gigedo, Is. 21 A3
Rey 10 D2
Reyaiyeh 10 C2
Reza'iyeh, Lake of 10 C2
Rezekne 7 C2
Rhine 4 A3
Rhode Island 20 F1
Rhodes I. 6 F-G3
Rhodes, City 6 F-G3
Rhodesia see Zimbabwe
Rhône 4 A4/5 E1-2
Riau Is. 13 B3
Ribeirao Prêto 24 E2
Riberalta 23 C4
Richmond 20 F2
Ried 4 C3
Rieti 6 C2
Riga 7 C2
Riga, G. of 7 B2
Riihimäki 2 F3
Rijeka 6 C1
Rimini 6 C1
Rîmnicu-Vîlcea 6 E-F1
Rincon 20 C2
Ringkobing 4 A-B1
Ringvassoy 2 D1
Rio Cuarto 24 C3
Rio de Janeiro 24 E2
Rio Gallegos 24 C5
Rio Grande 24 D3
Rio Grande do Norte 23 F3
Rio Grande do Sul 24 D2
Risor 2 B4
Rivas 21 D3
Rivera 24 D3
Rivière du Loup 19 K5
Riyadh 10 C3
Rjukan 2 A-B4
Roanne 3 D-E5
Roanoke 20 E2
Robertsport 15 B4
Robinson Crusoe 24 B3
Robson, Mont. 19 D-E4
Roca, C. da 5 A3
Roçadas 17 B3
Roca Partida Island 21 A3
Rocas 23 F3
Rocha 24 D3
Rochester 20 F1
Rockall 3 A2
Rockhampton 25 C4
Rock Island 20 D1

Rock Springs 20 C1
Rocky Mtns. 19 D-E4-5/20
  B-C1-2
Rodez 5 D1
Roebourne 25a A2
Roes Welcome Sound 19
  H3
Rogacov 7 D3
Roman 4 F4
Romania 5 E1
Romans 5 E1
Roma 25a D2
Rome 6 B-C2
Romny 7 E4
Ronda 5 B3
Rondônia 23 C4
Ronne 4 C2
Ronne Land 27 R-S1
Roosevelt 23 C3-4
Roosevelt I. 27 M-L2
Roques Los: see Los
  Roques
Roraima 23 C2
Roros 2 B3
Rosa, Mt. 6 A1
Rosario 24 C3
Rosario de la Frontera 24
  C2
Rosa Santa 24 C3
Rosebery 25a D4
Rosenheim 4 B-C4
Rosiori-de-Vede 6 E-F1
Roslavl' 7 E3
Ross Ice Barrier 27 M-L2
Ross Sea 27 M-L2
Ross Ice Shelf 27 L-M1
Rosso 15 B3
Rossos 7 F-G4
Rostock 4 C2
Rostov 7 F-G2
Rostov-na-Donu 7 F-G5
Roswell 20 C2
Roti 13 D5
Rotterdam 3 D-E4
Roubaix 3 D4
Rouen 3 D4
Rovaniemi 2 F2
Rovno 7 C3
Roxas 13 D2
Royan 5 C1
Rtiscevo 7 G3
Ruapehu, Mount 25a G5
Rub'al-Khali 10 C-D3-4
Rubtsovsk 9 D-E3
Rudbar 11 B2
Rudn'a 7 D3
Rudolf, Lake: see Turkana,
  L.
Rufiji 17 D2
Rufino 24 C3
Rufisque 15 B3
Rügen 4 C2
Rukwa, L. 17 D2
Rumbek 16 C-D4
Rum Jungle 25a C1
Rumoi 12 G2
Rumpi 17 D3
Rungwa 17 D2
Rungwe 17 D2
Ruse 6 F2
Russian Soviet Federal
  Socialist
  Republic 9 C-F2
Rutshuru 17 C2
Ruvuma 17 D3
Ruwenzori 17 C1
Ruzomberok 4 D-E3
Rwanda 14 E6
Rybachi Pen 2 H1
Rybac'ye 9 D3
Rybinsk City 7 F2
Rybinsk, Resr. 7 F2
Rybnica 7 D5
Ryazsk 4 E3
Ryukyu Islands 12 E4
Rzeszów 4 E3
Ržev 7 E2

S

Saale 4 B-C3
Saarbrücken 4 A3
Saaremaa 7 B2
Sabac 6 D1
Sabadell 5 D2
Sabah 13 C3
Sabhah 16 B2
Sabine, M. 26 L2
Sabie, Cape (Can.) 19 K5
Sable, Cape (U.S.) 20 E3
Sabnitz 4 C2
Sabya 10 C4
Sabzevar 10 D2
Sabzevar 10 D2
Sachigo 19 G4
Sacramento 20 A2
Sacramento, R. 20 A1-2

Sà da Bandeira: see
  Lubango
Sa'dah 10 C4
Sadiya 11 D3
Sado, River 5 A3
Sado Island 12 F3
Saestved 4 C2
Safi 15 C1
Safonovo 7 E3
Sagar 11 C3
Sagua la Grande 21 D-E2
Sagunto 5 C3
Sahara 15 C-D-E-F3
Saharanpur 11 C3
Saidpur 11 D-E3
Saigon: see Ho Chi Minh
  City
Saimaa 2 F-G3
Sain-Sand 12 C-D2
St. Brieuc 3 C4
St. Croix 21 F3
St. Denis 17 F4
St. Dié 3 E4
St. Dizier 3 E4
St. Elias, Mtns. 20 D-E6-7
Saint-Etienne 5 E1
St. Gallen 4 B4
St. George, Gulf of 24 C4
St. George's 23 C1
St. George's Channel 3
  B3-4
St. Helena 14 B7
St. Helena Bay 17 B5
Saint John 19 K5
St. Kitts 23 C1
St. Lawrence, Gulf of 19 K5
St. Lawrence Island 20 a6
St. Lawrence, River 19 K5
St.-Lô 3 C4
St. Louis 15 B3
St. Louis 20 D2
St. Lucia 23 C-D1
St. Malo 3 C4
St. Malo Golfe de 3 C4
St. Marthieu, P.te de 3 B4
St.-Matthew I. 20 a6
St.-Nazaire 3 C5
St. Paul 20 D1
St. Petersburg 20 E3
St. Pierre 17 F2
St. Pierre 19 L5
Saint Pölten 4 C3
St. Quentin 3 D4
St. Vincent, C. 5 A3
St. Vincent I. 23 C1
Ste. Marie I. 17 F3
Ste. Marie C. 17 E4
Saipan 25 C3
Sakai 12 F3
Sakashima Islands 12 E4
Sakhty 7 G5
Sakhalin 9 H3
Sal 15 A3
Salado 21 B2
Salado R. 24 C2-3
Salalah 10 D4
Salamanca 5 B2
Salavat 9 C3
Salawati 13 D-E4
Saldanha 17 B5
Salekhard 9 D2
Salem (India) 11 C4
Salem (U.S.) 20 A1
Sälen 2 C3
Salerno 6 C2
Salerno, G. of 6 C2
Salina 20 D2
Salina Cruz 21 C3
Salinas 23 A3
Saljany 10 C2
Salmi 7 E1
Salo 2 E3
Salonika 6 E2
Sal'sk 7 G5
Salta 24 C2
Saltillo 21 B2
Salt Lake City 20 B1
Salto 24 D3
Salūm 16 C1
Salvador 23 F4
Salween 13 A1
Salzburg 4 C4
Salzgitter 4 B2-3
Sambalpur 11 D3
Sambor 7 B4
Samcheok 12 E-F3
Samar 13 D2
Samarai 25 C3
Samarinda 13 C3-4
Samarkand 9 D4
Sambalpur 11 D3
Sámos 6 F3
Samothrace 6 F2

Sampit 13 C4
Samsun 10 B1
Samui 11 D3
San 15 C3
San'a 10 C4
S. Ambrosio 24 B2
Sanandaj 10 C2
San Andrés Island 21 D3
San Angelo 20 D2
S. Antioco 6 B3
San Antonio 20 D3
S. Antonio (Chile) 24 C2
S. Antonio, Cape (Cuba) 21
  D2
S. Antonio, Cape (Arg.) 24
  D3
S. Benedetto del Tronto 6
  C2
S. Benedicto I. 21 A-B3
San Bernardino 20 B2
San Blas, Cape 20 E3
S. Carlos (Argentina) 24 C3
S. Carlos (Philippines) 13
  D2-3
San Carlos de Bariloche 24
  B4
Sánchez 21 F2-3
S. Cristóbal 24 C2-3
S. Cristobal, Island 25 D3
S. Cristóbal de las Casas 21
  C3
Sandakan 13 C3
Sanday 3 C2
San Diego 20 B2
S. Diego, Cape 24 C5
Sandoa 17 C2
Sandviken 2 C-D3
Sandy, Cape 25a E2
S. Felipe (Chile) 24 B3
S. Felipe (Venez.) 23 B-C1
San Félix, I. 24 A-B2
S. Fernando (Chile) 24 B3
S. Fernando (Philipp.) 13
  C-D2
S. Fernando (Venez.) 23 C2
San Fernando (Trin. and
  Tob.)
  23 C-D2
S. Fernando de Apure 23
  C2
San Francisco 20 A2
Sangar 9 G2
Sangha 17 B1-2
Sangihe, Archip. 13 D3
S. Ignacio 23 C-D4
S. Joaquin 20 A2
S. José (Costa Rica) 21 D4
S. José (Colombia) 23 B2
S. José (Brazil) 23 C3
S. José (Bolivia) 23 C-D4
S. José de Jáchal 24 C3
S. Juan, River 20 C2
S. Juan (Puerto Rico) 21 F3
San Juan (Arg.) 24 C3
S. Juan del Norte 21 D3
S. Juan del Sur 21 D3-4
S. Julián 24 C4
Sankuru 17 C2
S. Lorenzo (Hond.) 21 D3
S. Lorenzo (Ec.) 23 A-B2
S. Luis Potosi 21 B-C2
S. Lourenco, River 23 D4
S. Lucas, Cape 21 A-B2
San Luis 24 C3
S. Marino 6 C2
S. Martin, L. 24 B4
San Mateo, Gulf of 24 C4
San Miguel de Tucumán 24
  C2
Sanok 4 E3
S. Pablo 13 D2
S. Pedro (Ivory Coast) 15
  C4
San Pedro (Parag.) 24 D2
S. Pietro 6 B3
San Rafael 24 C3
San Remo 6 A-B2
San Salvador de Jujuy 24
  C2
S. Salvador or Watling I. 21
  E2
S. Sebastián 5 C2
S. Severo 6 C2
Santa Ana 20 B2
Sta. Ana 21 D3
Sta. Barbara 20 A-B2
Sta. Catarina 24 D-E2
Sta. Catarina, I. 24 E2
Sta. Clara 21 D2
Sta. Cruz (U.S.) 20 A2
Sta. Cruz (Boliv.) 23 C4
Sta. Cruz (Arg.) 24 C4
Sta. Cruz, Islands 25 D3
Sta. Cruz de Tenerife 15 B2
Santa Fé (Arg.) 24 C3
Santa Fé (U.S.) 20 C2
Sta. Genoveva 21 A2

125

Santai 12 C3
Sta. Ines 24 B5
Sta. Isabel 25 C-D3
Sta. Maria (Brazil) 24 D2-3
Sta. Marta 23 B1
Santander 5 C2
Sant'Antonio Oeste 24 C4
Santar Is. 9 G-H3
Santarém (Port.) 5 A3
Santarém (Brazil) 23 D3
Sta. Rosa (Hond.) 21 C-D3
Sta. Rosa (Brazil.) 24 D2
Santiago I. 15 A3
Santiago (Panamá) 21 D4
Santiago (Dom. Rep.) 21 E3
Santiago (Chile) 24 B3
Santiago, R. 23 B3
Santiago de Compostela 5 A2
Santiago de Cuba 21 E3
Santiago del Estero 24 C2
Santo Antao 15 A3
Santo Antônio (Amazonas) 23 C3
Santo Antônio (Rondônia) 23 C3
Santo Domingo 21 E-F3
Santos 24 E2
S. Vicente 15 A3
Sanyuan 12 C3
Sao Borja 24 D2
Sao Francisco, River 23 E-F3-4
Sao Francisco do Sul 24 E2
S. Joao del Rei 24 E2
S. Joao do Araguaia 23 D-E3
Sao Luis 23 E3
Saône 3 E5
Sao Paulo de Olivença 23 C3
Sao Paulo, Island 22 G-H3
Sao Paulo, State 24 D-E2
Sao Paulo City 24 E2
Sao Roque, C. 23 F3
Sao Tiago 15 A3
Sao Tomé 17 A1
Sao Tomé and Principe 15 D4
Sao Tomé, C. 24 E2
Sapporo 12 F-G2
Saragossa: see Zaragoza
Sarajevo 6 D2
Saransk 9 C3
Saratov 9 D2-3
Saratsi 12 C-D2-3
Sarawak 13 C3
Sardinia 6 B2
Sargodha 11 C2
Sarh 16 B4
Sari 10 D2
Sarir 16 C2
Sarja 7 H2
Sarmiento 24 B-C4
Särna 2 C3
Sarny 7 C4
Saros, Gulf of 6 F2
Sarra 16 C2
Sartène 5 F2
Sary-Sagan 9 D3
Sasebo 12 E3
Saskatchewan 19 F4
Saskatoon 19 F4
Sasovo 7 G3
Sassandra 15 C4
Sassari 6 B2
S'as'stroj 7 E1
Satu-Mare 4 E4
Sauda 2 A4
Saudi Arabia 8 C-D4-5
Sault Ste. Marie 20 E1
Sava 6 C-D1
Savannah 20 E-F2
Savannakhet 13 B2
Savona 6 B1
Savonlinna 2 F-G3
Savukoski 2 G2
Sawahlunto 13 B4
Sawakin 16 D3
Sawknah 15 E2
Sawu 13 D5
Sawu Sea 13 D4
Say 15 D3
Sayan: Ra 9 E3
Sayhut 10 D4
Scarborough 3 C-D3
Scekino 7 F3
Schefferville 19 K4
Schwäbisch Hall 4 B3
Schwaner Range 13 C4
Schwangyashan 12 F2
Schwerin 4 B-C2
Schwyz 4 B4
Scilly, Isles of 3 B4
Scors 7 D-E4
Scotland 3 B-C2
Scott, Is. 27 L2
Scranton 20 F1

Seattle 20 A1
Sebastián Vizcaino, B. 21 A2
Sebastiao, I. de S. 24 E2
Sebastopo' 10 B1
Sebez 7 C-D2
Sedan 3 E4
Seeheim 17 B4
Ségou 15 C3
Segovia 5 C2
Segre 5 C-D2
Segura 5 C3
Seiland 2 E1
Seinäjoki 2 E3
Seine 3 D-E4
Seine, Baie de la 3 C4
Sejm 7 E4
Seksna 7 F2
Sekaju 13 B4
Sekondi-Takoradi 15 C4
Selaru 13 E4
Selatan, C. 13 C4
Selb 4 B3
Selenga 12 C2
Sélibaby 15 B3
Selkirk 24 A3
Selvagens Is. 15 B1
Semara 15 B-C2
Semarang 13 C4
Semeru 13 C4
Semipalatinsk 9 D3
Sem'onov 7 H2
Sem'onovka 7 E3
Sena 17 D2
Sena Madureira 23 B-C3
Sendai 12 F-G3
Senegal 14 A4
Senegal, River 15 B3
Senhor do Bonfim 23 E-F4
Senja 2 C-D1
Senkaku, Is. 12 E4
Sens 3 D4
Seoul 12 E3
Sepetovka 7 C-D4
Sept-Iles 19 K4
Serafimovic 7 G4
Seram, Island 13 D4
Seram, Sea 14 D-E4
Serang 13 B4
Seremban 13 B3
Sergino 9 D2
Sergipe 23 F4
Seria 13 C3
Sérifos 6 F3
Serov 9 D2-3
Serowe 17 C4
Serpukhov 7 E-F3
Sérrai 6 E2
Serui 13 E4
Sesfontein 17 B3
Sestoreck 7 D1
Sète 5 D2
Sétif 15 D1
Setúbal 5 A3
Sevastopol' 7 E5
Sevcenko 9 C3
Severn, River (U.K.) 3 C4
Severn, River (Canada.) 19 H4
Severnaja Zemlya 9 F1-2
Severodvinsk 9 C2
Severomorsk 9 B-C2
Seville 5 B2
Seward 20 d7
Seward, Mount 27 R2
Seward, Peninsula 20 B6
Seychelles 17 F2
Seydhisfjordhur 1 B-C2
Seymour 25a D3
Sfax 15 D-E1
S'Gravenhage 3 D-E3
Shaba 17 C4
Shabani 17 C4
Shagra 10 C3
Shahjahanpur 11 D3
Shalsund 4 C2
Shanghai 12 E3
Shangjao 12 D4
Shangkiu 12 D3
Shangshui 12 D3
Shannon, River 3 A3
Shanho 9 D4
Shansi 12 D3
Shantung 12 D-E3
Shaohing 12 E3-4
Shaoyang 12 C-D4
Sharjah 10 D3
Shark Bay 25a A2
Shasi 12 D3
Shasta, Mt. 20 A-B1
Shaykh 'Uthman 10 C4
Sheboygan 20 E1
Sheffield 3 C3
Shendi 16 D3
Shensi 12 C3
Shentza 11 D2
Sherbro I. 15 B4
Sherridon 19 G4

Shetland Islands 3 C1
Shibam 10 C4
Shibeli 16 E4
Shigatse 11 D2
Shihkiachwang 12 D3
Shihtsui-shan 12 C3
Shikoku 12 F3
Shillong 11 E3
Shimoga 11 C4
Shimonoseki 12 E-F3
Shinyanga 17 D2
Shiraz 10 D3
Shiukwan 12 D4
Shizuoka 12 F3
Shkodër 6 D-E2
Shkodër, Lake 6 D2
Sholapur 11 C3
Shreveport 20 D2
Shrewsbury 3 C3
Shuqra 10 C4
Shwangliao 12 E2
Sialkot 11 C2
Siam: see Thailand
Siam, Gulf of 13 B1-2
Sian 12 C3
Siangfan 12 D3
Siangtan 12 D4
Siaokan 12 D3
Siauliai 7 B3
Sibenik 6 C-D2
Siberia 9 D-E-F-G-H2
Siberian Plain 9 D-E2-3
Siberut 13 A4
Sibi 11 B3
Sibiti 17 B2
Sibiu 6 F1
Sibolga 13 A3
Sibu 13 C3
Sibut 16 B4
Sibuyan Sea 13 D2
Sicily 6 C3
Sichang 12 C4
Sidi Barrani 16 C1
Sidi-Bel-Abbès 15 C-D1
Sidi Ifni 15 B2
Siedlce 4 E2
Siegen 4 A-B3
Siem Reap 13 B2
Siena 6 B2
Sierra Blanca 20 C2
Sierra Colorada 24 C4
Sierra Leone 14 A5
Sierra Madre, Eastern 21 B-C2
Sierra Madre, Western 21 B2
Sifnos 6 F3
Sighet 4 E-F4
Sighisoara 6 F1
Siguiri 15 C3
Sikar 11 C3
Sikasso 15 C3
Sikhote Alin 12 F2
Si Kiang 12 D4
Sikkim 8 F4
Sil 5 B2
Siliguri 11 D3
Silinhot 12 D2
Silistra 6 F1
Siljan 2 C3
Silka 9 F-G3
Silovo 7 G3
Silva Porto: see Bié
Silvânia 23 E4
Silvassa 11 C3
Simanovsk 9 G3
Simeuluë 13 A3
Simferopol' 7 E5
Simla 11 C2
Simpson Desert 25a C2
Simusir 9 H3
Sinai Peninsula 16 D2
Sines 5 A3
Sineviju 12 E3
Singa 16 D3
Singapore 8 G5
Singaradja 13 C4
Singida 17 D2
Singkawang 13 B3
Sinhailien 12 D-E3
Sining 12 C3
Sinkiang 11 D1
Sinkiang Uighur 11 C-D1-2
Sinmin 12 E2
Sinoja 18 D3
Sinop 10 B1
Sinsiang 12 D3
Sintang 13 C3-4
Sinyang 12 D3
Sion 4 A4
Sioux City 20 D1
Sioux Falls 20 D1
Sioux Lookout 19 G-H4
Siple, Mt. 27 O2
Sipora 13 A4
Sir Edward Pellew Groups 25a C1
Siret 4 F4, 6 F1

Sirjan 10 D3
Siros 6 F3
Sisak 6 D1
Sisak 6 D1
Sitia 6 F3
Sittwe 11 E3
Sivas 10 B2
Sivrihisar 10 B2
Siwa 16 C2
Skadovsk 7 E5
Skagen 4 B1
Skagerrak 2 B4
Skagway 20 E7
Skellefte 2 D2
Skelleftea 2 E2
Skibotn 2 E1
Skien 2 B4
Skikda 15 D1
Skiros 6 F3
Skópelos 6 E-F3
Skopin 7 F3
Skopje 6 E2
Skövde 2 C4
Skovorodino 9 G3
Skrira 7 D4
Skye 3 B2
Slamet 13 B4
Slancy 7 C-D2
Slatina 6 F1
Slav'ansk 7 F4
Slav'ansk-na-Kubani 7 F5
Slavgorod 9 D3
Slavuta 7 C4
Sligo 3 A3
Sliven 6 F2
Slonim 7 C3
Sluck 7 C3
Slupsk 4 D2
Smithton 25a D4
Smola 7 E2
Smolensk 7 C-D3
Smolevici 7 C-D3
Smoljan 6 F2
Snake 20 B1
Snares, The 25a F6
Snasa 2 C2
Sniardwy, L. 4 E2
Soasiu 13 D3
Sobat 16 D4
Sobral 23 E3
Society Islands 25 F3
Socorro 20 C2
Socorro, I. 21 A-B3
Socotra 10 D4
Sodankylä 2 F2
Söderhamn 2 D3
Södertalje 2 D4
Sofia 2 A4
Sogne Fjord 2 A3
Sohag 16 D2
Sokodé 15 D4
Sokol 7 G2
Sokoto 15 D3
Sol'cy 7 D2
Solgótarján 4 D-E4
Soligalic 7 G2
Soligorsk 7 C3
Solleftea 2 D3
Solomon Islands 25 C-D3
Solway Firth 3 B-C3
Sombor 6 D1
Sombrerete 21 B2
Somerset I. 19 G2
Somerset West 17 B-C5
Somes 4 E-F4
Son 11 D3
Sondrio 6 B1
Songea 17 D3
Songkhla 13 B3
Sonsorol Island 13 E3
Soochow 12 E3
Sopron 4 D4
Soria 5 C2
Sor Kvaloy 2 D1
Sorocaba 24 E2
Soroki 7 D4
Sorong 13 E4
Soroy 2 E1
Sorsele 2 D2
Sortavala 7 D1
Sossi Bé 17 E3
Sostka 7 E4
Sotkamo 2 G2
Sousse 15 E1
South Africa 14 D-F8-9
South Andaman 11 E4
South Australia 25 B4 25a C2
South Bend 20 E1
South Carolina 20 E-F2
South Dakota 20 C-D1
South East Cape 25a D4
South Georgia 24 F5
South Island 25 D-E5
South Orkney Islands 27 S2

South Sandwich Islands 27 A3
South Shetland Islands 27 R-S3
South West Africa 14 D-E7-8
Southampton 3 C4
Southampton Island 19 H3
Southend-on-Sea 3 D4
Souther Alps 25a F-G6
South Island 25a G6
South Plate 20 C1
South Saskatchewan 19 E-F4
Southwest, Cape 25a F-G6
Sovietskaja Gavan 9 G-H3
Soya C. 12 G2
Spain 1 C4
Spartanburg 20 E2
Spárti 6 E3
Spartivento, C. 6 D3
Spas-Demensk 7 E3
Spassk-Dalni 9 G3
Spatha, C. 6 E-F4
Spencer Gulf 25a C3
Spitsbergen Is.: see Svalbard Islands
Split 6 D2
Spokane 20 B1
Spola 7 D4
Sporades 6 E-F3
Springbok 17 B4-5
Springfield (Illinois) 20 D-E1-2
Springfield (Missouri) 20 D1
Springs 17 C4
Srednekolymsk 9 H2
Sretensk 9 F3
Sri Lanka 8 F5
Srinagar 11 C2
Stalowa Wola 4 E3
Stanke Dimitrov 6 E2
Stanley 24 D5
Stanovoj Ra.9 G3
Stara Zagora 6 F2
Starbuck 25 F3
Stargard 4 C2
Starica 7 E2
Starobel'sk 7 F-G4
Starogard 4 D2
Staro-Konstantinov 7 C4
Staryi Oskol 7 F4
Staten Island: see Estados, I. de los
Stavanger 2 A4
Stavropol 7 G5
Steenkool 13 E4
Steep Point 25a A2
Steinkjer 2 B-C3
Stendal 4 B2
Sterlitamak 9 C3
Stettin: see Szczecin
Stewart Island 25 D5 25a F-G6
Stip 6 E2
Stockolm 2 D4
Stockton 20 A-B2
Stojba 9 G3
Stoke-on-Trent 3 C3
Stolin 7 C3-4
Stony Tunguska 9 E2
Store Baelt 4 B2
Stören 2 B3
Storsjö 2 C3
Storsjön 2 C3
Storuman 2 C-D2
Stranraer 3 B3
Strasbourg 3 E4
Straubing 4 C3
Streaky Bay 25a C3
Strimon, Gulf of 6 E2
Strömsund 2 C3
Strugi-Krasnyje 7 D2
Struma 6 E2
Stryi 7 B-C4
Stung Treng 13 B2
Stura 5 E1
Stuttgart 4 B3
Suanhwa 12 D2
Suarez, C.nel: see Coronel Suarez
Subar-Kuduk 9 C3
Subotica 6 D1
Suceava 4 F4
Suchan 9 G3
Suchbaatar 9 F3
Suchinici 7 E3
Suchow 12 D3
Suchumi 10 C1
Sucre 23 C4
Sucuriú 24 D1
Suda 7 F2
Sudan Des 14 E-F4
Sudan, State 16 A-B-C-D3
Sudbury 19 H5
Suez 16 D1
Suez, G. of 16 D2

Suhar 10 D3
Suhsien 12 D3
Suihwa 12 E2
Suiteh 12 C-D3
Suja 7 G2
Sukabumi 13 B4
Sukhona 7 G-H1
Sukhumi 10 B-C1
Sukkertoppen 19 L-M3
Sukkur 11 B3
Sula Archip. 13 D4
Sulina 6 G1
Sulitjelma 2 D2
Sulu Archip. 13 C-D3
Sulu Sea 13 C-D3
Suluq 16 C1
Sumatra 13 A-B3-4
Sumba 13 D4
Sumbawa 13 C4
Sumbawa-Besar 13 C-D4
Sumgait 10 C-D1
Sumilino 7 D3
Sumen 6 F2
Sumy 7 E4
Sunan 13 D4
Sunda Islands, Lesser 86
Sunda Strait 13 B4
Sunderland 3 C3
Sundsvall 2 D3
Sungari 12 F2
Suniteyuchi 12 C-D2
Sunndalsora 2 B3
Sunyani 15 C4
Suolahti 2 F3
Suomussalmi 2 F-G2
Superieur 20 D1
Superior, L. 20 E1
Sùqutra 10 D4
Sur 10 D3
Surabaja 13 C4
Surakarta 13 C4
Surat 11 C3
Surat Thani 13 A3
Suraz 7 D-E3
Surgut 9 D2
Surigao 13 D3
Surinam 22 E3
Surt 16 B1
Susuman 9 H2
Sutlej 11 C3
Suva 25 D-E3
Suwatki 4 E2
Suweon 12 E3
Svalbard Islands 9 A2
Svappavaara 2 D-E2
Svatovo 7 F4
Svealand 2 C-D4
Sveg 2 C3
Sverdlovsk 9 C-D3
Sverdrup Islands 19 F-G2
Svetogorsk 7 D1
Svistov 6 F2
Svolvaer 2 C1
Swain Reef 25a E2
Swakopmund 17 B4
Swatow 12 D4
Swaziland 14 F8
Swindon 3 C4
Swansea 3 B-C4
Sweden 1 E2-3
Swinoujscie 4 C2
Switzerland 1 D4
Sycovka 7 E2
Sydney (Austr.) 25 C4 25a E3
Sydney (Can.) 19 K-L5
Syktyvkar 9 C2
Sylt 1 A-B2
Syracuse 6 C3
Syr Darya 9 D3
Syria 8 C2
Szczecin (Stettin) 4 C2
Szczecinek 4 C-D2
Szechwan 12 C3
Szeged 4 D-E4
Székesfehérvár 4 D4
Szekszard 4 D4
Szeping 12 E2
Szolnok 4 E4
Szombatheley 4 D4

T

Tabarka 5 F3
Tabor 4 C3
Tabora 17 D2
Tabou 15 C4
Tabriz 10 C2
Tabuk 10 B3
Tacloban 13 D2
Tacna 23 B4
Tacoma 20 A1
Tadzhikistan 9 D4
Taegu 12 E-F3
Taejon 12 E3
Taganrog 7 F5

Tagus 5 A-B3
Tahat 15 D2
Tahcheng 11 D1
Tahiti 25 F3
Tahoua 15 D3
Tahsien 12 C3
Taichung 12 E4
Taimyr, Lake 9 F2
Taimyr Pen. 9 E-F2
Tain 3 B2
Tainan 12 D-E4
Taipei 12 E4
Taiping 13 A-B3
Taitao Peninsula 24 B4
Taivalkoski 2 G2
Taiwan, (Formosa) 12 E4
Taiyüan 12 D3
Ta'izz 10 C4
Tajset 9 E3
Tajuna 5 C2
Tak 13 A2
Takamatsu 12 F3
Takaungu 17 E2
Takla-Makan 11 C-D2
Talaud Islands 13 D3
Talca 24 B3
Taldy Kurgan 9 D3
Tali 12 B-C4
Taliabu 13 D4
Tallahassee 20 E2
Tallinn 7 C2
Tal'noe 7 D4
Taltal 24 B2
Tamale 15 C-D4
Tamanrasset 15 D2
Tamatave 17 E-F3
Tambacounda 15 B3
Tambelan Islands 13 B3
Tambov 7 G3
Tambura 16 C4
Támega 5 A-B2
Tampa 20 D3
Tampere 2 E-F3
Tampico 21 C2
Tamsag-Bulak 12 D2
Tamworth 25a E3
Tana 2 F-G1
Tana, Lake 16 D3
Tana, River (Kenya) 17 D2
Tana, River (Norway) 2 F1
Tanacross 20 D6
Tanami Desert 25a C2
Tanana 20 c-d6
Tanana, River 20 d6
Tanaro 6 A-B1
Tandil 24 D3
Tandjung 13 C4
Tandjungkarang 13 B4
Tanezrouft 15 C2
Tang 11 E2
Tanga 17 D2
Tanganyika 17 D2
Tanganyika, Lake 17 C-D2
Tangchi Pass 12 B3
Tangier 15 C2
Tanglha Range 11 D-E2
T'angshan 12 D-E3
Tanimbar Islands 13 E4
Tannu-Ola 12 B1
Tanout 15 D3
Tanta 16 D1
Tanzania 14 F6
Taoan 12 E2
Taoudenni 15 C2
Tapa 7 C2
Tapachula 21 C3
Tapajós 21 C3
Tapti 11 C3
Taquari 23 D4
Tara 9 D3
Tarakan 13 C3
Taranto 6 D2
Taranto, G. of 6 D2-3
Tarare 5 E1
Tarawa 25 D2
Tarbes 5 D2
Tardin 12 B3
Taree 25a E3
Tarif 11 D3
Tarifa, C. 5 B3
Tarija 24 C2
Tarim 10 C4
Tarim, River 11 D1
Tarko-Sale 9 D-E2
Tarlac 13 C-D2
Tarn 5 D1-2
Tärnaby 2 C2
Tarnavo 6 F1
Tarnów 4 E3
Tarragona 5 D2
Tarrasa 5 D2
Tartari, Str. of 12 G1-2
Tartu 7 C2
Tartus 10 B2
Tasauz 9 C3
Tashigong 11 C2
Taskent 9 D3
Tas-Kumyr 11 C?

Tasman Sea 25 D4, 25a E3, 25a F-G5-6
Tasmania 25 B-C5, 25a D-E4
Tatabánya 4 D4
Tatra 4 E3
Tatsaitan 12 B3
Tatta 11 B3
Tatung 12 D3
Taufikia 16 D4
Taung-gyi 13 A1
Taunton 3 C4
Taupo, Lake 25a G5
Tauragè 7 B3
Taurus Mountains 10 B2
Tavoy 13 A2
Tawau 13 C3
Tawitawi 13 D3
Taytay 13 C-D2
Taz 9 E2
Tazovskiy 9 D2
Tbilisi 10 C1
Tchibanga 17 B2
Tchien 15 C4
Tebes 16 D2
Tecuci 6 F-G1
Tedzhen 9 C-D4
Teesside: see
   Middleosbrogh
Tegucigalpa 21 D3
Tehran 10 D2
Tehuantepec 21 C3
Tehuantepec, G. of 21 C3
Tekeli 9 D-E3
Tekirdag 6 F2
Teikovo 7 F-G2
Tel Aviv 10 B2
Telegraph Creek 19 C-D4
Telén 24 C3
Teles Pires R. 23 D3-4
Telingha 12 B3
Telsiai 7 B2
Telukbetung 13 B4
Temir 10 D1
Temirtau 9 D3
Temr'uk 7 F5
Temuco 24 B3
Tenasserim 13 A2
Ten Degree Channel 11 E5
Ténéré 15 E2-3
Tenerife 15 B2
Ténès 5 D3
Tengchung 12 B4
Tengiz, L. 9 D3
Tengkow 12 C2
Tenke 17 C3
Tennant Creek 25a C1
Tennessee 20 E2
Tenosique 21 C3
Teófilo Otoni 23 E4
Teramo 6 C2
Terengganu 13 B3
Teresina 23 E3
Termez 9 D4
Termini Imerese 6 C3
Ternate 13 D3
Terni 6 C2
Ternopol' 7 C4
Terracina 6 C2
Terre Haute 20 E2
Teruel 5 C2
Tessalit 15 C-D2
Testa del Gargano 6 D2
Tete 17 D3
Tetjukhe 9 G3
Tetovo 6 E2
Tétouan 15 C1
Teulada, C. 6 B3
Texarkana 20 D2
Texas 20 C-D2
Texeira de Sousa see Luau
Thailand 8 F-G5
Thakhek 13 B2
Thames (Austr.) 25a G5
Thames (U.K.) 3 C4
Thamud 10 D4
Thana 11 C4
Thanh Hoa 13 B2
Thanjavur 11 C-D4
Thar Desert 11 C3
Thásos 6 F3
The Hague: see
   S'Gravenhage
The Sound 4 C2
Thessaloniki, G. of 6 E2-3
Thiers 5 D1
Thiés 15 B3
Thiewiaza 19 G3
Thimbu 11 E3
Thira 6 F3
Thisted 4 A-B1
Thok Daurakpa 11 D2
Thon Buri 13 A-B2
Three Kings Island 25a G5
Thule 19 K2
Thun 4 A-B3
Thunder Bay 19 G-H5
Thurso 3 B-C2

Thurston, Pen. 27 Q2
Tibati 15 E4
Tibesti 16 B2
Tibet 11 D-E2-3
Tibet, Plateau of 11 D2
Tichitt 15 C3
Tichla 15 B2
Tichoreck 7 G5
Tichyin 7 E2
Ticino 6 B1
Tidjikja 15 B3
Tien Shan 11 C-D1
Tienshui 12 C3
Tientsin 12 D3
Tierra del Fuego 24 C5
Tigre 23 B3
Tigris 10 C2
Tijuana 20 B2
Tiksi 9 G2
Timaru 25a F-G6
Timimoun 15 D2
Timis 6 E1
Timisoara 6 E1
Timmins 19 H-I5
Timor 13 D4
Timor Sea 13 D5 25a B1
Tinaca, Point 13 D4
Tindouf 15 C2
Tingo Maria 23 B3
Tinogasta 24 C2
Tinos 6 F3
Tipperary 3 B3
Tiran 10 B3
Tirana 6 D2
Tiraspol' 7 D5
Tirgoviste 6 F1
Tirgu-Jiu 6 E1
Tirgu-Mures 4 F4
Tirich Mir 11 C2
Tirnava 4 D3
Tiruchirappalli 11 C-D4-5
Tisza 4 E4
Tit-Ary 9 G2
Titicaca, L. 23 C4
Titograd 6 D2
Titov Veles 6 E2
Titule 16 C4
Tjendrawasih 13 D3
Tjepu 13 C4
Tjirebon 13 B4
Tlemcen 15 C-D1
Toba L. 13 A3
Tobago 23 C1
Tobi 13 E3
Tobol'sk 9 D3
Tocantinopólis 23 E3
Tocantins 23 E3
Tocopilla 24 B2
Tocorpuri, Cerros de 24 C2
Togian Islands 13 D4
Togo 14 C5
Tokar 16 D4
Tokara Islands 12 E3-4
Tokchen 11 D2
Tokelau Islands 25 E3
Tokmak 7 E-F5
Tokyo 12 F3
Tolbuhin 6 F-G2
Toledo (Sp.) 5 B3
Toledo (U.S) 20 E1
Tolo, G. of 13 D4
Toluca 21 B3
Tomini 13 D3
Tomini, G. of 13 D4
Tommot 9 G3
Tomsk 9 E3
Tonalá 21 C3
Tonder 4 B2
Tonking 13 B1
Tonking, G. of 13 B1-2
Tonga 25 E3
Tonlé Sap. 13 B2
Tonopah 20 B2
Toowoomba 25a D-E2
Top, Lake 2 G2
Topeka 20 D2
Torbat-e-Heydariyeh 10
   D-E2
Torne 2 E2
Tornio, River 2 E2
Toropec 7 D2
Tororo 17 D1
Torquay 3 C4
Torrens, Lake 25a C3
Torreón 21 B2
Torres Strait 25 C3 25a D1
Torsby 2 C3
Tortosa 5 D2
Tortosa, C.de 5 D2
Tortuga 23 C1
Toruń 4 D2
Torzok 7 E2
Tosno 7 D2
T'osovo-Netyl'skiy 7 D2
Tot'ma 7 G1
Tottori 12 F3
Toubkal 15 C1

Touggourt 15 D1
Toulon 5 E2
Toulouse 5 D2
Toungo 13 A2
Tours 3 D5
Townsville 25 C3 25a D1
Tozeur 15 D1
Trabzon 10 B1
Tradom 11 D3
Transkei 14 E-F9
Transvaal 17 C-D4
Trapani 6 C3
Treinta-y-Tres 24 D3
Trelew 24 C3
Trelleborg 2 C5
Tremiti Islands 6 C2
Tremp 5 D2
Trencín 4 D3
Trento 6 B1
Trenton 20 F-I2
Tres Arroyos 24 C-D3
Trés Lagoas 24 D2
Tres Marias Island 21 B2
Tres Puntas, C. 24 C4
Treviso 6 C1
Trier 4 A3
Trieste 6 C1
Trikkala 6 E3
Trincomalee 11 D5
Trindade 24 F2
Trinidad 23 C4
Trinidad I. 23 C-D1
Trinidad and Tobago 22
   D-E2-3
Tripoli 16 B1
Tripolis 6 E3
Tripolitania 16 B1
Tripura 11 E3
Trivandrum 11 C5
Trois Rivières 19 I5
Trollhättan 2 C4
Tromelin 17 F3
Tromso 2 D1
Trondheim 2 B3
Trondheim Fjord 2 B2-3
Troyes 3 E4
Trudovoy 9 D3
Trujillo (Perù) 23 B3
Trujillo (Sp.) 5 B3
Truk Is. 25 C2
Truro 19 K5
Trutnov 4 C3
Tsaratanana 17 E-F3
Tsau 17 C3
Tsetserleg 12 C2
Tshabong 17 C4
Tshele 17 B2
Tshikapa 17 C2
Tshuapa 17 C2
Tsiaotso 12 D3
Tsinan 12 D3
Tsinghai 12 B3
Tsingshih 12 C-D4
Tsingtao 12 E3
Tsining 12 D2
Tsitsihar 12 E2
Tsitsilin 12 C3
Tsugaru, Str. 12 G2
Tsumeb 17 B3
Tsunyi 12 C4
Tsushima 12 E-F3
Tuamotu, Archipelago 25
   F-G3
Tübingen 4 B3
Tubruq 16 C1
Tubuai, I. 25 F4
Tubuai Islands (Austral
   Islands):
   25 F4
Tucavaca 23 D4
Tucson 20 B2
Tucuarembó 24 D3
Tucuepala 23 B-C4
Tucupita 23 C2
Tucurui 23 E3
Tukangbesi Islands 13 D4
Tukums 17 B2
Tula 7 F3
Tulcea 6 G1
Tuléar 17 E4
Tulle 5 D1
Tulsa 20 D2
Tulun 9 F3
Tumaco 23 A-B2
Tumbes 23 A3
Tummo 15 E2
Tundra 6 F2
Tungchuan 12 C-D3
Tunghwa 12 E2
Tungliao 12 E2
Tungpu 12 B-C3
Tungsha Tao 12 D4
Tung Ting, L. 12 D3
Tungtze 12 C4

Tunguska Lower 9 E2
Tunhwa 12 E2
Tunhwang 12 B2
Tunis 15 D-E1
Tunisia 14 C2
Tunja 23 B2
Tunki 12 D4
Turabah 10 C3
Turayf 10 B2
Turbat 11 B3
Turbio, El: see El Turbio
Turda 4 E4
Turfan 11 E1
Turgaj 9 D3
Turia 5 C2-3
Turin 6 A1
Turkana, Lake 16 D4
Turkestan 9 D3
Turkey 8 C-D4
Turkmenistan 9 C-D4
Turks and Caicos, Is. 21
   E-F2
Turku 2 E3
Turnu-Severin 6 E1
Turukhansk 9 E2
Tu-shan-tzu 11 D1
Tutajev 7 F2
Tuticorin 11 C5
Tutrakan 6 F2
Tuvalu 25 D3
Tuxpan 21 C2
Tuxtla Gutiérrez 21 C3
Tuyun 12 C4
Tuz, Lake 10 B2
Tuzla 6 D1
Tuzugu 16 B2
Tyrrhenian Sea 6 B-C2-3
Tyube 11 B2
Tyumen 9 D3
Tzekung 12 C4
Tzepo 12 D3

U

Uaupés 23 C3
Ubaitaba 23 F4
Ubangi 16 B4
Ubeda 5 C3
Uberaba 24 E1
Ubundu 17 C2
Udaipur 11 C3
Uddevalla 2 B4
Udine 6 C1
Udon Thani 13 B2
Uele 16 C4
Uelen 9 K2
Uelzen 4 B2
Ufa 9 C3
Uganda 14 F5
Uglegorsk 9 G-H3
Uglic 7 F2
Uglovka 7 E2
Ujiji 17 D2
Ujjain 11 C3
Ukhta 9 C2
Ukmergé 7 C3
Ukraine 9 B3
Ulan-Bator 12 C2
Ulangom 12 B2
Ulanhot 12 E2
Ulan-Ude 9 F3
Uleeheue 13 A3
Uleges 13 B4
Ulhasnagar 11 C4
Ulithi Is. 25 C2
Uljanovsk 9 C3
Uljastay 12 B2
Ullapool 3 B2
Ulm 4 B3
Uman' 7 D4
Umanak 19 L-M2
Ume 2 D2
Umea 2 D3
Umiat 20 c-d6
Umtali 17 D3
Umtata 17 C5
Umzimvubu 17 C-D5
Una 6 D1
Unalakleet 20 c6
Under-Han 12 D2
Uneca 7 E3
Ungava, Bay of 19 K4
Ungava, Pen. 19 I3
Union of Soviet Socialist
   Republics: see U.S.S.R.
United Arab Emirates 8 D4
United Kingdom 1 C-D3
United States of America 18
   I-M6
Unst 3 C1
Unza 7 G2
Upington 17 C4
Upper Volta 14 B-C4
Uppsala 2 D4
Ural, River 9 C3

Ural Mountains 9 C2-3
Uralsk 9 C3
Ural'skiy 9 D3
Uraricoera 23 C2
Urgenc 9 D3
Urubamba 23 B4
Uruguaiana 24 D2
Uruguay 22 E7
Uruguay, River 24 D2
Urumchi 11 D1
Urup 9 H3
Ur'upinsk 7 G4
Uruzgan 11 B2
Usak 10 A-B2
Usküdar 10 B1
U.S.S.R. 8 C-D-E-F-G-H3
Ussuri 12 F2
Ussurijsk 9 G3
Ust-Barguzin 9 F3
Ust-Cilma 9 C2
Usti 4 C3
Ustica 6 C3
Ust-Ilimsk 9 F3
Ustka 4 D2
Ust-Kamcatsk 9 I3
Ust-Kamenogorsk 9 D3
Ust-khayryuzov 9 H3
Ust-Kut 9 F3
Ust'-Labinsk 7 F-G5
Ust-Luga 7 D2
Ust-Maya 9 G2
Ust-Nera 9 G-H2
Ust-Olenëk 9 F-G2
Ust-Port 9 E2
Ustyurt 10 D1
Utah 20 B2
Utajärvi 2 F2
Utena 7 C3
Utete 17 D2
Utiariti 23 D4
Utrecht 3 E3-4
Utrera 5 B3
Utsjoki 2 F1
Utsunomiya 12 F3
Uttar Pradesh 11 C-D3
Uusikaupunki 2 E3
Uvarovo 7 G3
Uvs Nuus 12 B1
Uxituba 23 D3
Uyuni 24 C2
Uzbekistan 9 D3
Uzen' 9 C3
Uzgorod 7 B4

V

Vaal 17 C4
Vaasa 2 E3
Vác 4 D4
Vacaria 24 D-E2
Vadodara 11 C3
Vadso 2 G1
Vaduz 4 B4
Váh 4 D3
Valdaj 7 E2
Valdepeñas 5 C3
Valdés Peninsula 24 C4
Valdivia 24 B3
Valence 5 E1
Valencia (Sp.) 5 C3
Valencia (Venez.) 23 C2
Valencia, G. of 5 C-D3
Valga 7 C2
Valjevo 6 D-E1
Valka 7 C2
Valkeakoski 2 E3
Valladolid (Mexico) 21 D2
Valladolid (Sp.) 5 B2
Valle 2 A4
Vallenar 24 B2
Valletta 6 C4
Valmiera 7 C2
Valparaiso 24 B3
Valujki 7 F4
Van 10 C2
Van, Lake 10 C2
Vancouver 19 D5
Vancouver I. 19 C-D5
Van Diemen Gulf 25a B-C1
Vänern 2 C4
Vanna 2 D1
Vännäs 2 D2
Vannes 3 C5
Vansbro 2 C3
Vanua Levu 25 E3
Vanuatu 25 D3
Varanasi 11 D3
Varanger Fjord 2 G-H1
Varanger, Peninsula 2 G1
Varazdin 6 D1
Varberg 2 C4
Vardar 6 E2
Vardo 2 G-H1
Varena 7 C3
Varese 6 B1
Varginha 24 E2